TAKE ONE, ACTION!

TAKE ONE, ACTION!

ANDY WILKINSON

The Book Guild Ltd

First published in Great Britain in 2021 by
The Book Guild Ltd
9 Priory Business Park
Wistow Road, Kibworth
Leicestershire, LE8 0RX
Freephone: 0800 999 2982
www.bookguild.co.uk
Email: info@bookguild.co.uk
Twitter: @bookguild

Typeset in 11pt Minion Pro

Printed and bound in the UK by TJ Books Limited, Padstow, Cornwall

ISBN 978 1913551 353

British Library Cataloguing in Publication Data.
A catalogue record for this book is available from the British Library.

To my parents, George and Mary,
thank you for making me who I am.

To my sister and brothers,
Maureen, George, Garry and Scott,
for being there and making me smile.

To Katy,
the love of my life,
together we are whole.

To our two glorious sons,
Jake and Oscar,
our everlasting monuments.

To Professors Roy and Angela Goodall,
my sword masters.

A fencer's salute to you all.

Andy

CONTENTS

PROLOGUE

Dear film enthusiasts, duellists and fencers,

Hello, welcome and thank you for picking me up!

You may find my style of writing, if I have one, a little different from the other scholarly tomes you may read on the techniques and history of the film business and fencing. However, please indulge me with a chance to entertain you, as I have an interesting story to tell, whether you are a swashbuckling sword fighter or a film fan. You will enjoy this merry tale of real-life derring-do and swordsmanship and lots of fun along the way.

This is not a biography about someone just interested in film, or a wannabe. This story happened; it is my tale of how I ventured into the, sometimes alien, world of film-making.

I am certainly no Michael Caine, Roger Moore or Sean Connery. I am not even in their esteemed league. You may not know my name, but I'll wager you have probably seen me on the screen at either the cinema or on your television.

I am not, nor have I ever claimed to be, an actor or stuntman.

I am a world title-winning fight director, film sword master, qualified fencing coach, Honorary Professor of the British Academy of Fencing for theatrical fencing, voting member of BAFTA and full professional member of a number of guilds and entertainment unions. You will discover all this as you read on about my adventure.

Why read this memoir instead of that of another, more famous actor?

I am a credited film and theatre director and a writer and producer for radio who started from a working-class background, with no family connections in the film industry. Someone who has picked their own way to reach their personal dream.

Unlike what you read in other film biographies, I have had no lucky break; I have been in this business for thirty-five years and I am still waiting to be discovered! Everything you will read about I achieved through hard work and dedication. I have had 'Talk to the hand' thrust in my face many times on this journey, yet I have overcome these setbacks.

Like the writer Cormac McCarthy says in *No Country for Old Men* (2007), the line "You never know what worse luck your bad luck has saved you from" seems to tally with me. I hope this story will inspire you, in whatever life career you have chosen and give you strength to never give up. "If Andy did it, I can do it too."

Like the pressures one faces each day, such as heading off to school, the office or fencing salle each morning, all journeys need that first step to be taken, often outside your comfort zone.

These first steps always require a level of bravery depending on the individual; after all, you are heading into the unknown.

Is there a maths test I haven't prepared for? Have I failed to send that email to secure that contact? Will I have to give épée lessons all day?

You may be lucky and have a guide, a mentor, a fencing master – someone to show you where to place your feet so as not to stumble or fall. I have found those along the way, but this story begins as a solo adventure.

This story is about who I am, for better or worse.

My eyes were open and I had to make my choices alone, without a safety net, other than my loving family, who would comfort me through my mistakes and errors of judgement, with a sympathetic ear, yet were unable to offer any practical advice or give any solutions to my discomfort or often bewilderment as to what my next move should be. This journey was all new to me, as it was to them.

My ambition to join the film business was seen as my personal pipe dream, and with no financial support available, training in whatever avenue I decided on would be expensive and paid for by me. So, I not only had to work out what I wanted to do but how I was I going to fund it.

The film business is as hard to get into as Wonka's chocolate factory! I needed a golden ticket and, like Charlie, I needed to have a bit of luck and that was as hard as finding teeth on a chicken!

I come from working-class stock. My parents didn't even own a car, as neither could afford to learn how to drive. With five children, three square meals a day for us all (Mum and Dad too) was the main priority. Clothing four boys and my sister came next. It is often said that the war generation was the best. It certainly was in my family. My young life was my halcyon days. We had nothing extra and what we did have, we all shared.

I am not that ancient, honest I'm not, but technology has come along in leaps and bounds from when I started out. My children joke with me when I tell them what I had to do when I was their age and what life was like. They come back as quick as one of Roger Federer's returns, saying, "…this is not 1944, Dad!"

In those days, we rented the family television from DER. It was a huge box of furniture that took up a major part of our living room. Yet today my children can access a huge range of programming from the comfort of their bedrooms.

Jumping ahead a little, the first family computer was not bought in a store, or off Amazon. That didn't exist yet! No, our first very basic 16-bit MS-DOS computer was built by my older brother Garry. Yes, he built it! It was an Acorn Atom. Do you remember those?

Goodness, you're as old as me!

Yet now my children are part of the Xbox generation who take this advanced computer programming as a part of the natural world!

My journey started with the tentative steps of trying to work out who I was and who I wanted to be. My father gave all the Wilkinson children a bedrock, the foundation to understand who we were as people and our values. Our characters were left to our own design, with only the occasional swipe across the head with a damp tea towel by our very loving and devoted Irish mother to point us in the right direction, of course!

I am sure I won't win any prizes with this memoir. What I do hope, though, is that you will find it a useful and interesting personal insight to my experiences. I have written numerous articles over the past twenty years, mainly for the British Academy of Fencing journal, so my pen leans towards writing for friends and colleagues, for that small eclectic bunch of professionals, fencing coaches, fencers and stage-fighting actors. It is written from the heart and no ghostwriter has been engaged or used to correct my thoughts or beliefs.

Before we saddle up for the journey ahead of us, let me introduce myself properly, so we will no longer be strangers; my name is Andrew Adam Wilkinson. To be honest, the family of my birth are the only people who still call me Andrew. It was my fencing master, Professor Roy Goodall, back in 1984, who called me Andy for the first time when I attended Salle Goodall and today, I am known by that handle, in life, in the film business, in fencing and by friends and associates.

I am only called Andrew at home now by my wife and children when I am in trouble or have done something wrong, normally the telling of a bad joke.

Do you know the one about the boomerang?

No?

Don't worry, it will come back to you.

Or for my singing, which is normally in the morning and taken from the film *Singin' in the Rain*.

"Good morning. Good morning!"

You can understand why they shout out, "Andrew!"

I hope you enjoy reading this glimpse into the life of a big dreamer, have fun along the way with the interesting facts and trivia I have accumulated over my lifetime and, for those of you aspiring to work in the entertainment business, find some inspiration for your future success from someone who has never given up on the dream and has achieved a little something along the way.

I do thank my dear wife, Katy, for typing this book. My typing is not that bad, although perhaps my spelling and grammar could use a polish, from time to time.

Thanks to my dear children, Jake and Oscar, for keeping my feet on the ground and to those family members I speak to daily.

Thanks also to those in my heart whom I acknowledge for their love, especially those no longer able to stand by my side, who have never had the chance to smile or raise a glass to my endeavours, adventures and triumphs. It is to those departed I owe the most, thank you!

I am not an A-List actor or renowned Oscar-winning director (yet) and I have worked professionally in the film business for over thirty-five years. It is not always the money, the fame or the glory which is important (though some is always welcome!). It is the journey, the friendships you make along the way, the work you have done, your experiences and how you have entertained people.

"Memories, friends and 8x10s," as the old saying goes.

This is a story about a dream that came true and I hope it will inspire you to catch your dream. Before long I hope you will have new tales to tell and I look forward to hearing all about them.

See you on the red carpet!

Andy (Andrew) Wilkinson
Hertfordshire, England 2019

SCENE 1

TAKE ONE, ACTION!

FADE IN:

I am a film buff – '*buff*' definition: 'a person who knows a lot about and is very interested in a particular subject'.

Actually, I'm more than that, if that is possible. Not only am I a film buff, I am also a huge fan of the people who make them.

My lovely wife, Katy, has noted more than once that even if I have seen a particular film many times, I still run it in the background while reading a book or newspaper in hand, yet when the film finishes I lower the reading material to study the credits, once again, and comment on certain people who have worked on other films too.

Where did this infatuation come from? It is time to put me in the director's chair and ask some of those questions.

N

The tale of my journey into the film business is not going to be a 'remember when?' tale. I judge myself on my current endeavour or my next project. My past work is stored in my head and in my office, where it is used for reference. I am in a privileged position, having spent thirty-five years studying and getting practical experience to obtain my skills and knowledge.

Sourcing the photographs for this book was therefore a little uncomfortable for me. They are a record of my past, but I look forward – 'What's next?' is more of an accurate saying for me. As I said, this is not a 'remember when?' book. However, stories illustrate a point and as a child I loved stories. My mother would read them to me and my younger brother, Scott, every night before bed. I vividly remember our collection of Disney books, each with a different-coloured spine and each colour told a different tale, from the classics such as *Pinocchio* to world stories from Hans Christian Andersen.

We'd pick one and I was instantly transported to the land of the story. My brother and I would look at the beautifully drawn coloured pictures as Mum read the story. I would let my imagination run wild and create the other scenes in my head. This is how I know I dream in colour, apparently the sign of a creative – since I vividly remember dreaming about a red van, delivering bread.

The television was a box that dwelt in the living room. It told me stories too. I remember early children's programmes such as the Franco London production of *The Adventures of Robinson Crusoe* (1964), and *The White Horses*, a 1965 television series co-produced by RTV Ljubljana (now RTV Slovenija) of Yugoslavia and German *TV* (Südwestfunk). These were the stories of my school holidays and both had great musical themes, which are now my and your ear worms for the rest of the day if you remember them! *Whirlybirds* (1957) was also a favourite, which was a syndicated American adventure television series.

As I grew up watching these fabulous shows as a child, the concept of storytelling was imbedded into my inner self. I was a shy child and these stories and adventures were the formative basis of my very active imagination.

In 1965 there was a children's programme that aired for the first time which changed storytelling for children forever. It was packed full of drama, action and characters that I would emulate when I played with friends – Gerry Anderson's *Thunderbirds*.

Another ear worm!

Another integral element of the shows was dawning on me too and that was the music, with the grand themes that I would sing all day. I was hooked. For me, the path was set at this early age and I have only recently understood the effect my early childhood of storytelling was to have on my future.

"Thunderbirds are GO!"

In time I was old enough to watch certain films too. At Christmas, a favourite was *Rudolph the Red-Nosed Reindeer*, with Burl Ives, a 1964 Christmas stop motion animated television special.

As I grew to be a teenager, I would sit with my family and watch films together – this was, after all, the early days of television when it was what families did together. I loved watching their reactions to a scene within a film and working out why they responded as they did. *The Adventures of Robin Hood* (1938), Errol Flynn, Michael Curtiz directing particularly springs to mind on a Sunday afternoon. Little did I know that many years later it would still be part of my life, as in my office I have a photograph still of Errol Flynn as Robin Hood, framed and on my wall.

The Adventures of Robin Hood was a family favourite and funnily the score by Erich Wolfgang Korngold was obviously dancing to a different tune with Garry, my brother, who went on to become a composer, as Scott would too in years to follow.

Dramatic storytelling, I learned with my dad, especially in *Being There* (1979) with Peter Sellers, directed by Hal Ashby. This was a two-hour ten-minute film, which was very long for those times, and both Dad and I watched it several times, even with commercials!

At the other end of the spectrum, one of my mum's favourite films was *The Court Jester* (1955) with Danny Kaye, Melvin Frank directing. Of course, the fencing in it is outstanding, but what I remember the most is watching my mum laughing so hard, her toes curled up.

I also have a very clear memory of staying up late one weekend with my Uncle Bert to watch a Western comedy, *Advance to the Rear* (1964), with Glenn Ford, directed by George Marshall. This was such a popular film; it was turned into a television comedy show called *F Troop* (1965) with Forrest Tucker. *Advance to the Rear* was the start of me quoting from the screenplays of films that I had watched and liked. I used it for a comedic moment to describe something going wrong. "Mount up" – when Glenn Ford said this line in the film, he would turn his head to avoid seeing his cavalry attempting to mount their horses, always a comic catastrophe.

Films were magical to me and had the power to provoke such deep, unguarded reactions. The list of films I remember watching in my youth is extensive (I have put a list of over 300 films at the rear of this memoir that I either have in my collection or enjoy whenever I get the opportunity to screen them), but just to name a few more, as this is a cathartic exercise for me as I remember back to those halcyon days, these are some of the all-time classics:

- *The Wizard of Oz* – Judy Garland/Victor Fleming
- *The Searchers* – John Wayne/John Ford
- *The Quiet Man* – John Wayne/John Ford

- *Genevieve* – John Gregson, Dinah Sheridan/Henry Cornelius
- *Return of the Pink Panther* – Peter Sellers/Blake Edwards
- *The New Adventures of Don Juan* – Errol Flynn/Vincent Sherman
- *Scaramouche* – Stewart Granger/George Sidney
- *The Titfield Thunderbolt* – Stanley Holloway/Charles Crichton
- *Singin' in the Rain* – Gene Kelly/Stanley Donen

I'm sure my primary school teachers (the deputy head is still on my Christmas card list) would say I had an active imagination, and film and storytelling in general was my main source of entertainment. It consumed all my activities.

In secondary school, I would choose my school subject options on the basis of which film I had buzzing around in my head that day. One late evening, for me anyway, on television I watched *Marooned* (1969) with Gregory Peck, directed by John Sturges. An Oscar-winner, the story is all about astronauts being stranded in low earth orbit and NASA's rescue attempt. No Thunderbird 3 available in this movie, so on that day I wanted to be an astronaut and opted for maths and physics.

As I got older, I was tall for my age with a man's build already and could easily get into films that I was too young for, such as the re-release of *Dirty Harry* (1971 original release date), with Clint Eastwood, directed by Don Siegel. Now I wanted to be a policeman.

The futuristic story held no fear for my imagination either. In a re-release of a 1975 film, packed full of testosterone, as most boys are at that age, I went to see *Rollerball* with James Caan, directed by Norman Jewison. I was far too young to see this violent film. I know, I know, it would have been an 'AA' certificate, remember those?

Rollerball was the perfect adolescent film for an adrenaline-fuelled teenager. My friend and I would get our bicycles, doubling, of course, for the motorbikes in the film, put on roller skates and cricket gloves, with rubber spikes along the fingers as the metal studs Rollerballers wore. We spent hours cycling and skating, holding a cricket ball high in the air in our backyard or playground recreating the film's key moments. It was great fun.

I do believe that *Rollerball* was the very first film where the entire stunt team was credited. The director rightly said these guys deserved a credit because the action in the movie was so much part of the story.

Of course, the year 1977 to me is the best year for film-making. My favourite films, the ones I will watch over and over again, were all produced and released in 1977, including the film that has influenced me the most in my choices on this journey from a shy innocent to the man I have grown to be today.

In May 1977 I was just fourteen years old and *Star Wars* directed by George Lucas was released. I can remember telling my friends at the time, when I watched the advertisement for the opening of the film, that I wasn't interested and didn't think it would do any business at all. How wrong could I be?

I saw this film for the first time in the Gaumont Cinema in North Finchley. Sadly, it is no longer there. The film triggered something deep within me. I had seen many films even by this early stage of my film-watching life and enjoyed both film and television productions, yet *Star Wars* spoke to me, no one else in the cinema, just me, in ways other films had not done so before. Like every teenage boy who saw the film, I fell in love with Princess Leia. I was memorised by the entire fantasy. I asked myself what was all this stuff about lightsabers?

I had seen sword fights before, in films like *El Cid* (1961), Charlton Heston, directed by Anthony Mann, *The Adventures of Robin Hood* (1938), Errol Flynn, directed by Michael Curtiz, to name but two (of this much more later on). Yet this was something in a different realm. I am not ashamed when I tell you I saw *Star Wars* seventeen times in the cinema. In '77 I had no idea that this film was to play a major part in my life a mere seven years later.

Indulge me in a little sidetrack here for a moment, as this seems the place to talk about what I have in my mind. Have you seen the film *Signs* (2002), Mel Gibson, directed by M. Night Shyamalan? After first viewing it at a BAFTA screening, I really liked the plot and felt the script was very good too. Things happen for a reason and not by chance is the theme of film. As I planned this memoir, *Signs* has popped back into my head on more than one occasion. Spooky.

✘

Untimely, on June 18th 1984, Father's Day, eighteen days after my twenty-first birthday, my dear father, George Wilkinson, suddenly passed away, without any known illness or warning.

✘

This momentous event changed my world and life forever.

Who now was going to look after my family the way Dad did?

My brothers and sister were either too young to take on the mantle of looking after Mum, Mary Wilkinson, or were themselves married with their own children and had moved away from home.

The gauntlet had been thrown down in front of me and I picked it up, without hesitation.

You hear stories, I suspect apocryphal, of grandmas picking cars up off the tarmac when a child is trapped underneath and you read true heroic tales of Victory Cross awardees and their magnificent deeds.

To a lesser degree, but just as important and as real as a VC-winner, these deeds are within all of us. The questions are the same for everybody: What do I do now? How do I continue? Where do I start? How do I make everything okay again? Who can I blame for my world crumbling before my eyes?

I went through all these emotions, within a couple of minutes. No longer could I indulge them, though; I had things to do. I didn't grieve as most people do and my family tells me I carry my dad's spirit with me every day. All of us Wilkinsons do and it makes us whole, as a family.

⚡

If I were not to drown in my own dark thoughts, I needed to step up and do what I always said I would do.

Time is a great healer – it passes and you must get on with life. I was twenty-one now and decisions had to be made by me for my family. They wanted to know what I was up to and, besides that, my young brother Scott was still only sixteen.

The question 'What do I do now?' was booming in my head.

I did know this: that as a starting point, my first step into the world I wanted to be immersed in was to be found reading encyclopaedias and gaining the knowledge. My first encounter was in my school library, but we had a set of encyclopaedias at home, which I started reading avidly. These are rare books today. I believe the *Encyclopaedia Britannica*, first published in 1768, is no longer published in book form; it is an online publication only now. Why have they stopped printing it?

Google it!

I first learnt that the magic lantern was invented in the 1600s, probably by Christiaan Huygens, a Dutch scientist.

It was the earliest form of slide projector and was illuminated by candles and then, as technology evolved, was lit by increasingly powerful means.

In 1888 Thomas Edison, the America inventor, with his cinema collaborator Eadweard Muybridge, decided to combine their inventions, the phonograph and the zoopraxiscope, to create a short film synchronised with a recording.

This was the birth of cinema.

Then it came to me. I loved *Star Wars*, which had sword fights, and I loved sword fight movies, having seen so many in my youth.

Okay, sword fights in films. How do I go about doing that?

I would take up fencing. I was not a fencer's build – not slim, more like a rugby player and not from a public school; however, I needed to learn how to fence.

Please remember, dear reader, all this took place back in the caveman days of the early '80s. There was no such thing as the internet or Google; I had to read books and journals to find out the information I needed. I had no one to ask for help, so I went to a library.

Just to put this all into context, *2001: A Space Odyssey* (1968), directed by the master film-maker Stanley Kubrick, was shot a year before Neil Armstrong landed on the moon.

There was no such thing as computer-generated imagery (CGI) when this film was made. It was all achieved with practical magic or smoke and mirrors. I challenge you to watch this masterpiece and tell me you can see the strings (not that any were used).

I needed to get myself along to a fencing club first of all and yet my research also told me that to work in film you needed something called an Equity card.

I decided to think about that later – I was wearing too many hats at once so it was fencing first. I looked up my nearest fencing club in the telephone directory and came across the Amateur Fencing Association, now British Fencing. I called them and they told me the nearest club to me was run by a man called Professor Roy Goodall. Salle Goodall was the club name and it was very close to where I was living.

Being a bashful chap, I wrote him a letter after I bought a small Lilliput typewriter, to make it look professional. The letter told him that I wanted to learn how to fence and be in films and that I was working on how to get my Equity card, but I wanted to start fencing first.

Little did I know that I had stumbled across someone who had a connection with the film I saw as a fourteen-year-old at the Gaumont Theatre in Finchley, North London, in 1977. Not only that, I soon discovered that Roy was a founding member of the Society of British Fight Directors, a theatre-based organisation which taught actors swordplay and unarmed combat for stage productions.

Roy was one of many, including Henry Marshall and Derek Ware (a stuntman), who got together and founded the first home for fight directors. I saw Derek Ware on a children's TV show setting fire to himself and falling through a window. I was fascinated by that side of 'practical magic'. Years later when we worked together, I told him that story and that it had inspired me to try and get into the film business. "Sorry, Andy," was his reply.

Roy replied immediately to my letter, informing me that to work on films as a swordsman, I needed not only to get my Equity card but also to join a register held by Equity called the Stunt Register and, to do that, I needed to gain qualifications in six disciplines in various sports and activities related to stunting.

This was the first of the many hurdles I had to overcome to meet my goal. Not only did I need to learn how to fence and pay for those classes, now I also needed an Equity card and a further five skills, assuming I liked fencing, to work as a swordsman on films.

Should I give up now and save the worry and expense and get a proper job to support a future family?

No! I swallowed hard and bit the bullet. I drove to Salle Goodall and introduced myself to Professor Roy Goodall.

What an amazing man he was. I told him of my dream to be in the film business, fencing being my first step on this huge learning curve. He nodded and listened and then, like Obi Wan Kenobi in the film that got me into this business, he started my training.

Salle Goodall was a European championship-winning foil club. I then received a formatted letter from Equity on the requirements for joining the stunt register, founded in 1973. The committee of established stuntmen set out a list of sports and qualifications they thought summed up the qualities of a stunt candidate and at that time they required a Bronze Sabre Proficiency Award.

There I was at a foil club, needing to learn sabre and Roy was happy to oblige. For the first six weeks I took my sabre lessons from Roy, then stood at the end of the gym watching people fence foil. Then Roy, taking pity on this sad boy-man standing down one end of the gym, came over to me and said, "Andy, if you really want to be a swordsman, you need to study all the weapons, foil, épée and sabre, then study the historical weapons, rapier and dagger, broadsword, small sword and some unarmed combat."

Wait a minute, this all sounds fantastic, I said, but where do I go to study all this?

That is when he told me about his passion for theatrical fencing. Yes, there was such a thing, new to me, of course, yet, thinking about it, how else would all the historical films get made without people having studied the fighting of the era and learning how the fights were to be created?

I knew Roy was a founding member of The Society of British Fight Directors, but hadn't really understood that the organisation was created to offer theatrical fencing or stage combat to actors, in drama schools across the country, for the stage.

If I stayed with Roy, he would teach me the skills of a theatrical swordsman too, alongside my competitive training in what I would later call the Olympic Three – foil, épée and sabre.

Roy decided to teach me sabre first, as it was the closest to a lightsaber. He also told me he knew the person who did the fights in *Star Wars* personally. Professor Bob Anderson, who had been the national fencing coach for Great Britain during his career.

How fortunate was I?

I was not only working with a professor of fencing but a personal friend of Darth Vader!

Remember me mentioning 'signs'?

SCENE 2

A FUNNY THING HAPPENED ON THE WAY TO THE FORUM

My one-to-one sabre lessons with Roy at Salle Goodall would last twenty minutes, which was about ten minutes longer than everyone else, but I wasn't complaining. I loved it.

The sabre was then and is still the only cut-and-thrust weapon in Olympic fencing. I could see why the Stunt Register chose that weapon as one of their requirements.

The target area is everything above the waist, arms, head and back. All you could hit if you were a cavalry officer sitting on a horse, striking at a foot soldier with a sword.

I was like a sponge. I absorbed all the information Roy gave me. I asked loads of questions, which he encouraged, and I found the physical aspects of fencing, despite having a rugby player physique, quite easy and fun. The timing of a movement required some extra thought and it was clear that that would take a lifetime to master.

Our lessons, after a short while, became fast and exciting to watch; after all, this was sabre fencing in a foil club. Cut and thrust, with through cuts to chest, Molinello parries and flèches or running attacks (although these have now been stopped in sabre fencing).

The club would stop and watch me take my lesson from Roy. I was performing and I loved it! I was doing a fencing sequence with my master and, for a young man like me, it took only a small leap of imagination and I was on a film set, in costume and the club members watching me were my cinema audience.

I know, how sad am I?

After one such brilliant exhibition of sabre fencing, Roy asked if I would give an introduction lesson to sabre fencing to any club member who wanted to have a go. I said of course, I would welcome the chance. The first candidate was a young lady barrister, a foilist by nature.

Now I have always been a bit of an innocent, although not naïve, chivalrous in manner and not possessive by nature, perhaps a throwback to a different era. In my experience, this view of life does not fit well in the society we have created for ourselves. I'm not sure it ever did. In the world we live in today, I have often been taken as a fool or too polite and nice to go far. Yet I would rather be chivalrous and pay the price than conform to the majority. My acupuncturist tells me I am highly sensitive, not physically to the needles but emotionally. She is right. I am.

I can say that now, but being a sensitive person was not on my radar, especially after the passing of my father. My childhood was gone and I had to grow up overnight, so my sensitive side was buried deep inside. It didn't change my attitude to life; maybe it enhanced it. I needed to develop a hard outer skin on my work side of life – that of a rhinoceros. More on that later.

The young lady took her lesson from me and it went very well. I was able to teach in the same way Roy taught me. I took on other pupils too for both foil and sabre. She asked for another the following week and this continued for several weeks. Fencing etiquette requires that after a fencing lesson or bout, the two fencers shake hands with their non-sword hand. Of course, the historical reason for this is to show that you were not carrying a dagger or blade in your non-sword hand as you got close to your opponent.

Our handshakes got longer and longer – not so much a handshake, rather we were holding hands. Thinking back… no, it was not soppy – mind you, I am a sensitive soul these days.

I will not go into any more detail in this memoir regarding our courtship, suffice to say that the young lady was indeed Katy and we have been together for thirty-one years and married for twenty-two years. My immediate family is made up from this encounter in Salle Goodall, two children and a Labrador, Buster. This is my family.

It turned out that I was a natural at coaching fencing. I found it easy to explain to people how to complete fencing moves. I wanted them to do well and felt if they didn't, it was my fault, so I would find another way to explain. I was to put this to good use in later years at the Cutting Edge Fencing Club.

Roy too was impressed and urged me to get some formal qualifications. The course Roy found for me to attend was at the Army School of Physical Training (ASPT) in Aldershot, home of the British Army. Through Roy's connection I was billeted in the sergeants' mess and it was very kind of the army to host a civilian fencer. The coach in charge of the course was Warrant Officer Peter Whiteside. I was thrilled to be invited to attend. How fantastic was this! The ASPT was then, and I am sure still is, a unique establishment of outstanding quality. As a civilian, from the moment I parked my car I had to follow the army rules and regulations while on MOD property. For example, walking was something they didn't understand. It was not allowed for enlisted men. Everywhere you double time – you run, no walking allowed, whether from the fencing salle to the NAAFI (Navy, Army and Air Force Institute, in case you didn't know – or you can call it the canteen) or to get something from your car, you *ran*! I didn't mind this at all. The rugby fellow I was could have done with the extra training.

The course attendees were made up from regiments from across the globe. All ranks were represented, from privates to NCOs to officers. On my particular sabre course there was a major and I noticed that when we were sent for tea over at the NAFFI, though we'd all run over, the major would casually stroll behind us.

By the third day curiosity got the better of me and I asked why he wasn't running like the rest of us. Without missing a beat, without any further comment or smile on his face and in a most matter-of-fact way, he said, "Officers don't run, it panics the men!"

This was such a great title for a future film or book, it's a wonder I haven't used it for this tome!

The sergeants' mess was a great experience for a young man who hadn't been exposed to the real world outside of my training schedule and home responsibilities.

Looking after my own quarters was a chore I had been trained well in by my mother. Buying beers for others in the NCO bar was an easy task. The soldiers made my life there very comfortable.

I was telling them of my sudden awakening to life on the passing of my father and the struggle that lay ahead for me to gain an Equity card plus all the extra training I needed, with no one in a position to help me. There was a collective view every night in the NCO bar that I should change my direction. I could look after my family and have a great life, while being paid, if I joined the army.

"Get behind me, Satan!" I silently said to those smiling faces every night after training. I did not want to be a soldier as I was so focused about learning how films were made and becoming a sword master.

Coaching at ASPT was so different from the methods at Salle Goodall. At Salle Goodall I was encouraged to ask questions and constantly tested on my fencing vocabulary, by Roy and other senior fencers, so that to this day my vocabulary of fencing terminology is second to none.

In the army, Coach Whiteside would introduce his lessons by saying we were going to study a particular move in a particular way. Being a civilian and not understanding the army regime and how these classes worked, I would raise my hand and ask questions, mostly starting, "Why?" His reply was always the same: "Because I said so."

I gave up asking. I fully understand why the army teach this way. When an officer asks a soldier to jump, the answer is never, "Why?" It should always be, "How high, Sir?"

The fencing salle at the ASPT is steeped in history and there are centuries of tributes marked out in gold paint on white wooden boards and black and white photographs of fencers on courses throughout their noble history.

Fox Gym, just 200 yards from the fencing salle, was then the largest gymnasium in the world. It looks like you could park a jumbo jet inside with room to spare!

This was also the first time I came across bayonet fencing. There were long wooden rifles with a large, metal spring-loaded bayonet for practice, although they were not sharp as they had a rounded metal button on the end. I learnt how to bayonet fence, during our rest periods. An odd, but logical on guard (en guarde) stance is required. Most people are right-handed and the rifle butt goes in the right shoulder, so naturally your left foot is forward. This feels very odd compared to fencing, where you would lead with your right foot if you are right-handed.

Derek Everard, British Academy of Fencing (BAF), was the chief sabre examiner and I still have his book on sabre fencing in my collection. I was delighted to have passed the exam on my first attempt after all my hard work and study.

As part of the exam process, all B.A.F. examiners provide written comments on how to progress your training, areas that might need improvement and things you did well. It has been very helpful and is a practice I have followed when teaching too. When I got home exhausted, blisters on my feet, I turned up to Salle Goodall, showed Roy my exam papers, and he said, "Yes, not bad, do better next time," and handed me back the exam papers.

"Yes, Master…" but I passed my exam!

∕

The best analogy to describe what fencing is all about is this: "Fencing is physical chess. For every move there is a counter move and you must have the physical capability to execute that move within one twentieth of a second."

In the Olympic sport of fencing, any longer than one twentieth of a second is considered a delayed action and your opponent has the right to renew their attack. Of course, that does not apply in swordplay, except that the idea of physical chess is certainly important in choreographing a fight for the screen. Imagine my delight when Roy said to me, "Andy, if you want to learn how to do film sword-fighting, and be the best you can be, you need to study more than the sabre fencing required for membership of the Stunt Register. You need to learn all the weapons, foil and épée too, plus, rapier and dagger, court sword, broadsword and some unarmed combat. You are a natural coach. You are personable and the club members enjoy your company. Become a coach and you can pass on what you have learned to beginners."

I smiled from ear to ear!

Roy Goodall began my training. I was under his wing and became his assistant – a 'Padawan', if you'll excuse the *Star Wars* vernacular.

My library search for a fencing club eighteen months previously, not only found me Salle Goodall, but a fencing master who was also a founding member of The Society of British Fight Directors (SoBFD) and who could teach me so much about my chosen career. This information was not listed in the phone book!

'Signs', anyone?

The SoBFD was formed by fencing masters and fencers involved in theatre and film swordplay. Its mission was to teach the art of theatrical fencing to actors, mainly in drama schools, to a high standard and provide an accredited examination at the conclusion of the course, enabling them to show producers and agents they have trained and passed an exam in theatrical fencing, unarmed combat and swordplay.

SoBFD was a unique, pioneering organisation, run by professionals, on a volunteer basis. The formula of training and examination has been copied the world over. This role has now been taken up by a number of organisations in the UK, for example by a direct descendant of the SoBFD, The British Academy of Dramatic Combat (BADC).

Roy taught me foil fencing next. The foil is a thrusting weapon and you can only score with the point of the blade. The target is the torso excluding the arms and head, yet including the groin at the front with a horizontal line across your hips at the back. The foil originates in historical duelling where it was a creation of the ancient masters to teach rapier, safely. A practice weapon in effect, which has become the most popular fencing weapon coached in the world.

I enjoy foil fencing very much and in swordplay in films and in theatre terms, we fight directors use the foil to teach and coach actors' point control. I have included more on how, when and why you use certain fencing actions in later chapters and have added a useful reference section at the end of this adventure which clarifies fencing terms, if you are unfamiliar with them.

Épée was next on my to-do list. The king of the Sunday crossword puzzle. The épée is the closest to the rapier sword that you will find in Olympic sport. Like the foil, it is a thrusting weapon. You cannot score a point using the edge of a foil or épée, only with a sabre. However, in épée fencing the target area is the entire body – hands, feet, legs, head and torso, front and back.

⚡

Salle Goodall was not the place to learn the other weapons I needed such as rapier and dagger, broadsword, small sword, court sword, quarterstaff and so on. It was a competitive fencing club, not a drama school. At that time, Roy was the sword master in residence at the Webber Douglas Academy of Dramatic Art, known the world over as Webber D, and he very kindly allowed me to shadow him when he taught there.

Sadly, Webber D is no longer with us, closing its doors to the arts in 2005, however the alumni read like a Hollywood movie cast list. To name but a few: Stewart Granger, Angela Lansbury, Donald Sinden, Antony Sher, Minnie Driver, Hugh Bonneville, Steven Berkoff, Julian Fellowes, Terence Stamp and, an old friend, Kevin Howarth.

Roy was responsible for the majority of the alumni having a sword comfortably fit in their hand and I trained with him there for five years. I never missed a session and learnt something every day, and this was at the same time as my competitive training at Salle Goodall.

✴

As well as fencing three to four days a week, I was working hard on my other skills too, such as swimming and lifesaving, weightlifting and parachuting. I obtained my preliminary teacher's certificate for swimming while I was doing my fencing coaching certificate training.

All these classes and courses needed to be funded by myself too. I was living with my mother and though my father's pension helped keep the wolf from the door, that was all there was in the kitty. At the start of the summer, I decided I needed to get a job to finance my training.

That was fortunate, as Haven Holidays was running a course in Hale, Cornwall, and they needed a level-one fencing coach to teach the children fencing. I now had my foil as well as my sabre coaching award and a swimming teaching qualification too. I applied and got the job!

PGL courses were great fun. The children had their own name for them, PGL – 'Parents Get Lost' courses. Staying in the Haven camp gave my family relief from having to feed me over the summer too. However, after the summer, the bills kept coming in, so I needed a daytime job to continue the funding of my training.

I found an advert for a security company, Securicor, who were looking to hire drivers to deliver cash to and from banks. The wages were good and, after training, I became a driver with a senior custodian, the boss of the truck, assigned to me.

I was given a crash helmet with a padded neck guard and a bulletproof vest. My first job was to collect cash from the bank vaults and deliver it to Heathrow for the ATMs there. I kitted up, helmet and vest, but noticed the custodian didn't put on his bulletproof vest. As before when I was training at the Army School of Physical Training, curiosity got the better of me and I asked the question, "Why no vest, Guv?"

"No point," he calmly said, "they never shoot you in the chest anyway. They shoot you in the legs, so you can't chase after them."

I stopped asking him questions after that too.

✗

I started to get my portfolio of stunting requirements together. I had my BAF coaching qualifications, but to my horror as I double-checked Equity's requirements, I found they wanted the Amateur Fencing Association Bronze Sabre Proficiency Awards. I had been working within the BAF's professional coaches' system.

The AFA offered bronze, silver and gold in each Olympic weapon. Although the AFA syllabus was not an easy award to obtain, bronze was well within my capabilities at all three weapons. I showed Roy the Equity requirements and the AFA Awards details. He nodded in acknowledgement and said, "No problem, after our coffee, kit up."

I was so lucky he was able to examine these as well. AFA bronze was a common award, silver was rare and gold awards were pretty much unheard of. Happily, Roy got me to gold standard in all three weapons.

According to the issue numbers on the certificates, I was the first ever to attain the épée gold, the second to attain the sabre and the twenty-eighth to attain the foil award.

After four years of training with Roy at Salle Goodall, he advised me to join the BAF as a member. He would sponsor my application and I was honoured that he felt I would be a good candidate.

The Academy is an ancient order of fencing masters founded in 1540 by Henry VIII. Its letters patent are still available in the Public Record Office, I believe. I was accepted and made a member in 1988 and it has been a large part of my life for much of that time as a member of the committee and for Golden and Diamond Swords, of which more later.

⚡

I was progressing well with my skills and now looked to getting my Equity card. To become a member then, you had to have, I think, three Equity contracts. Three decades ago, when I was trying to obtain membership, Equity was functioning as a closed shop. An unwritten agreement under which the film companies would hire only union members in good standing. This resulted in a 'Catch 22' situation, named after the book by Joseph Heller, later the 1970 film of the same name, starring Alan Arkin and directed by Mike Nichols. You could not get an Equity-related job, which you needed to get enough credits to obtain Equity membership, without first having done enough Equity-related contracts to become a member. Catch 22.

How on earth could you possibly then ever become an Equity member? No end in sight, no way out. After all my training, there was just no way I could jump that last hurdle.

Give up and go home?

No, there had to be another way. Was everyone on a film an Equity member?

Back to my library search. I read David Niven's biography *The Moon's a Balloon,* published in 1971. He talks eloquently about his start in Hollywood as a film extra which had its own union. You were not a fully accredited actor but you at least had access to a film set. That was a thread I needed to follow. There must be a union or guild for the making of British films with extras. I found that it was the Film Artistes Association, better known as the FAA.

I took the Tube into central London where their head office was based. I had no appointment and I didn't even know who I wanted to talk to, but I had to start somewhere. I found the offices and I entered. There was only one person in the entire building, an older gentleman. I explained my intentions and he listened to the entire saga.

When I stopped to take a breath, he jumped in and said he was the number one FAA member, the chair. He must have felt sorry for me since he signed me up on the spot. I was now a member of the FAA, with the telephone number of their agency, Central Casting, which would call once they had some work for me. I do believe that Sir Michael Caine is still a member. My journey was no longer a gentle stroll on my path to being a film swordsman, I was about to flèche!

↗

Central Casting was good to me and I got plenty of work. I remember my first job. It was for Tennents lager and I was a customer in a pub.

The first day I walked onto a film set, the smell of the hot lights and the atmosphere, the smoke machines they used in the scene, struck me like an arrow immediately and my first thought was, *I am home. This is where I belong.* The first assistant director (AD) set up the scene and I received my instructions. I wasn't allowed to have the glass with the product name facing the camera, since if I did I would I get an extra fee, which the production company did not want to pay. I wasn't to look at the camera, rather to look through it, as if it wasn't there. I had to turn a certain way and wasn't allowed to make any noise. I was to look as if I was speaking to those around me, silently. This was my first real experience of the practical side of film-making. The main cast were getting the money for the dialogue.

I was as happy as a sandboy.

Unknown to me on that day, the director, regrettably never introduced to me by name, liked my face. No comments, please. The scene we were working on was to incorporate the spilling of a drink over a customer in a comic moment and that customer was going to get wet. The director looked at all the people around the actors and stopped at me. He said, "I like this man's face." The first AD stood next to me. "…This is the one I want to have the drink spill over."

For me it was a 'stunt moment', though really it was just a little piece of action, on a commercial, for which I got a little extra money on top of my daily fee. The money for the day's work was very good. There were no residuals – the payments you get for each showing of your 'performance' – for this, however, they 'bought me out', which was reflected in my higher day's salary. Even if it were shown over and over again on television, I wouldn't get any more money. But I didn't care; I was on the set with a film camera, lights and action. I was on the set and I had got there on my own!

This first day rewarded my dedication and confirmed that I was on the right path. I had got there myself, the first Wilkinson to work in the film business and to be on television. I was very pleased. The journey had reached its first station, even if my family and friends still didn't quite understand that I had arrived; after all, it was still a pipe dream, wasn't it?

I did learn something else that day. The more they asked of me, the more money I could get. That came true on my second job. This was a Monty Python co-production with BBC Wales for a children's television show. I was to play a tattooed truck driver.

I have no tattoos, so on arrival at the location I was ushered to the make-up department. The lovely lady there sat me down and began to shave the hair on my arms. She then stencilled tattoos on to my arms. You honestly couldn't tell they were not real ones. The scene was for me, the truck driver, to discover a stowaway in the back of my lorry. I had dialogue too, both in English and, due to this being a co-production with BBC Wales, in Welsh. My daily rate was calculated by Central Casting as 'Dialogue, Tattoos and arm shaved'. No residual fee, as I was still working on my FAA card, not an Equity card. Nonetheless, it was a great day's work!

All the work I was offered was not on an Equity contract and FAA work is not eligible for consideration for Equity membership. However, I was learning something that no one could teach me, something that you can only learn by experience and being there on set, watching and listening. For me, this was a golden opportunity to learn things which I still use every day when I work – *film set etiquette.*

I can say this with authority as someone who has worked up from the bottom of this business, with experience of almost every job in front and behind the camera under my belt: you will not progress far if you do not understand and respect film set etiquette.

I cannot teach all of it; film courses and drama schools cannot teach all of it. It is the understanding of how a film is made, the knowledge of who is there on the set and how to respect them, which you can only learn when you are there. For example, you should never hang your coat on an empty light stand. Everyone from the man sweeping the set to the A-list star getting out of make-up for their scene will understand and respect it.

N

I was attending a course one summer at Missenden Abbey. This was a great sideline for Professor Goodall, as he was holding a theatrical combat course there which I would also attend, learning both theatre and film fighting.

On this particular course, an established veteran stuntman, whom I knew of but had never met before, was attending. He was small in stature, very agile, very fit, an acrobatic type of stuntman who worked doubling many film and TV stars; you'll know him from his work on *Last of the Summer Wine*. On the course, he would do lots of tricks with the swords – flipping them from his foot to his hands, juggling them, but not fencing with them. Roy, as the course director, asked him if he had any advice for his assistant, me, and he said, "Andy? I don't think he'd make a stuntman or work as a film swordsman, because he's too posh, he speaks too nice."

I was too nice to be a swordsman?

Roy couldn't understand or believe what he was hearing and his lovely wife, Professor Angela Goodall, added some colourful metaphors to Roy's comments. The film action world of swordsmen and stunts, according to this active and working stuntman, had an unwritten class system and only the working class could be stuntmen. Yet hang on a minute, despite that BS, I am working class!

You will hear me say this more than once in this memoir, to succeed in this business you will need to have a skin as thick as a rhinoceros to maintain your focus.

This was my first hard knock. I have no problem working hard, struggling even, to find the funds to train, but I had no answer, no argument, no skill to tackle a totally biased attitude to my professional behaviour and the way I spoke! I started growing my rhinoceros's skin that very day.

I met a horseman on a subsequent Missenden course who also had an early encounter with working stuntmen and he too didn't fit in. This time nothing to do with how he spoke, but personality. He was advising on setting up a jousting show at Camelot Theme Parks in Preston, where Equity card contracts would be available. My ears pricked up.

At this point in the journey, please let me introduce you to my elder sister, Maureen (Muzzy) Wilkinson-Till. Muzzy and I are particularly close, the only girl in the family, apart from my mother. She was a horsewoman who started at the bottom, mucking out stables and earning her tuition. She became a qualified riding instructor with the British Horse Society (BHS). Muzzy taught me how to ride and I still have the scars to prove it, so I have been riding and caring for horses since I was a teenager. Traditional English riding, of course – both hands on the reins, rising trot, all very proper, yet not what is needed for film.

Have you ever watched the jousting scenes in *El Cid*, for example? Have you wondered, if a rider holds the reins with two hands, how he also holds the lance, or a sword and shield? There had to be something else, another way to ride.

Back to my telephone directory and the library I went before I applied for a job at the theme park. I needed to know more about jousting and what it was I was required to learn. I found there was actually an organisation called the British Jousting Federation (BJF) based at Leeds Castle, in Kent, run by a man called Max Diamond.

I really just wanted to be a swordsman, yet I was being forced by the closed shop rule at Equity to explore essentially what I needed to qualify as a stuntman. Nonetheless, I gritted my teeth and drove to Kent to meet with Max. His jousting base in Leeds Castle was a hive of activity, full of horses, armour and swords, with training fights going on everywhere. I told Max my story and he said, immediately and with no hesitation, that I was too posh to be a stuntman. Imagine that. In the space of a couple of months two people had told me that all my training, all my hard work and expense, was for nothing, as I would never be accepted as I spoke 'too posh'.

I got a flavour of what the stunt register was all about then in the late 1980s and I never wanted to be a stuntman... a sword master, yes! I was the new kid on the block. I was getting qualifications in sports that were on the register but to a much higher standard, as I wanted to be a sword master.

However, I was very fond of Max. He was a lovely rogue of a character and had a wonderful way of talking to people that surprisingly put them at ease. He used to shout in a big, bellowing voice, frequently, in the yard around the horses and all the noise before a show, particularly when something didn't go quite as he wanted. I especially remember him shouting, "I love you dearly, but don't f**k me about!"

I never rode for Max, as he was not geared up for training people, but he gave me lots of good, sound advice, for which I thank him. It is hard to imagine, especially for my children and their peers, but I was doing all this background checking and research on how to become a swordsman in the movies before the internet, when Google and other search engines were not even a twinkle in Tim Berners-Lee's eye. In case you don't know, he is credited as the inventor of the World Wide Web!

I would write at least one letter a day to keep my journey moving forward and booking the next part of the trip. I might get one or two replies each month, if I were lucky.

After seeing the John Wayne film *Hellfighters* (1968), directed by Andrew V. McLaglen (the actor Victor's son), I fancied trying my hand at oil well firefighting, just to keep me busy and off the streets, so I wrote to Red Adair in 1985. The film *Hellfighters* is based on his life and exploits. I still have his reply; for some reason I can even recall the address: Paul N. (Red) Adair, Katy Freeway. *Katy* freeway? 'Signs' again?

There is no chapter about me being an oil well firefighter. Sadly, although the letter was very friendly, as you would expect, there was no job invitation attached!

I know that the fairer sex likes to claim they have the skill of multi-tasking down to a fine art, compared to us drone bees. However, my early years of study, learning and working to fund my journey to the practical magic station of film were tasks with few acknowledgments of a job well done. You have to keep going and have faith in yourself and your abilities and believe that, despite the solo adventure, the dream will come true.

𝄪

With all these activities and skills under my belt, I still needed an Equity card to be taken seriously as a professional. Thus, it was I drove up to Preston, Lancashire, to visit my colleague from the Missenden course. Although Camelot Theme Park is now no more, it was a thriving theme park at that time. My visit to Max Diamond of the British Jousting Federation in Leeds Castle was useful and I rode a few horses for them at Camelot. By falling off horses, and despite a few bruises, I got my Equity card!

I was moving forwards, having started my training and gained several qualifications. I had my FAA card and now my Equity membership showed I was a professional in the film world. With no foresight when Equity asked me my name, I gave them my full birth name and that is now the name on my Equity card. With a little thought, I could have been known as 'Andy Hunky Swordsman Wilkinson', but, alas, it was not to be.

SCENE 3

"A LITTLE TOUCH OF HARRY IN THE NIGHT", SHAKESPEARE, *HENRY V*

Having discovered this drive and focus, I did feel like I was the only one on the planet striving as hard as I was. Of course, this was absolute rubbish. However, compared to me, my friends, for various reasons, seemed to be content with their lot in life. The grass for me was always greener over the fence.

As I pushed for more and more, my fencing master, Prof Roy Goodall, quietly got on with being a sword master on films.

In 1985 Roy was engaged to choreograph and train the young cast in Barry Levinson's great adventure *Young Sherlock Holmes*, starring Nicholas Rowe. Roy choreographed a number of exciting swordplay sequences for this film and I recall being his stooge partner, off set, working through the routines before Roy would go to train the cast at the studio. Nicholas Rowe, a fine, underused actor, is left-handed, so being right-handed myself, I had to swap hands when we were working out the opponent moves for the film.

Young Sherlock Holmes is one of my favourite films, not just for the swordplay, which is just what the director wanted, but there is a wonderful twist at the end of the film. You have to watch the credits to see it – it is well worth it.

Sadly, this film raised an issue that was new to me back then, but one I am very familiar with even today. *Young Sherlock Holmes* was a Hollywood feature film produced by Mr Steven Spielberg's company, Amblin Entertainment, and Roy was the assigned fight director. However, his credits were mainly in theatre work. Roy, founder of the Society of British Fight Directors, a three-weapon competitive fencing master, professor of the British Academy of Fencing and instructor at numerous drama schools, did not receive a credit for all his fabulous work on this film.

Equity at that time was apparently not aware that theatre fight directors and stuntmen were two totally different breeds of people, in the eyes of the people who were in the business of stunting and fight direction. I learned on my journey to be a sword master, as early as 1985, that the saying 'never the twain shall meet' applied to film and theatre action or, perhaps more dramatically, they would never work together, much to my bewilderment.

I heard this directly while working on another film, as an unknown swordsman, having been found to be handy with a sword on an earlier film and not yet labelled as being from one side or the other by the people involved. They were proud that Roy had been prevented from receiving his credit, even though they were unworthy to be labelled as fight directors on either side of the fence.

This was an unwritten rule and you will not find it in any Equity documents, which hosts both stage and film members, but nonetheless this is a fact. I will leave it to others to say whether the situation has changed since 1985 and professionalism now rules over ego. Let us hope so.

N

The next film I was called for was *Slipstream* (1989) with Mark Hamill, directed by Steven Lisberger. I recall the film as having a super, international cast. My role was to be killed off in the opening sequence, nothing new here, I soon discovered, by a machine gun and then to be crushed by a stone column (not a real stone, of course) falling on top of me.

This was my introduction to visual effects on film. To simulate me being shot, the special effects team attached a few squibs or blood-filled capsules to me. These were wired to an electronic board, programmed to go off on the call "ACTION", when the bullets hit.

That's all I remember from this film, except I became aware of a simple yet, very important fact. If you want to be employable in this business, any business come to that, you *must* show and prove your indispensability to the company or unit. Be useful, on time, do what you're asked to do the best you possibly can and be polite, to everyone, when working. It's easy to be big-headed and rude: "I'm in the movies, I'm being paid, I am someone, get out of my face," and so on. It is much harder to be a good, hard-working, nice person, which I endeavour to do daily.

Ian Hickinbotham, who was the second assistant director (AD) on this film, was also second AD on *Young Sherlock Holmes* in 1985, and he remembered my association with Roy and how poorly he had been treated on that film, not by the production company but by those less qualified who were protecting their jobs.

Ian asked if I had kept up my fencing and, of course, I gave him my résumé on the spot. A helpful piece of advice is never to ask an actor how they are doing, unless, of course, you are prepared to hear a full résumé of their work in response.

Ian said they were about to go into production on a new telling of Shakespeare's *Henry V* and he would keep me in mind for the battle scenes. I thanked him very much. The first AD on *Slipstream* was David Tringham, who would be the first AD on *Henry V* too. A charming man with a huge amount of experience, including work as second AD on *Lawrence of Arabia* directed by Sir David Lean.

'Signs', anyone? I must stop doing that... Sorry.

✗

In between my working on *Slipstream* and *Henry V*, I worked on *Mountains of the Moon*, starring Patrick Bergin and directed by Bob Rafelson. The release date was 1990, as it was released late, and there are tales on film distribution which belong in another book!

This was the first time I met the legendary stunt coordinator Alf Joint. I had studied everything there was to learn on Alf Joint's work from books and by watching films he had worked on. I first came across his name when I was studying the grandfather of stunting on films, Yakima Canutt. Yak's list of film credits is simply amazing. He started to show all stuntmen how to do their work and, more importantly, how they could do it to come back another day to work again, raise a family, buy a house and be as safe as they could be.

Yak also changed how animals were used and treated in films. The turning point for the entire industry, worldwide, was the 1936 *Charge of the Light Brigade.* In one particular action sequence the stars of the film, Errol Flynn and David Niven, were horrified at the amount of injury and death the horses were suffering as they were brought down by trip wires and ditches to simulate being shot for the action sequences to be filmed. Errol Flynn called Yakima Canutt personally and asked for him to come out and sort out the action: "...too many horses were being hurt." Yak arrived and stopped the practices, instead using his team of horse-wranglers and horses that had been trained to fall without injury to work on the film.

Thanks to Yak, organisations such as MAP – Movie Animals Protected – and PETA – People for the Ethical Treatment of Animals – were allowed to establish groups to oversee films. Actually, I think I am right in saying that animal rights were in place in Hollywood before child protection was enforced.

Why is Yakima considered by many in the business as the grandfather of stunting?

If I list a few, and it is only a few, films for which he was the stunt coordinator, you might get the idea:

- *Gone with the Wind* (1939) – he doubled Clark Gable in the burning of Atlanta sequence. (The giant wall burning in this sequence was actually the giant doors from the 1933 original *King Kong* film.)
- *Ben-Hur* (1959)
- *Spartacus* (1960)
- *El Cid* (1961)
- *The Fall of the Roman Empire* (1964)
- *Cat Ballou* (1965)
- *Khartoum* (1966)
- *Where Eagles Dare* (1968)

In *Where Eagles Dare* (1968) with Richard Burton, directed by Brian G. Hutton, Yak had a cable car stunt to film. The location for filming this was in Austria, and before I met Alf Joint, I visited the location as part of my study. I wanted to see the mountains and the scene of this dangerous stunt for myself. I went with a school friend, Michael Smith, who would later play the 'Padre' in *Birth of a Legend*, but more on that later. It was an exciting sequence and one of his stuntmen was Alf. I am not sure if what I was told by a fencing student is true or not, however, he said some years later that he had the chance to meet Alf, told Alf he knew me and that I was teaching him how to fence and swordplay. To my delight Alf said, "Andy, a top hand. I gave him his first job!"

/

While I was on the set of *Mountains of the Moon*, Kenneth Branagh's *Henry V* was now in full pre-production and at the studio I bumped into Ian Hickinbotham, who was to be the second AD on *Henry V*. He was heading over to the costume department and said he was meeting with Phyllis Dalton, the costume designer. I tagged along.

I was bowled over by the sight of the king's tabard on a mannequin and have to say the work of the entire department was breath-taking. It was no surprise that Phyllis Dalton won the 1990 Oscar for Best Costume design for *Henry V* and I was so honoured to see the costume in the studio that day.

Shepperton Studios was to be *Henry V*'s base. A field on the studio grounds was set aside for the battle scene rehearsals and it was here that all the soldiers for the Battle of Agincourt assembled. Ian met me on arrival and introduced me to Vic Armstrong, the stunt coordinator. This was our first meeting. Vic is the natural and obvious torchbearer for stuntmen, who can stand side by side with Yakima Canutt. He is a prolific stunt coordinator and many of the signature films in the latter half of the twentieth century are Vic Armstrong films. We shook hands and he said, "Ian tells me you're great with swords. Fancy taking this bunch and turning them into an army?"

I said, "Nah, I'm fine thanks…"

HA! No, I didn't say that, of course. I'm not an idiot. It's just the way I comb my hair (thanks, Mr Bob Hope).

The soldiers for the Battle of Agincourt were real soldiers from 2 Parachute Regiment – Territorial Army. Having been to the ASPT in Aldershot I knew they would take instruction, and they did. They were brilliant – enthusiastic, keen and followed my instruction without hesitation.

Using canes only at this stage, I taught them the eight guards first. Then after a while, I taught them some simple attacks, nothing fancy. Once they were happy with all that, I said okay, break up into pairs, threes too. Now have a sword fight, but remember what you are doing, so you can repeat it! I will come around and mark you out of ten. The best of you will be in the foreground, the others will be used to fill up gaps. I can tell you now, I could have put them all in the foreground; they were an army of medieval soldiers. Vic was impressed.

I too got to be a soldier, both French and English, and loved every day I worked on that film. Working with Vic Armstrong was one of my golden ambitions and it came true. I learnt a huge amount from him. We still keep in touch and his book is a must-read.

There is one moment I would like to share with you. In Act 4 Scene 7 the English children, back at the camp, are murdered by the French knights on horseback and this horror is discovered at the close of the battle: "Kill the poys [sic] and the luggage! 'Tis expressly against the law of arms."

This scene was filmed with the king, Branagh, picking up and carrying one of the slain children, Christian Bale (yes, Batman), to a cart at the far side of the battlefield. A long tracking shot was used, the camera on a dolly that is on a trackway. Now, what Mr Branagh chose to do then was very clever. He choreographed the action to move with the camera, riders on horses as well as the foot soldiers and women grieving their losses, all to the music of Patrick Doyle's version of 'Non Nobis Domine'. For filming, he placed a dozen or so very large audio speakers behind the camera and out of shot so that stirring music could be heard by all.

It was a very emotional scene to film, let alone watch! Big butch stuntmen could be seen after David Tringham yelled,

"Cut," wiping their eyes, claiming the field was dusty. It was muddy not dusty, but I too was wiping the 'dust' out of my eyes.

If you do not know Patrick Doyle's version of 'Non Nobis Domine' from this film, then please do listen to it. Every time I hear it, I am immediately a knight waiting to go into battle.

This piece of music is so important to me, Katy and I had it sung by a choir in the church when we got married. It is that important to both of us.

※

The entire Armstrong family are all involved in the stunting world. Vic's lovely wife, Wendy Armstrong, *née* Leech, is a stunt woman and Vic's brother, Andy Armstrong, is also a stuntman.

My next encounter with the Armstrong 'Stunts Incorporated' team was on *Nightbreed* (1990), with Craig Sheffer, directed and written by Clive Barker. I had the opportunity to work closely with Andy on this film, almost from beginning to end. I had multiple roles and characters to play.

The story is about the monsters of the night, a fantasy horror adaptation of the Clive Barker novel; the story was about where the monsters hid. Median was a complex of catacombs that hosted the fabulous creatures at night, and this was built on the back lot of Pinewood Studios.

My first role was to play an armed posse member, who was tracking down the monsters and firing AK47s at anything that moved in the night. Then I played one of the two 'Berserkers', a massive monstrosity with grotesquely misshapen heads and heavily muscled. In one scene, towards the end of the film, Midian, the home of the Nightbreed, is blown up, releasing the Berserkers to revenge the attack. Jesse Johnson, Vic and Andy's nephew, and I were dressed as Berserkers in a full body suit and head/mask. Since we were going to use explosions and fire, this was a night shoot. Fire or flames always look best at night. On "Action", the first couple of explosions went off, using explosive cork tiles, and gasoline made the flames. Jess and I then attacked the fleeing posse.

We then strode over to a police car parked inside the catacombs where the actor Charles Haid (Andy Renko from *Hill Street Blues*) was barking orders to the posse to stand their ground. Mr Haid was the only actor I ever doubled for.

Jesse and I, with help from the visual effects team, threw the police car over the wall, with the police chief still inside. Then, and this is a clever bit of smoke and mirrors, the film cuts to a posse member, the Rocket Man, played by me. I took position by a burning tree with a hand-held rocket launcher, took aim at the two Berserkers, fired and missed. I then strode to camera as a Berserker to kill the Rocket Man – myself!

A clawed hand, worn by the designer of the suit, then tore my face off in close-up. You can see the continuity photos of the make-up later in this book.

N

Once again, I enjoyed the experiences of working with the Armstrong family immensely and there was talk that they might need me on their next production out in Mexico, *Total Recall* (1990), with Arnold Schwarzenegger.

Unbeknown to me, and I still don't really know the full story, there was a problem with the team of UK stuntmen travelling out to Mexico. I'm sure Vic picked the best he could, but my name was not on the list. Besides, I wasn't really a stuntman; I was a swordsman, but working for and with the Armstrongs I felt I had become a 'useful hand', and when the job needed to be done, I would have done it.

N

My next swordplay film came along almost immediately. *Robin Hood: Prince of Thieves* (1991), Kevin Costner, directed by Kevin Reynolds. Word of my work on *Henry V* obviously got out, although I was never told by anyone outside the *Henry V* family that that was why I was hired. I was asked to teach swordplay to Celts and Merry Men; some of them came from *Henry V* and some were new to swordplay.

In one scene, Morgan Freeman had to show the Merry Men how to use swords, so I had the pleasure of showing Morgan Freeman a few moves with a sword to look good for camera, and if you look at the film, it is me he is teaching! I also have a little knowledge, through my studying of all aspects of battle scenes, of how to make fletchings, the wings of an arrow, and again, if you look in the film, you see me doing just that.

I had a recurring role as an unnamed Merry Man and this made me available to coach any swordplay to the extras as and when I was required to, especially in the numerous battle scenes. I even played a captured Merry Man, a tortured soul, back at Shepperton Studios.

It was at Shepperton Studios, after a long, thankless day, being ignored by the stuntpeople I was supposed to assist, that I had a flashback to what had happened to Professor Roy Goodall on *Young Sherlock Holmes* six years earlier. Nothing had changed; I was a qualified swordsman, yet I was never going to be accepted as such. I was being forced to be a jack of all trades, someone to be plugged in anywhere. Despite being useful and never turning down an assignment on film, I was not going to be allowed to move on from this position.

After work, with nothing for me on the call sheet for the following day, a few swordplay fighting actors and I went for a cool beer in the Shepperton bar. I came to a major conclusion on my journey. I told them of my decision. I was going to get off this train and change platforms. Go in another direction, still in the film business but with a different hat on. They were all startled and all tried to persuade me to remain, as I was employable and valuable to them, at least, as I was training them and giving them skills which they found it hard to find elsewhere. I had spent many weeks on *Robin Hood: Prince of Thieves*. It wasn't as fun as *Henry V* or *Nightbreed*. I felt I was used beyond the call of my duty, although I of course delivered every time I was asked.

This is not paranoia on my part. Please forgive my moaning here, but this is important, as it was the reason I became a director and writer. The great stunt coordinator and second unit director Max Kleven, a tall, American cowboy I had learned about while studying Yak and Alf, noticed there was an atmosphere between me and one stuntman in particular. I had remembered him as one of the stuntmen from *Nightbreed* that Andy Armstrong asked me to replace for a scene. Max suggested that I could move on from what I was doing; try America, he said, I 'would be snapped up there'.

Indeed, my contributions were not always welcome by some, but I remained professional and the unit directors knew that.

✕

It was time. There had been a number of sword films over the past six years, all productions based in the United Kingdom, and thankfully I had had an involvement, in one capacity or another, in all of them. I was not interested in being anything other than being a sword master.

The films that were now in favour did not require European classical swordplay. *Crouching Tiger, Hidden Dragon* (2000) was becoming the norm in Hollywood too.

The producers doing the hiring forgot about our ancient history of sword-fighting and jumped on the wagon of the Eastern style. Don't believe me?

Look at the new *Star Wars* films; can you see classical swordplay with the lightsaber? Is it what Obi Wan Kenobi described as, *"...the weapon of a Jedi Knight. Not as clumsy or random as a blaster. An elegant weapon... for a more civilised age."*

As well-trained swordsmen and historians of European sword-fighting, ignored by Hollywood for too long, Ralph Faulkner and Fred Cavens must be spinning in their graves, looking down on these new sword films.

The CGI sword fights are unrealistic, unbelievable and nonsensical. Any live action is now mainly achieved with actors on wires, suspended in the air, and in disbelief, they fight, spinning and twirling with swords in hand, sometimes two!

The choreographed swordplay from the likes of *The Mask of Zorro* or *Scaramouche* has been washed over for now. Please, please do not misunderstand me. There is a place for the Eastern-style martial art form of swordplay, but to sacrifice entirely our own classical form of swordplay is a price too high to pay. I was a highly qualified swordsman and I needed to express this the best way I could. In the bar at Shepperton Studios I decided to become a film and theatre director and a screenwriter.

Now, how the bloomin' heck was I going to do this?

SCENE 4

SWORDSMEN OF
THE SILVER SCREEN

Despite all the action films I had been involved with, my passion was still very much in the world of swordplay, and I brought that baggage with me when I changed track.

My own research unearthed a name, a man whom I had never heard of before, yet he was instrumental in the life and career of the first celebrity of Hollywood, Douglas Fairbanks Snr. The name I discovered was that of Henri J Uyttenhove, Hollywood's first film sword master.

Who were these unsung heroes calling themselves sword masters, I wondered, and can I be one?

That simple find, in a dusty old book on Hollywood, piqued my curiosity and lead me to gain a little authority on the subject that I bring before you today.

Uyttenhove was born in 1878, in Herch-La-Ville, Belgium. Although he only worked as a fencing advisor on ten films from 1917 to 1923, his collaboration with Douglas Fairbanks on three films, *The Mark of Zorro* (1920), *The Three Musketeers* (1921) and *Robin Hood* (1922), established Uyttenhove as the pre-eminent silent film sword master.

Uyttenhove led the way where other fencing masters would follow. With the evolution of camera design and techniques, sound and film stock quality, plus new dynamic storylines, the action sequence, as we know it today, was born.

N

Sadly, as I have mentioned, the European style of swordplay has been replaced by an Eastern style of martial art sword-fighting. The ancient history of the European duel has, in the movie business, anyway, been abandoned and forgotten.

If you look at the new series of films, they are without question in the style of martial art swordplay. No graceful conversations between the blades, duels of technique by experts or empathic routines reaching a crescendo. All frenetic, fancy, jumping and bouncy ball-fighting, bashing the weapons together now and again. Not the weapon or style of a Jedi Knight. A Jedi would still be elegant and quick, even if he were fighting someone who was not a fencer. Is this the writer's misunderstanding of the concept of a lightsaber or the fight choreographer's, or simply tailoring for Eastern audiences?

Phew, I feel better now that is off my chest! I would welcome a chat, Mr Lucas, if you're interested in reviving the blades of a Jedi Knight...

N

Uyttenhove gave grace and skill to such silent film stars as Fairbanks, Alan Hale, Robert McKim and Bert Lytell, underpinning their legendary swashbuckling credentials that survive to the present day.

On the other side of the camera, the first actor to reach superstar status in the halcyon days of the silent film era was the self-proclaimed King of Hollywood, Douglas Fairbanks. It was Uyttenhove and Fairbanks that first used the science of ergonomics, the designing and arranging of the set, including furniture, so that people could use them easily and safely in an action sequence. A trick that does not go unnoticed by modern-day action stars, such as Tom Cruise.

If you watch a Fairbanks film carefully, you will think all his actions in the film were effortless and that was because the whole set, staircases, balconies, ropes, for example, were designed to be within his easy grasp or reach. Fairbanks was able to slide down a staircase with his hands on the bannisters, looking graceful and elegant, as it was designed that way. He certainly could not have made the same entrance down the magnificent, yet wide, staircase at Tara in *Gone with the Wind.*

Ergonomics can also be seen in Gene Kelly's version of *The Three Musketeers* (1948), directed by George Sidney. Kelly was a dancer first and foremost and then learnt the swordplay. He was so elegant and gymnastic; the swordplay was almost like a ballet. All he did was in his physical boundaries and beautiful to watch.

✄

Frederic Adolphe Cavens was born to French parents in Lacken, Belgium in 1882; aged seven he was enrolled into the prestigious Military Institute of Physical Education and Fencing (Belgium), where he was first introduced to the art of fencing.

Fencing struck a chord with the young cadet and by the time he was fifteen, Cavens knew he wanted to be a fencing master, and by the age of just twenty-one he had achieved his ambition.

Around this time, Cavens met and fell in love with a ballet dancer from the Belgium Opera Company; marrying her, he decided to emigrate to the United States, where he would set up a fencing school in Hollywood to train fencers as well as budding actors.

Fairbanks was so impressed with Cavens' work on *The Three Must-Get-Theres* (1922), directed by Max Linder, he engaged Cavens as fencing master (the term sword master was yet to be coined) on his subsequent films *Don Q, The Son of Zorro* (1925), *The Black Pirate* (1926) and *The Iron Mask* (1929).

Fred Cavens defined the work of the film sword master as surely as Yakima Canutt is credited with defining the work of the stuntman.

Cavens laid down the essential characteristics of the screen duel, perhaps for the first time:

> "All movements – instead of being as small as possible, as in competitive fencing – must be large, but nevertheless correct. Magnified is the word. The routine should contain the most spectacular attacks and parries it is possible to execute while remaining logical to the situation. In other words, the duel should be a fight and not a fencing exhibition, and should disregard at times classically correct guards and lunges. The attitudes arising naturally out of fighting instinct should predominate. When this occurs, the whole performance will leave an impression of strength, skill and manly grace."

Cavens tutored many stars in their swashbuckling films: Douglas Fairbanks Snr and Junior, Errol Flynn, Louis Hayward, Cornel Wilde, Basil Rathbone and Tyrone Power, to name just a few.

Cavens' son, Albert, born in 1906, assumed his father's role and doubled for Power extensively in *The Mark of Zorro* (1940).

For me, the sabre duel in this film is perhaps the finest

example of theatrical sabre duelling currently on film – the cadence, accuracy and the choreography are outstanding. You really believe they are having a fight.

N

When I started my training as a fencing coach under the guidance of Professors Roy and Angela Goodall, the name of Ralph Faulkner would often crop up in our sessions.

Faulkner's achievements as a sabre world champion (1928), a two-time member of the American Olympic Fencing Team (1928 and 1932) and then as a swashbuckling film swordsman and fight choreographer were inspirational to me, especially at that early time of my training and study.

Faulkner was born in Texas, at the time a US state known more for the Alamo, cattle trails and cowboys than for world championship fencers.

Coming from Texas, Faulkner not only had a fencing career to build, but he also had to face the challenges of doing so despite what he refers to in an interview in 1983 as 'the elite of the East Coast fencing Salles', who at the time, "…didn't feel a savage from out West could be superior."

Echoes of the words I was hearing from the established stuntmen working in England at the time, that I was 'too posh', don't you think?

Faulkner entered films as a fight double and choreographer in 1921 and for the next thirty years, Faulkner's movie list reads as a history of Hollywood's halcyon years of swashbuckling films that included *Anne of Little Smoky* (1921) to *The Three Musketeers* (1935), *Captain Blood* (1935) and *The Sea Hawk* (1940).

Faulkner's skills were still in demand in his ninetieth year, working for MGM once again on *Clash of the Titans* (1981). A career spanning well over forty films in sixty years.

It is noteworthy to mention here that not once did Faulkner or any of his contemporaries ever receive an on-screen credit for their work as fight choreographers or doubles for the stars of these films. Don't forget that this was the time of the studio system in Hollywood, when the off-screen reputation of the stars was tightly controlled and publicity had the film-going public believing that the stars could do everything they saw on film. Faulkner did some acting as a sideline, twenty-three films and television productions in total, where he did get screen credit. Actors had a stronger union, I guess!

Faulkner never stopped coaching competitive fencers while working in films, opening his fencing school 'Faulkner's Falcon Studio' on Hollywood Boulevard. He attracted both fencers and actors, especially those actors looking to pad out their résumés or just train with the master fight choreographer himself.

Faulkner would later reflect on some of the more famous of his students with footnotes on their personal performance. Here are a few to amuse you:

Errol Flynn	"he could memorise every movement in a sword script and remember them six weeks later."
Ronald Colman	"not the athlete Flynn was."
Basil Rathbone	"an accomplished swordsman."
and	
Douglas Fairbanks Jr	"he got into fights because he tended to be a little mouthy."

In a full and productive life, Ralph Faulkner could not only claim to be a world-class fencer, a legendary fight choreographer but also a childhood business partner of Dwight D. Eisenhower, as he and the future five-star general and President of the United States fished for carp and sold them for twenty cents apiece.

To the day of his death, Faulkner was known for his decorous posture and the time-honoured courtly and stern visage of the fencing master. His students knew him as a disciplinarian who brooked no nonsense, whether they were famous or not.

⚔

The last swordsman of the silver screen I would like to mention is Professor Robert (Bob) Anderson.

My two sons Jake and Oscar met Bob while I was directing *Diamond Swords* at Warwick Castle. Bob was the guest of honour. The boys had just finished a taster fencing session and showed Bob their certificates. Without missing a beat, Bob asked for a pen and he signed the certificates. They are treasured possessions, from Darth Vader himself, since Professor Bob Anderson was the sword master on the original three *Star Wars* films and played Darth Vader in the fight scenes.

Professor Anderson was the national fencing coach for Great Britain. He was a past President of the British Academy of Fencing. His film works include choreographing fights for Errol Flynn, the *Star Wars* films and a Bond film. He also worked as a stuntman.

As you may remember, I was moaning earlier about how martial art swordplay has eroded European swordplay in the *Star Wars* franchise and I can pinpoint when this event occurred. When Bob was too ill to work on the new films and unavailable, no qualified sword master substitute was hired.

Fencing masters such as Uyttenhove, Cavens, Faulkner and Anderson all excelled in the disciplines of all three weapons and were champions themselves.

↗

In the classic John Ford Western, *The Man Who Shot Liberty Valance* (1962), Senator Ransom Stoddard (James Stewart) returns home to Shinbone for the funeral of Tom Doniphon, (John Wayne). Stoddard recounts to a local newspaper editor Maxwell Scott (Carleton Young) the true story behind his early life in Shinbone as a lawyer. Scott is shocked to learn the truth about who actually shot Valance:

Ransom Stoddard:	*You're not going to use the story, Mr Scott?*
Maxwell Scott:	*No, Sir. This is the West, Sir. When the legend becomes fact, print the legend.*

This maxim must be applied liberally to the stories that surround Errol Flynn. Separating the wheat from the chaff is a difficult task since so much misrepresentation has been printed and broadcast since Flynn's first emergence on screen as Fletcher Christian, *In the Wake of the Bounty* (1933).

It is safe to assume, however, that his swashbuckling persona spilled over from the silver screen and it followed Flynn for the rest of his life, like a technicolor phantom, haunting his off-screen life as he tried in vain to live up to his own screen image. No matter how ridiculous the accusation or scandal surrounding his personal life, the public believed in the legend and the story stuck to him like cocklebur.

What can one say about Flynn's *Robin Hood* that has not already been said by better critics than I? It is a fabulous adventure story on every level and is my favourite Robin Hood film depiction, this coming from the man who contributed to the sword work on Kevin Costner's version, *Robin Hood – Prince of Thieves* (1991).

If you have not seen Flynn's *Robin Hood*, you have missed a wonderful film experience.

A bit of a diversion now; the horse Olivia de Havilland rides in the film is a Palomino. (The breed was, in fact, not found in England in that period of history. We will skip over that lack of attention to detail, shall we?) The horse was called Golden Cloud. Golden Cloud was later bought by Roy Rogers and renamed Trigger – 'the smartest horse in the movies'. Trigger lived a great life until he died in 1965 aged thirty-three.

Stuntmen too had their well-trained steeds close to their hearts and home. John Wayne's stunt double, Cliff Robertson, had a horse named Cocaine; Hal Needham's was called Zorro. All these stuntmen loved their animals and were broken-hearted when they died.

Good falling horses in the film business created by Yakima Canutt could earn more than a bank manager, it was said.

I digress a little, but to finish the point, when Trigger died Rogers did not have the heart to bury him, so he had him stuffed instead, in a rearing stance no less!

Errol Flynn's first starring role was in the classic Michael Curtiz-directed film *Captain Blood* (1935). The endorsement of Flynn by Fred Cavens, sword master on *Captain Blood*, helped to promote Flynn as the true heir apparent to Douglas Fairbanks. The die was cast and a string of swashbucklers followed, all produced by Warner Bros and with the same troupe of actors reprising roles that were little different to the previous films. The public loved them and they were the golden fleece of the box office. The name Errol Flynn became synonymous with the swashbuckler genre, yet he only ever made a half dozen or so in his film career. It is a testament to his skill, enthusiasm and passion that he will forever be remembered as a swaggering swordsman, soldier, adventurer and daredevil.

Two of my favourite films are *The Adventures of Robin Hood* and *The New Adventures of Don Juan* (1948). In Robin Hood, Olivia de Havilland shone as Maid Marion and as I write she is a sprightly 102-year-old, living in Paris, and the last of that acting dynasty.

A great fight is like a tsunami – it starts shallow and then grows and grows until it reaches its crescendo. The wave length and height can be short or long, rise and fall, be interrupted or hold its breath – unlike a real fight, where you would just hit them!

In *Robin Hood*, Rathbone is killed by Errol Flynn. The move is a compound attack, point to chest, feint to head, hit to chest. A classic fencing movement and a fitting end to the Sheriff.

Where Fairbanks' style was always graceful, using ergodynamic sets and lesser 'skilled' opponents, Flynn's style of swordsmanship was, in my humble opinion, often clunky. His swordplay punctuated his dialogue with large exclamation marks of movement followed by a change in rhythm, often to allow him to negotiate the obstacles of set design and props. Flynn obviously had a bad back and you can see it in his stance in *Robin Hood*, sticking his bum out all the time! He was, though, a real professional, learning every element of his fights and replicating it over and over again.

Flynn's nemesis in almost all of his swashbuckling films was, of course, Basil Rathbone, who was an outstanding fencer in his own right, winning a British Army Fencing Championship. He maintained his high standards of fitness, fencing knowledge and practice throughout his life. This made Flynn's epic climactic duels with Rathbone that little bit more special and believable, as you had two swordsmen capable of winning, making their fights more edgy, whereas you were left in no doubt at all that Fairbanks was always going to win.

The New Adventures of Don Juan has everything, even a synchronised fencing class sequence. The swordplay is fun, light for Flynn, and exciting. I would have to say the final duel between Flynn and Robert Douglas, a wonderful English actor, is outstanding and brilliantly filmed by Vincent Sherman.

In this final duel, which takes place on a magnificent staircase, the final death thrust is delivered by Flynn, in truth doubled by stuntman Jock Mahoney (Oscar-winning actress Sally Field's stepfather), leaping from high up on the staircase to floor level – it is a breath-taking leap that brings an end to the dastardly Duke de Lorca.

Also, you should never underestimate the musical score to Flynn's films, an advantage Flynn had over the silent era of Fairbanks. Erich Wolfgang Korngold's (1897–1957) magnificent Oscar-winning score for *The Adventures of Robin Hood* underscored the magical events taking place on the screen.

Flynn was just fifty years old when he died in Vancouver, Canada, suffering a heart attack after what was said to be a last binge-drinking party. Who is to say what the truth is other than this – a candle that burns twice as bright burns for half as long.

※

One of the best proponents of the sword, much underrated and often forgotten by swordplay historians, is, of course, Stewart Granger.

Granger was born James Lablache Stewart in London in 1913, taking his middle name from his great-great-grandfather, the actor and opera singer Luigi Lablache. A man blessed with a magnificent bass voice, a skilled performer in the *Commedia dell'Arte* style of performance, one in which Granger would reprise for his own performance as Scaramouche in the film of the same title (1952).

The duel in *Scaramouche* was at one time the longest on film. I would need to check to see if that has been bested by the numerous *Game of Thrones* and *Vikings* television series now on. I doubt it, however, as screen time is valuable on television.

As a young man, Granger attended Epsom College as a medical student, but that Lablache gene was far too strong to be ignored and Granger soon abandoned his medical career seeking employment as an actor. As mentioned above, it came as a surprise to me that out of the sixty-four films credited in Flynn's filmography, only a handful are actual swashbucklers. Similarly, Granger only made a handful of swashbuckling films in a career spanning fifty-six years.

Those he did make are noteworthy for many reasons. *Scaramouche*, *The Prisoner of Zenda* (1952), directed by Richard Thorpe, and a decade later the lesser-known *Swordsman of Siena* (1962), Baccio Bandini, stand out for me.

The main theme and soundtrack from *Swordsman of Siena* is, in my opinion, one of the best swashbuckling themes ever penned by composer Mario Nascimbene.

Granger was so dedicated to the art of fencing that he worked for months with the sword master Jean Heremans and it was said, "Granger took so many fencing lessons, the practice made him wear out a dozen or so pairs of fencing shoes."

On the release of *Zenda*, Stewart Granger even adorned the cover of *Life* magazine; the title was 'Stewart Granger: Swashbuckler'.

Perhaps the only actor superior to him in fencing at that time was Basil Rathbone, who has been the opponent to so many of the stars. Never the good guy, save perhaps when playing Sherlock Holmes.

Yet another side note here. Of all the films and television productions I have been associated with, I never won a sword fight or a fist fight. I was always the loser, the bad guy, never the hero. Life can be tough! HA!

The fencing sequences in *Scaramouche* and *The Prisoner of Zenda* are, for any sword master, the foundation on which the understanding of how to train, stage and film a dramatic sword fight is built.

Comedy swordplay is notoriously difficult to choreograph well. Ralph Faulkner set the standard in *The Court Jester* (1955) and, though many have tried to imitate it, few have accomplished the ideal.

As a child growing up watching swashbucklers on the television with my dad and younger brother, probably on a lazy Sunday afternoon, I didn't realise that Robin Hood or the Sheriff of Nottingham had to train to be swordsmen. Fencing… what's that? The actors placed in these magnificent sets and costumes had the task of bringing to life the weeks and weeks of training for the screen.

In fact, I did not think about their swordsmanship at all. I just loved watching them fight exciting duels, often to the death, in castles magically lit by half a dozen candles!

✳

I cannot fail to mention in this part of the memoir the art of the duel. *The Duelists* (1977), Harvey Keitel, Ridley Scott directing, is an excellent story of the duel, as is *Le Bossu* (1997), Daniel Auteuil, Philippe de Broca directing, which is a full-on sword flick!

The Duel of Honour has a code by which all must abide. The code consists of twenty-six written-down rules – the first three (for pistol duels) are this:

I. The first offence requires the first apology, though the retort may have been more offensive than the insult. Example: A tells B he is impudent, etc. B retorts that he lies; yet A must make the first apology, because he gave the first offence, and (after one fire) B may explain away the retort by subsequent apology.

II. But if the parties would rather fight on, then, after two shots each (but in no case before) B may explain first and A apologise afterwards.

III. If a double exists who gave the first offence, the decision rests with the seconds. If they will not decide or cannot agree, the matter must proceed to two shots, or to a hit if the challenge requires it.

A further twenty-three rules are in the code. It resembles STEAM or non-electronic fencing as there were four judges, your seconds, to ensure fair play. It is fair to say it is a lengthy code and presents a complicated etiquette for drawing first blood and even killing someone.

The question that I am sure has crossed your mind is, why are fencers historically considered the best fight choreographers, not just your enthusiastic sword-thumper?

I do have an answer for you; my one-word answer will, however, require explanation if you are not a fencer, yet.

A fencer should be able to say, "Aha! Of course." The word is… drum roll please… is…

Vocabulary…

Okay, "What the heck is he on about now?" I hear you cry.

In film action, scenes may seem chaotic and random, but they are not. They are choreographed so that the cast know what is going to happen in the sequence, when it is going to happen, what their reaction is to what is happening, how to do it safely, *and* the camera needs to film the action, so that the editor has some good footage to cut together to make the film.

Now think about a sword fight and all its variations – offensive moves, like an attack; defensive moves, like a parry; movements, such as steps or running, close up or further away... all of the sequence will need to be executed with the same amount of energy levels as the first time. Not only that, exactly the same movements have to be recreated multiple times to film the whole scene from all the camera angles required for continuity, the edit and the lighting.

As the fight director or sword master, you can train the cast to do all the physical movements, but you need to record all the action so it can be repeated. Fight notation is therefore vital. This is the common language between the fencing masters and those who execute the fight sequences so well.

You could write it out in long hand, but it is much better to use the language of fencing and swordplay. The vocabulary of the weapons describes the blade actions and physical movements designed in the sequence. You can then share this common language. Scribbles, arrows and dots mean nothing but a bunch of scribbles, arrows and dots to the reader who is not familiar with your language. Using the vocabulary, you then describe the fight in the notation. There are many formulas for fight notation and there has to be more than one of you who can read and understand it or it has to have a Rosetta Stone as the key. Choreographing fights for a ballet, for example, I have seen various methods. Personally, I use musical staves, which are a set of five horizontal lines with four spaces that each represent a different musical pitch. I simply substitute the musical notes with parts of the body, starting above the top stave, which is metaphysically then associated with a simple blade or body movement, thrust, parry, head, duck, lunge and so on. This is then symbiotically connected with the musical score.

As I continue my endeavour to emulate Cavens' magical duels on screen, two of his films remain my *raison d'être* – *The Mark of Zorro* and *Scaramouche.*

If Fred Cavens was the kindling for me becoming a swordsman and later, in a kind of meandering, eclectic way, a director, then Ralph Faulkner was certainly my inspiration to keep that flame going.

If I have learnt anything at all, it is that the very best theatrical fencers, Fairbanks, Flynn, Power and Granger, learned their craft from fencing masters.

Fred Cavens died a year before I was born. He left an indelible legacy of sheer magic on the films he worked on and he inspired me to take up the sword, under my fencing master and mentor Professor Roy Goodall (also sadly no longer with us).

SCENE 5

IN DAYS OF OLD...

As you have probably realised by now, and rightly so, I am a bit of an anorak when it comes to fight choreography, period weapons, period styles of fencing and swordplay.

When I first picked up a sword, quarterstaff, chain and ball or shield, I had had no training other than my own study. I had not yet had the pleasure of working with Professor Goodall.

I found a job providing the entertainment at banquets. I was the white knight, champion to the king, who was a budding comedian. Dressed as a knight, I would walk round the banquet being the host, talking and laughing with the guests, whilst my friend acted the black knight, stealing their food and wine. At the end of the evening, we would provide the climax to the dinner with a massive fight set to the music of *El Cid*, using broadswords, chain and ball, shields, quarterstaffs and just fists, with crushed polo mints being spat out as the lost teeth! Needless to say, the guests roared for both sides and loved the entertainment. I won, of course, and, as the guests cheered, I took my bow and delighted in having thrilled them all with my knowledge and understanding of the history of what we had portrayed.

This little job started my interest in the world of the chivalrous knight. The named swords of the great knights, Arthur's Excalibur, Charlemagne's Joyeuse and the two swords of El Cid – Tizona and Colada.

I enjoyed my detailed study of the medieval period. I was surprised to learn that King Arthur's famous table where his knights gathered at Camelot was built by a knight for that sole purpose. The builder's name was Sir Cumference!

What do you mean, "ouch"?!

I wish I had had the time to study theatrical plays as much as I wanted to. I have dabbled as often as I can in Shakespearian plays and can honestly say I know most of the fights. However, my knowledge of the rest of the stories is rather sketchy, to my shame.

My knowledge of film swordplay and routines is much better and of a higher quality, much to the annoyance of those who are sitting near me watching a classic piece of swordplay. The running commentary is the price you pay when I am in the room.

The study of historical swordplay covers a wide spectrum of topics from weapon design and their use, to political and military history, through global campaigns, political geography and architecture. The study of defensive structures, from Iron Age hill forts such as Maiden Castle in Dorset, to castles such as Arundel, a medieval example in West Sussex or the Tower of London, is fascinating. There are so many magnificent forts and castles, and it is a pleasant duty for me to visit them all. In the hallway of my house, I have prints of castle fortifications. Have you ever noticed that many Europeans castles have arrowhead-shaped battlements rather than the square or round turrets we are familiar with in the UK and in Disney movies? The round ones I think are more aesthetically pleasing and being extremely thick were very effective, yet the arrowheads provided a really different defence perspective and were adopted as functional and cost effective.

My study has not, therefore, been restricted just to the United Kingdom's fine history. European history is equally as fascinating. *Golden Swords©*, which was staged at the Globe Theatre, London (of which more later) covered European swordplay from 1540 to the modern day.

That show, although comprehensive, is a shadow only of the study and the number of books I have read on weaponry, fencing, knights, horsemanship, film production, fight choreography, stunting and stunt people, castles, history, combat, conflicts and battles. I have combed second-hand bookshops up and down the country, for many of the older books are no longer in print, especially on weapons and how to use them, castles and structures, history from Roman to medieval times, and the weapons and fighting styles of gladiators. I have a respectable library and it has been a wonderful way to spend weekends, looking in old bookshops and at castles.

I'm thinking back as I write this memoir about how I felt when I would visit a castle, often with Katy. I always knew instinctively I was a swordsman when entering the grounds of the castle, fortification or walking on the sacred grounds of a battlefield. A knight or swordsman, not a king, ready to defend my castle keep. I was not an Olympic-style fencer, although I had spent three decades of my life learning the art. I was a swordsman; this I felt in my core.

Ask anyone who knows me and they will happily tell you I don't look like a fencer. However, as casting agents will tell you, with a broadsword, small sword, lance or mace in my hand, I really look the part, totally at home in chainmail and armour.

To this very day, I feel drawn to a different era or age quite strongly. I am not a religious man; however, I feel I would have thrived in the medieval period. I don't believe in reincarnation or past lives, but my wife and family have said I was born in the wrong historical time. This I believe is the residual imprint of immersing myself in these textbooks over many years, as the best Hollywood sword masters have done before me.

I am curious, however, so here is a question for all of you, especially my friends and colleagues. Do you feel the same way as I do when you visit somewhere historic, a castle or fort or a battlefield, not just a manor house? What are your emotions?

✎

Grabbing a handful of topics, as you would as a kid in Woolworths when buying your sweets for the week ahead from the pick 'n' mix, I have put together an 'Andy mix' of some interesting and tasty bits on the development of swords and sword-fighting. I am not a historian and each area of this might be a lifetime's study in its own right. Yet as a sword master, I have found it fascinating to learn how the development of swords, shields, armour and even fashion were intertwined and led to the development of different styles of fencing. I have found you must be knowledgeable about as many types of swordplay as possible, so you can understand how to recreate these for film. It seems to me that these are at least some of the major stages on the evolution of swordplay.

Are your fingers ready to get those sticky, chunky bits out of your molars? Then here we go.

At the start, Bronze Age swords couldn't take a sharp edge and would have to be re-hammered after each use. They were therefore largely percussion or beating weapons, relying on force to create disabling injuries. The introduction of iron to metallurgy made a huge difference as it enabled a sharp edge to be maintained easily by the sword wielder, making them more portable across distances, yet they were still not primarily thrusting weapons. Perhaps the best and earliest known use of the small sword was by the Roman army. Their small sword, or *gladiolus* (after which my favourite flower to give to Katy is named – gladioli), had a style of fighting in which the non-sword arm and shoulder were covered with padding and used as a shield to deflect blows. How their fighters were trained has been of particular interest to me. *Spartacus* (1960), Kirk Douglas, Stanley Kubrick directing, gives you a great example of gladiatorial training, as does *Gladiator* (2000), Russell Crowe, Ridley Scott directing, which also amply demonstrates the entire armoury of weapons and fighting skills which had to be learned. Not only the gladioli, but also the trident with net, spear/lance, axe and mace (although these were not used widely within the legions themselves).

The Roman legions were also experts in shield defence and movability as a unit. For example, in the Roman tortoise, or *testudo*, the soldiers at the front and sides interlocked their shields, with the remainder placing their shields over their heads to form a protective shell in a very strong, tight formation. Likewise, the phalanx or (pl. phalanges) was a rectangular formation, usually composed entirely of heavy infantry armed with spears or pikes or sarissas, which were 4–6m (13–20ft) in length, making it impossible to get near them.

The percussion style of fighting with swords changed little over the centuries, although by the time of the medieval knights the broadsword had evolved into a very heavy percussion weapon, with a hand and a half hilt assembly, often called a bastard grip. The guard position was solid to support the weight of the weapon and involved the left foot being forward for a right-handed person, with the sword held upright over the now back leg (right foot). This would be reversed in years to come when thrusting weapons evolved.

It was Sir Laurence Olivier who created the myth that a knight in armour needed to be winched onto his horse in *Henry V* (1944). Knights were trained from an early age and were in fact strong and fit. I mentioned the padding used by the Romans for the non-sword arm and as a defensive shield. This idea evolved and improved as weapons became sharper and techniques more sophisticated. Chainmail, for example, is believed to date back to antiquity and, in the West, was adopted by the Romans after they realised its potential after fighting the Celts. It is a type of armour consisting of small metal rings linked together in a pattern to form a mesh, which gives obvious protection against a percussion but not thrusting weapon. Together with full suits of armour, they would have been very time-consuming to make, expensive to buy and heavy to wear and so in antiquity, only the rich could afford to wear them. Although costumers like Berman and Nathan or Angels produce a very authentic-looking chainmail (essentially a thick knit like string of very heavy gauge and sprayed silver or metallic), it should not be used too liberally on sets for that reason.

The mobility of chainmail is extraordinary against the protection it offered. In a double bonus for me, whilst researching the science of the manned spaceflight programme for my documentary *False Dawn: The Promise of Apollo* ©, I found that engineers from the US National Aeronautical Space Administration (NASA) studied the suits of armour in the Tower of London. They looked at how well the metal suits plated together, covering a great percentage of the body, and yet how flexible it was. Did you know you can lunge in a full suit of armour (although the lunge was not used in mediaeval times)? NASA used these ideas to develop the space suits for the moon walkers.

In reality, a knight was able to move about and mount a horse easily using a block step up and whilst on his horse, he was all but invincible, favouring an axe, mace or flail when in battle, as less skill and control was required. Once toppled, you could spend ten minutes hacking away with a big sword at someone wrapped up in thick plate armour and be exposed to attack yourself while doing so, without really getting anywhere on the downed knight. Thus, it was the unmounted squires, following the battle, who, if they saw a knight fallen and unable to move quickly, would find a flap or gap in their armour and dispatch the knight with a thin blade or dagger. That is where the saying 'a chink in your armour' hails from.

Those who could not afford the luxury of metal resorted to leather, although this too was expensive due to the tanning process. Living next to a tannery was always smelly as they used urine to soften the leather. The urine was collected in pots or buckets and you were paid for the amount you delivered to the tannery. The poorest of the poor were those who didn't even have a 'pot to piss in' to earn money this way.

At the lowest end of the scale, thick padded and quilted cloth was quite common, very similar to the costume I am wearing in the Battle of Agincourt photo in this memoir, for which the costumers won awards. As a fighter wearing quilted padding, it would be easier to thrust with a sword rather than raise your arms to wield a percussion weapon, as the material would restrict your movement, yet the swords were not designed for this. It would also make any fight much slower, which is something to bear in mind when recreating such scenes.

Surprisingly, not everyone got a helmet either. Again, you would have been rich or a favoured fighter to afford a metal helmet or perhaps have acquired it from a downed adversary. Instead, you might have a hood or coif (a close-fitting cap) made of chainmail or material, depending on your status.

Shields too were used for personal defence and came in various shapes and sizes depending on your resources and the period you came from. They were your calling card and announced your allegiance or country or, in later years, your personal coat of arms or heraldic family crest. You can easily imagine how the large defensive shields of the Roman or Norman foot soldiers developed into the knight's shield which was large, heavy and tapered to a heart shape so it could be carried on a horse. To beat that shield, the broadsword needed to be of reasonable weight and that in turn required two hands to wield it. Since that was not possible whilst on horseback and carrying the shield, a single-handed axe or a chain and ball or mace was developed. The latter was also known as a holy water sprinkler – to brain and bless you at the same time!

Knights were still vulnerable to archers, of course. There are people more qualified than I to talk about archery, although I know a little about the history of the longbow as I have had some practical training and read about their use in battle, especially at the Battle of Agincourt.

What I did discover, and this too is in my memory box, is that to be an archer you would have to be well nourished and a fit individual to be useful. This was not for the desk-bound! When the *Mary Rose* was recovered, a cargo of longbows was found which was on board when she sank. When these were tested, they found a force of 90–110 pounds (400–490 newtons) was needed to draw them – that's like pulling someone weighing six and a half stone across your chest every time you fire an arrow. An archer's game to show off his prowess was to fire ten arrows before the first one landed!

Recent archaeological digs have found what are believed to be the remains of archers of the period, with distorted spines due to the tremendous forces required to let loose an arrow from a longbow and differences in diet compared to the foot soldiers.

There is great debate over whether the sticking up of two fingers or V sign insult derives from the Battle of Crécy, which was fought on 26 August 1346 in northern France, where captured archers had their draw fingers amputated to prevent them from drawing their bows. The two-finger salute being to show their adversaries that they were still able to fight and draw their longbows. I hope it is true, as when driving, I am just showing the other drivers who have been naughty that I am just an active archer – nothing else, honest, officer!

What really ended the era of the knight was gunpowder, which, according to a ninth-century text, was probably discovered in the East by alchemists as an accidental by-product from experiments seeking to create the elixir of life.

It was the Silk Road that allowed the news about gunpowder to travel and made it available in warfare to everyone who was interested, for a price. This was the terrestrial trade route, connecting East Asia and Southeast Asia with East Africa, West Asia and Southern Europe, along which the lucrative trade in silk and other goods was carried out some 200 years BC. The first military applications of gunpowder were developed around 1000 AD, although the use of it was prevalent in the East centuries before it was used in cannons in Europe.

It sounded the death knell for the armoured knight, as the explosive and accurate nature of the powder and projectiles could penetrate his armour with ease. It also put the archer and the longbow into the shadows of warfare, despite their success at the Battle of Crécy. At that battle, an army of English, Welsh, and allied mercenary troops led by Edward III of England, engaged and defeated a much larger army of French, Genoese and Majorcan troops led by Philip VI of France. Some sixty-nine years later, the Battle of Agincourt, 1415 (which of course I fought in, *Henry V*) was famous for the use of the longbow too. However, it was the Battle of Flodden in 1513 that is noted as the last battle on English soil to be fought with the longbow.

Time moved on and, in the same way that suits of armour had evolved, there were a lot of overlapping sword designs and it took time for one style to win out over the other. Sword design is an oxymoron, mixing inspirational and enlightened design with a bewilderment of practicalities, social etiquette and fashion, all thrown together.

Percussion fighting was still championed in England during the late sixteenth and early seventeenth centuries by a swordsman and writer, George Silver, who was born in 1550. A true gentleman of England, his most famous writing on the art of swordsmanship was entitled *Paradoxes of Defence* in 1599. In this tome, you will read comprehensive arguments for the percussion, or blow, approach and how he thought that the transition to pointed or thrusting weapons was ambiguous at best.

The move to pointing or thrusting weapons was affected by a small change in how you held the sword. Imagine you are holding a sword in your fist to strike a downward blow on your opponent. Now from that closed fist, extend the index finger of your sword hand and allow the sword to rest along that finger and your thumb. You can now hold a sword, depending on design, between your hand and index finger with the ability to thrust and to direct the point accurately. This is the European style of fencing. It eventually evolved into the rapier, a little longer than the modern-day épée at just under 100cm. In later times, smaller shields like a buckler were used with these smaller (compared to broadswords) thrusting weapons. Swords and shields are intimately connected, and different fights require different movements with hand weapons.

Swashbuckling is a commonly used term to describe the colourful, romantic Hollywood movies I described earlier. In fact, the 'swash' was the noise made as sixteenth-century swordsmen whirled their long swords in the air and the 'buckler' was the shield they hit with the end of their sword. They used this sound as a drunken way to challenge people to fight in the streets and inns of the harbour town or hamlet they were frequenting that day. They were hardly the romantic Errol Flynn loveable rogues, more sixteenth-century yobs.

Court swords were dictated by fashion and a need to reduce the number of duels. In the time of the Renaissance, everyone carried a sword in the royal courts. If you did not wear a sword, you were considered undressed. To carry a sword and not know how to use it was like carrying a book and not knowing how to read. Teachers of the sword were prized individuals and only men with means were able to afford their tuition. As rapier blades grew ever longer, they had no scabbard (a blade sheath or cover) and were normally worn in a *baldric,* which was a belt worn over one shoulder and often also used to carry a weapon, a sword or another implement such as a bugle or drum. These long rapier blades would often catch people unaware, in busy court rooms and antechambers. The blades would cut and rip clothing, especially ladies' dresses, or, in extreme cases, draw blood and a fight would ensue.

To avoid these problems, a new sword was required just for wearing at court on official business. The blade had to be no longer than the length of an average man's leg. The sword would be fully functional, but it was smaller so less dangerous and fewer arguments were caused, which pleased the court.

Yet this posed another problem, since the court sword could be concealed by the voluminous cloaks of the time. Sword etiquette therefore decreed that the wearing of a court sword should be accompanied by a dagger to show you were armed. This additional weapon brought in an entirely new form of swordplay – sword and dagger fighting. The stance was the same as for the broadsword to bring the points of both weapons together at the same distance (sword arm back and dagger forward).

This additional weapon allowed the teachers of swordsmanship to invent a more elaborate and more spectacular defence. Sword and dagger parries, which involved crossing the two at the forté of the blades (the widest part of the blade by the guard) to defend against blows to vital areas of the body, were instigated and taught. Affectionately and accurately called in the twentieth century 'spectacles, testicles, wallet and watch' parries for the valuable items they protected. My study included rapier and buckler, rapier and dagger, rapier and lantern, rapier and cape – actually you could fight with a rapier and anything that came to hand.

As Silver was changing the way you held the sword, the swordsman and fencer Ridolfo Capo Ferro in 1610 designed a new footwork movement that enhanced the use of the rapier, which today we call the lunge. Up until then, all hits were accomplished on the pass, where the rear foot (if right-handed the left foot) crossed the leading foot, to pass, and cover the measure to target to hit.

Capo Ferro wrote about this new movement in his book, *Italian Rapier Combat*. He thought there must be a quicker way to hit the target than just crossing over, on the pass, and he was right. Instead of taking a step forward with your rear foot, you extend the sword arm to target first, then immediately take a big step with the front leading leg. This is the lunge that is taught to every fencer in a beginners' class.

Changing to this style meant that the sword became the forerunner of thrusting weapons. This meant too that the weapons changed style and the evolution of metallurgy allowed them to become much lighter.

This reduced the teaching of the George Silver percussion style dramatically and brought forward the pointing weapon. This change also meant that the arm and leg movements also became smaller. The effort to move a broadsword is large. It takes fencing time to move the blade and requires strength and energy compared to the agile, light and fast movements of keeping the blade work small, tidy and, excuse the pun, to the point.

George Silver once said, "Show me a fencer and I'll cut him down with some good English blows." Alas, circumstances laid to rest this style of fencing to the books and movies that showed them in historical context.

The mythological battle between the percussion style of George Silver and the thrusting weapons was fought throughout the fifteenth and sixteenth centuries and was settled, without blades ever being crossed, although some would say that it is immortalised in *Romeo and Juliet* as the duel between the Capulets and Montagues.

Similar to today's population, the majority of people were right-handed. The Latin for left was *sinistra* and also took on meanings of 'evil' or 'unlucky'. Rarely would you find a left-handed swordsman.

The House of Domenico Angelo was established in Carlisle House, Soho, London in 1761, with the patronage of the Earl of Pembroke. This was a fencing school that we could recognise today. Thrusting weapons now became very widespread, mainly inspired by those able to partake in the Grand Tour of European capitals for the art, languages and cultural learning. These were very popular, especially with the Romantics of the early nineteenth century such as Byron and Shelley, who travelled Europe extensively, later writing about them and the world of the fencing master.

N

I am often asked my opinions on gunfights and indeed have a number of books in my library on gunfighters, guns of all ages and types and the history of gunsmithing, rifles and shotguns. I am always prepared as I never know what my agent may bring to me! Indeed, in *Nightbreed* I played both a posse member and a Berserker, and fired a number of guns, from a SPAS 12 to an AK47.

However, I have to say that gunfights are not really my cup of tea and although I love directing and watching Westerns and John Wayne is my favourite actor (yes, actor), I think guns are easy to use and there is little skill or thought required in firing one. There is a wonderful line in *Freebie and the Bean* (1974), James Caan, Alan Arkin directed by Richard Rush when Freebie (Caan) pulls his .38 Smith & Wesson on a huge American football fan, who is drunk and out of control in a hotel lobby on the eve of the Superbowl. The football fan ignores the gun and continues to be rowdy. Freebie turns and says to camera, "These things are useless, unless you use them," and he holsters the gun. He and the Bean (Arkin) then 'attempt' to arrest the American football fan using hand-to-hand force.

Likewise, I am afraid that I have never felt Oriental and martial arts were really my cup of Lapsang Souchong either, although I was good at judo in my youth. I am interested in the samurai and their philosophy, though not necessarily their style of combat, find kendo great to watch, and admire and am fascinated by their use of armour, especially how the plate of armour moulds to the wearer inside.

For me, the European style of fencing and swordplay and its history is where I belong. Swordplay or fencing requires training and the best sword fights are a conversation between two blades by two skilled, trained people.

There is one community I have not mentioned thus far in this memoir, simply due to the fact that I have had no practical contact with them. It is appropriate for my final words in this scene to reflect that our history is flush with historically important events, which resonate even today in these political times, and to mention the re-enactment societies. The pageantry of these great moments in our history is recreated for us today by groups of well-educated, skilled and dedicated re-enactors. If you have a chance, one of the best I have seen is the re-enactment group that recreates the Battle of Bosworth Field of 1485 which was the last significant battle of the Wars of the Roses in England.

In the early days, the re-enactment groups were looked upon by the film community as nothing more than weekend warriors and, frankly, that was often the case. They were beer-drinking men who just fancied a sword fight with someone at weekends. No film company could use these groups, as they were uncontrollable. I heard from senior assistant directors of problems such as wearing their watches when filming, taking weapons off set, drinking at lunchtime and not taking direction from the stunt coordinator or fight director.

Thankfully, this is no longer the case. Health and safety at public events has stepped in and I have to say the re-enactment groups have stepped up to the mark. They are outstanding in their accurate historical interpretations of the period and they are expert in the costumes and accompanying camps, which are extensively researched and recreated. The weapons and metallurgy of the weapons are accurate too, often with blacksmiths showing the visitors how the weapons were made. Their understanding of archery and use of weapons in battle is textbook. These professional groups, who are all marshalled and organised, are an asset to any period film now and totally underused.

SCENE 6

THE CUTTING EDGE
FENCING CLUB

The year of my changing track from film sword fighter to theatre and film director and screenwriter was 1991. I had a clean slate in front of me, with a few years of unbelievable valuable film experience behind me and some new friends and contacts.

Back to the books and study was the only option I had. To keep the wolf from the door, I decided to open my very own fencing club and teach the three Olympic weapons to both adults and children.

This was the birth of the Cutting Edge Fencing Club, London.

In 1993, we lived in Highgate, North London and just fifteen minutes' walk away was Highgate School, a private school with a purpose-built fencing salle attached to its sports hall.

I introduced myself to the director of sport and their sports centre manager. We all hit it off and I was asked to teach a course of fencing that year at their summer camp, which I jumped at. I taught at those Highgate summer camps for two years, then the resident fencing master at the school was to retire and I was approached to take over from him. This was perfect; I would be the fencing coach at Highgate School and run my own fencing club at weekends and in the evenings, while working on becoming a screenwriter and director. I could easily fill the pages of my memoir with just my exploits of teaching at Highgate, the students I taught and the lifelong friends I made there and at the club.

The Cutting Edge was a three-weapon (foil, épée and sabre) club and I chose to teach everyone from six years old. There was no upper age limit. I held children's classes at the weekends and adult classes during the evenings on Mondays and Wednesdays, while teaching at the school during the day. As I cast a torch over the depths of my dusty memory, the light falls across some boxes full of trivia and memories stacked in there.

Highgate School, while I was coach, won the Public Schools' Fencing Championship, which I believe still is the largest fencing competition in Europe. The competition is so big it requires the use of the entire Crystal Palace arena, mezzanine floor too, for an entire week!

The fencing salle produced junior national champions in all three weapons, a London junior épée champion and welcomed fencers from other schools too.

A small number of City of London girls joined us at what was an all-boys school at that time; it was groundbreaking. This amalgamation really enhanced every student's capability to fence and undertake further training, as the fencing salle had use of the gym and pool for supervised training sessions by other staff. It was quickly becoming a club of note.

My after-school club, the Cutting Edge, was open to all, regardless of their schooling background. That was not important to me at all; having fun while learning to fence was. Children's classes were open to both sexes and were a unique experience. Fencing as a sport has a predominantly public school, upper-class elitism about it. My club opened the doors to everyone and we had an eclectic bunch of enthusiastic, talented children who just wanted to take part in the sport or who wanted to be a ninja or *Star Wars* character and learn how to use a sword properly. I welcomed them all to the club and because of my experience on the other side of fencing – the film side – I was able to make the class so much more enjoyable and relevant to them.

The club grew and I had approximately sixty students a week, spread over a number of classes. Four school club sessions during the week, three on a Saturday for my junior students and two adult evening sessions a week. It was exhausting but fun.

I was not an elitist, despite some stuntmen on films telling me how posh I was. Highgate is in the borough of Haringey and we had a multi-racial, multi-ability super bunch of children and adults attending. The understanding of a complex sport like fencing should not be stuck in a formula of old ideology and outdated stigma.

My philosophy is simple; if a student does not understand the instruction, it is the coach's fault for not explaining it more clearly.

I*D*E*A – Introduction, Demonstration, Explanation and Application.

As a coach you need to have flexible thinking, to be able to find another way to explain want you are looking for.

Over time, I discovered more about my students from their parents. The problems they were having at school, about learning certain topics, with discipline, fitting in, social mixing and I discovered that many of the children had body image issues, attention deficit and attention seeking, not just puberty!!

As a nation, we like to label things and it can be useful in some cases, but I do feel we are too quick to label people. First impressions are not all they are cracked up to be, in my opinion. Look at my story, for example. At my primary school, I was considered a slow learner; a day dreamer. At my secondary school, my careers advisor said I should think about becoming a labourer. Yet, I was labelled posh and elitist by the stuntmen I later encountered. The very people I wanted to be professionally associated with as a swordsman.

Yes, I am proud to say I am a dreamer, but on the whole, as a swordsman, world champion title-winner, film director, writer and audio executive, I think I have proved them all wrong in their labelling of me as a day-dreaming labourer.

Children are labelled far too quickly; they are not allowed to grow at their own pace and I find the current rise in mental health concerns hardly surprising given the social pressures and need to conform to academic standards within the school environment. They have to be 'normal' or their boxes are not ticked.

Please don't misunderstand me. There have to be rules, as in my fencing classes, but once the rules are set and not abused by either side, I allow the freedom of youth to mature and shine. Fencing is not a panacea for all problems, but the club, with all the other fencers attending, creates a safe place to learn from those with similar issues and allows the young to bloom.

A man's reach should exceed his grasp. This was a huge learning curve for me; I think it made me a better coach and human being.

I ensured there was no pressure at the Cutting Edge, unlike other clubs where results were the key to your remaining at the club. No bullying was tolerated, at all. Friendly, educational and fun so that everybody relaxed, got along with each other, learnt fencing and came back for more of the same, every week.

My personality and style of coaching, especially with children, attracted a wide selection of younglings (sorry, *Star Wars* crept in again). Some had mild physical issues and some just needed a 'big brother' to get another point of view on their daily life, especially when their parents were struggling a tad with their relationships and students with two bedrooms, one at Mum's house and one at Dad's, were common.

I had a number of young people who had to deal with dyspraxia, which is a form of developmental coordination disorder. It is a common disorder affecting fine and/or gross motor coordination, in children and adults too.

These people found all sport difficult. I would listen to their similar stories of trying different sports, all with no fun involved or ones they lacked the ability to do. They were the last ones to be picked in team sports, where a smile and a laugh hid their 'shame'. I have coached at other secondary schools where the PE department would collect all the children who didn't enjoy sport into one group and called the class 'The Undatables'. I had no formal training in medicine or psychology, but I knew the children in this class realised what they were called. It was just negative reinforcement of what was probably dyspraxia or shyness or a plethora of other mild mental health issues.

When I was asked to coach a group of these students, I found a group of disheartened, disillusioned and unhappy people. This should have been their 'best of times' in their young lives and produced the very best memories but, no, it was taken away from them. I hated that, and I made sure that, while they were with me, I treated them all the same. We had great fun and they learnt basic fencing in the short time they had with me. I hope they will remember that fencing class fondly. Fencing was perhaps their last chance at finding a sport and I hope many of them are still fencing today.

This memoir is not a fencing reference book or manual, but I thought it might be interesting for you to illustrate how I taught fencing to all, including dyspraxic children.

This is just one example. One of the basic lessons to teach the class was a circular parry of sixte (moving the blade 360 degrees on the right-hand side of the body for right-handers), followed by a direct riposte (thrust the weapon forward to hit your opponent on target). After I used my I*D*E*A approach to the class and sent them away to practise, I then would coach the action, watching at how they were getting on. A good coach will notice the fencers who are struggling.

Looking around the room I could see those for whom my terminology had not worked. 'A circular parry of sixte with a direct riposte'? The words and practice of the other fencers did not match anything understandable they were looking at. It was not their fault or error; it was mine. I didn't explain it in a way they could understand and master. Fencing terminology is complicated and they needed another way of imagining what I was asking them to do. I replaced 'circular parry of sixte with a direct riposte' with 'wrap it round and stick it in'!

It was a light-bulb moment for them and me, and I could see it in their eyes and their smiles that they now understood what they had to do. Any difficulties they had simply fell away.

When I have some spare time, I would love to speak to an expert on how the brain works, as there are what I would call 'join the dot' moments in my understanding of how things work. For example, I know that Megan Washington, a fabulous songwriter and singer from Australia, is a stutterer, but does not when she sings, and some cannot visualise actions in space, when others can. There are links to be made, I am sure, so if you know them, please forgive my ignorance.

Now I enjoy inventing different ways of explaining fencing actions. My own mantra is that it is not my students who did not understand what I was asking of them. It was my fault for not explaining it in a way that made it easy to grasp. This is not rocket science, after all. It is just fencing.

I am so pleased to tell you that many of the six-year-old fencers I knew back then still keep in contact with me today.

One, an accomplished artist, does a few commissioning jobs for me today, storyboards and posters for my projects. One is a doctor, although it still feels strange that he qualified and old enough to deliver babies in his work for a medical charity, somewhere in Africa. He is London-based now, and his mum and I share a birthday! When I first met him, his junior foil was almost as big as him!

As for the grown-ups, well, a few of the young adults are married and have families, and being invited to weddings and christenings by my students has been a wonderful bonus to being their coach. Both Katy and I enjoy seeing them as often as we can.

Two of my regular students at the Cutting Edge Fencing Club were natives of Sweden and very much involved in the performing arts, in particular circus skills. They were expert on high-rigs and acrobatics on the rings and went on to perform at the opening ceremony of the Øresund Bridge between Sweden and Denmark. They were inspired to set up a student stunt school in Ystad, Sweden, with Janne Lindquist as their chief instructor. Janne is a member of the Swedish Stunt Company Stuntmakers, a prolific stunt team, founded by Peter Lundberg, famous most recently for their work on *Wallander* and *The Bridge* TV series and involved in my *Birth of a Legend: Billy The Kid & The Lincoln County War*.

My two fencers needed sword training for their students and since they trained with me in the UK, they asked me to go to Sweden to give block lessons over several months in their stunt school, and I of course obliged.

My philosophy at Cutting Edge of stage/film fighting and fencing fitted together perfectly and I taught all their students. This enabled me to travel to Sweden and to visit Hässleholm years later, scouting for locations for a feature film I had in mind about Billy the Kid.

The Cutting Edge Club was very important to the fencers and to me too, as it developed my teaching skills and my knowledge and understanding of designing stage and film swordplay and unarmed combat sequences.

Competitive fencing teaches you about the fencing measure; that is, the distance between two fencers where one would have to move to hit the target, either by stepping in or with a blade action. You break the measure to hit. I used to tell the children to think of the Ready Brek advert. "Central heating for kids," they used to call it, and the eaters of Ready Brek would have a beautiful red glow surrounding them after they had the cereal, even when walking around in all weathers.

It was an easy way to explain to the students that when they were fighting, if the Ready Brek boundary was broken, a hit would be scored against them and in swordplay you could create an accident-free environment by maintaining a Ready Brek zone.

For those of you not of a certain age, without a clue what I am talking about, may I suggest you YouTube the advert and feel sorry for this old geezer, as I have been doing coaching for such a long time!

In stage and film fighting, the skill in the swordplay is knowing how to make the fight look realistic and achieve your movements but outside the fencing measure for safety. For example, there is no threat if I present my blade to you, vaguely pointing it at your ear or your shoelaces. It is just not convincing. The skill is to choreograph a routine that looks dangerous *but* is safe and outside the fencing measure.

Safety is essential, no matter what you are doing. You should always protect yourself when training at any level and there is no excuse for not doing it. The fencing mask is the number one piece of kit – your eyes are not replaceable. When coaching competitive fencing, the only time you will hear me shout in a club is if I see anyone fencing without a mask on. I have a very loud voice.

Although when you come to filming or the actual play, you won't have it on, the fact that you have previously been kitted out properly will heighten your awareness. Wear it all – gloves, plastron, breast protectors, jacket and breaches, and mask. Jacket, gauntlet, tracksuit bottoms and mask are minimum for stage fighting training.

I have attended many stage school examinations and showcases and have always found them a pleasure to watch, whether for RADA or E15 or school drama classes. The people are charming and the productions are always very well done. The cast résumés include lots of sports under hobbies, such as archery, horse-riding, rugby, dance, martial arts and swimming. Sadly, today rarely is fencing ever mentioned, despite the brilliant rapier and dagger, small sword and sabre routines I watch. They are all very well-trained, with well-coordinated routines and a sprinkling of unarmed combat and acrobatics thrown into the mix.

"Why do you not attend a fencing club?" I ask. Sadly, the replies I get are always the same no matter where I go in the country.

"You just cannot find the right coaches. They cannot relate the two skills, competitive fencing to theatrical swordplay. Plus, it is far too expensive to get all the kit; we are cash-poor students. We have to buy it, as the clubs are either school clubs and they cannot lend us the kit or all the other fencers come with kit. Frankly, the attitude of the sport is so negative to us. Fencing was an easy option to drop."

I have now heard this from so many top-flight drama schools and academies throughout the UK over my thirty-five years teaching competitive fencing and theatrical swordplay. We seem to be losing friends and supporters at an alarming rate.

We've lost so much funding in competitive fencing, are we now losing friends in the arts too?

When I delve deeper, they pretty much say the same thing.

"Fencing coaches are not relevant," or, "The coach was too snooty," or, "Clubs were unwelcoming," or, "When other club members found out who we were and what we were doing, they ignored us."

I think there is a real opportunity here, not to become one of the 'snooty' coaches, but instead to become one of the sword masters I have spoken about like Fred Cavens, Ralph Faulkner, Henri Uyttenhove, or, even closer to home, Professor Bob Anderson or Professor Roy Goodall, who were the best their countries had to offer. I never won an Olympic medal; however, I did win a world title in my chosen sport of Theatrical Fencing.

This is what I believe the arts are looking for: teachers, coaches, swordsmen and women to continue carrying our torch forward, for the sport we love so much, onto the stage and silver screen.

The adults at the Cutting Edge were an eclectic bunch: city workers, medical doctors, architects, builders and people who just wanted to learn how to fence. As I have said, all were welcome and all were taught the same way as the kids. However, the adults would often ask me one question which the kids never did… if I were in a fight with a sword, would I win? My considered reply would be, yes, because I don't fight fair.

What does that mean?

It means I wouldn't fight to the conventions of fencing. In a real fight, like the ones in the new *Star Wars* films, while they are spinning around, jumping up, waving their lightsaber about at my ears or shoes, a swordsman would just stick it in!

As the wise old master says, "I may have taught you everything you know, but not everything I know"!

SCENE 7

THE PEN IS MIGHTIER
THAN THE SWORD

In my spare time, my brother Scott and I talk movies and television shows. He is as much a film buff as I am, but, as I said previously, Scott is an extraordinarily talented musician.

In fact, both of my brothers Garry and Scott are naturally gifted musicians and my late brother George, who died of leukemia aged fifty, was also a talented guitarist.

Moi? I played the double bass at school; I wasn't too bad at it either. However, putting the base under my chin got too much for me after a while, so I turned to sport and judo.

I can read music, though, and have a good ear, having produced the musical CD for one of our shows with the Bournemouth Symphony Orchestra. More of that later too. Gosh, I hope I remember everything I've said I will talk about later!

I still play the bass guitar when the house is empty, so rare now.

On a summer break, Katy and I went down to East Devon, where her architect father had converted the old village bakery and flour loft into houses, keeping a small cottage for Katy's grandfather to live in. When he passed, the family kept the cottage as a summer holiday bolthole.

We would often sit in the Hook & Parrot public house, in Seaton, enjoying the late afternoon sun with a glass of ale for me and a glass of wine for Katy, looking out over Lyme Bay. Beer Head is to the west of Seaton and on this special, warm evening, during what the film business calls the magic hour, just before sunset, I looked across at Beer Head and in my mind's eye I saw a Spanish galleon's bow break around the cliffs.

From this daydream I created a story, or at least a rough outline of one, anyway. I told my brother Scott the story when we got back to London and he seemed to like it. Our joint enthusiasm for the story and the characters we created brought us both back to our childhood nights and the wonderful stories Mum would read to us before bedtime. We started work on our very first screenplay together, a family adventure we called *Fortune's Luck* ©.

The main character is a young, athletic, handsome, agent provocateur called Jake Fortune. Many years later when Katy and I had our first son, we named him Jake, after the character in the film. Scott is his godfather.

Fortune's Luck ©, we decided, was to be a family-oriented story about lost Inca treasure and the curse that it brought on all who touched it. No sex, no violence, no swearing, but packed full of drama, action and sword fights and with great humour. This was an original story, inspired by the stories and films of our childhood and that evening in Devon; *Fortune's Luck* © was written in 1989 and did the rounds with agents, but was not picked up. *Pirates of the Caribbean* was and the rest is history, yet there are more than a few similarities between *Fortune's Luck* © and these other films. Neither Scott nor I can watch them and never have. Great soundtracks, though!

What we did learn through writing the original screenplay of *Fortune's Luck* © was simply how to write a screenplay, for example knowing the correct format to use, how to structure it and how a script should flow and make sense. As I have mentioned, it was packed full of swordplay, heroic deeds, romance and a witty, fast-paced story. It was to be the first of many screenplays we would write together.

⚡

Although I had an FAA card, an Equity card and I had worked on many, many film and television productions, looking back as I write this memoir, I realise I was incredibly naïve about the entire business I was aiming to join. I guess I just didn't know how it all worked, and I use the word 'worked' loosely. It was a jigsaw puzzle with no picture or box lid for me to peek at. I didn't know how disjointed the entire entertainment business was at that time and indeed still is.

In order to act, to work in swordplay, to direct, in either theatre or film, or to write, you need to be a member of a guild or union. This list doesn't include all the set designers, painters, carpenters, wardrobe and make-up artistes, electricians – the list goes on and on. There is a whole range of people who make a film or production happen, and, yes, all these people need to be members of a guild or union so that they can be represented.

I have not even touched on agents, performing or literary yet, but all of us have one or have needed one. I wanted to be a writer, to be a professional writer, not just a guy sitting in a shed with a pencil, a sharpener and a ream of A4 paper. Forgive me, as I doff my hat to the wonderful Roald Dahl, who wrote his stories in his shed! Nevertheless, for us mere mortals, it was necessary to prove that we could write before anyone would read our machinations.

Again, what the heck was I going to do next?

Scott and I got our thinking caps on. What did we enjoy and what could we write about? We both enjoyed reading science fiction, Robert A. Heinlein, Arthur C. Clarke and Isaac Asimov in particular. We also both watched *Star Trek* (1966–1969), (reruns, of course), and the latter reincarnations on television *Star Trek: The Next Generation* (1987–1994), *Deep Space Nine* (1993–1999) and *Voyager* (1995–2001). I had read in my copy of *The Writers' and Artists' Yearbook* that there was a thing called a speculative script. This is abbreviated to a spec script. It means a script that is not commissioned or requested by a studio or agent and there is a very small, a very, very small chance, that a studio might pick up and read one of these spec scripts and an even smaller chance that they like it and it gets greenlit to be made. I had no other option. I hadn't written anything, apart from *Fortune's Luck* ©, a postcard home from holiday once a year and some Christmas and birthday cards! What could they say? Nothing or, "No, thanks."

With *Fortune's Luck* © under our belts, Scott and I knew we could write scripts and thought it had strengths – a well-balanced shooting script for a film. Why not give a spec script a shot, but who or what were we going to take aim at?

Deep Space Nine, perhaps?

Why not? Scott and I were new to spec scripts. You may be surprised to learn that there are quite a few books specifically about writing scripts for the *Star Trek* franchise, including *Deep Space Nine*. We bought them all and read them all. I studied them meticulously and we started work on our first television script.

After a few months of some creative blue-sky thinking, we came up with an exciting, character-led story. We thought it was quite rare not to be situation-led for a televisual screenplay and, a few redrafts later, we produced a script for *Deep Space Nine* called *Out of Bounds* ©. Not convinced one spec script would be enough to show off our writing skills, we ploughed on and wrote another called *Leap of Faith* ©.

We bit the bullet and posted them, snail mail (remember, the internet was still fledgling) to Paramount Studios, Hollywood, with a return-to-sender paid envelope inside. Nothing ventured, nothing gained. We waited and waited. The summer came and went. I was fencing and Scott was playing his music. Then we got the scripts back in our big envelope. A deep breath. If they liked them, they would have kept them, surely, and sent a small letter to acknowledge their wonder at these two beautiful stories and scripts?

Taking out the scripts one at a time I noticed that they both had a Paramount Studio 'READ' stamp on. Accompanying them was a brilliant letter written by Lolita Fatjo, pre-production assistant, saying they had read the scripts, liked them, but there was no room in their schedule to proceed with them so returned them. A disclaimer stated that nothing would be used in any forthcoming episodes for these spec scrips; any similarities will be coincidental.

I didn't mind that at all. An acknowledgement from Paramount Studios no less that we could write was enough, plus, all this would go into the file at the Writers' Guild of Great Britain as points to gaining my WGGB membership. Scott liked writing, but he was a musician, so joining guilds and unions was not his cup of tea.

N

Time does pass when you're busy and having fun. I was fencing almost every day of the week at Highgate School, the Cutting Edge and a primary school nearby. I was then appointed to the British Academy of Fencing (BAF) Committee. If you are following the time frame of this journey, it was still the '90s. I was appointed to the committee of the BAF and I was Members' Representative.

The President of the Academy then was Professor David Austin, whom I didn't know well then, but is a close family friend today. The British Academy of Fencing was founded in 1540 by King Henry VIII and wisely it took a hiatus during World War II, thus it was reformed in 1949 after the war when everyone was home. The golden anniversary of the reformation of the Academy after World War II was in 1999. David asked Roy Goodall to think about what form of celebration we should undertake to mark this event. Roy came up with a wonderful idea. The History of European Swordsmanship from 1540 to the Modern Day. Roy asked if I would like to be involved; I jumped at the opportunity.

The crowning glory was a series of meetings and discussions with Mark Rylance, the then director of Shakespeare's Globe Theatre, London. Mark approved the concept of the show. We had a stage!

Roy and Angela Goodall and I wrote the script. King Henry VIII was to be the golden thread to pull all the stories and ages together. Of course, after 1547 the king appeared on stage as a ghost. This worked beautifully, as well as comically.

When King Henry VIII founded the British Academy in 1540, the prize fights, the means by which promotion through the ranks were judged and awarded, certainly had a flair of the theatrical about them. The prize fights drew crowds from across London to witness the skills of the swordsmen and pugilists taking part. Samuel Pepys, in his famous diary, wrote about the prize fights in detail, explaining how and where it was possible to gain your provostship and professorships from the ancient masters, as they were called.

There has always been a symbiotic relationship between fencing masters and theatrical fencers. Roy had all the contacts required to ask all the drama schools in the UK if they would be interested in selecting a period of history, ending with the Olympics, and a style of swordplay to perform in the show. The response was overwhelming and enthusiastic as expected. The story showcased the history of quarterstaffs, small sword, broadsword, rapier and dagger and Spanish circle, as well as restaging famous duels such as Sheridan's and the first recorded female duel.

Logistically, this was a huge, spectacular event. The cast and crew numbered approximately 100 people. All had to be marshalled with military precision, on and off stage with weapons. We had a regimental sergeant organising backstage as the performers, arriving in script order, were ushered to costume and make-up, collected their weapons, lined up and went on stage to give their performance and then reversed the process to hand in their weapons, remove their costumes and exit at the back of theatre. It all ran like the smoothest clockwork you have ever seen! This was done for the entire production over the weekend – as I said, around 100 people in total, hundreds of weapons, music from Dragon's Fire, sound effects for horse and carriages and WWII air raids at one of the world's most prestigious theatrical venues. No pressure on any of us then!

On Sunday October 10th 1999, *Golden Swords* played to a packed house of invited international guests, fencers and the general public. It was a tremendous success and a highlight of the BAF fifty-year anniversary celebrations.

I directed the performance and, as far as we are aware, it is still the largest live action swordplay spectacular ever staged. We should have got it into the *Guinness Book of Records*!

To cap it off, I had a credit for co-writing the show and with that I applied to the Writers' Guild of Great Britain, hoping that I had enough points to be recognised and offered membership.

I was delighted when I was made a full member and I am still a proud member of the WGGB today.

✗

The new millennium was just around the corner and more global celebrations were being planned. In London, at Greenwich, a new building called the Dome was being designed and built specifically for the events. There was to be a dramatic acrobatic show to be placed for an extended period, in the centre ring of the Dome, after the official opening for Her Majesty and the press. All the performers were either professionals or students working towards a career in entertainment. Their jobs at the Dome required them to be there for all performances of the show, which allowed little or no time for their own training. The performers together came up with a solution. They would ask the management to engage specialist coaches to continue their training in between show performances, to be undertaken at the Dome, in the training room high in the steel rafters of the building.

A number of show performers knew me, either from fencing at the Cutting Edge or through my work in film and the Dome management gave me a call. Would I be interested in being the fencing coach at the Millennium Dome?

I said I would be delighted to coach there.

My classes were exciting and great fun to teach. A super bunch of extraordinarily fit people. Let's face it, the show included them bungee jumping from the roof of the Dome on stilts, unclipping their harnesses and performing an act, still on stilts! I know, I know, amazing people.

✗

The year 2000 had just started and I was getting serious. If I wasn't serious enough about my journey into the film business already, I decided to form a production company, Wilkinson Productions Ltd, to realise all my projects – written, directed and acted in – while I kept my fencing going. The year 2000 was about to become *awesome*.

⚡

I was attending a BAF committee meeting and, as usual, all the Academy business was taken care of, professionally and with a sense of humour, under David's chairmanship.

Any other business (AOB) was the last item. On my agenda I saw there was nothing written down for AOB. *Home early today*, I thought. Then I noticed the room went very quiet. I looked up from my notes and the entire committee was looking at me, with big smiles on their faces. I looked to David.

I said, "If I were standing up right now, I'd check my flies. What's up?"

David, in a most serious voice, said, "You know who the FIE and AAI are, don't you?"

I replied, "Yes, the International Academy of Arms and the International Federation of Fencing."

"Well, every four years, in an Olympic year, the FIE/AAI hold an international competition called the Artistic Theatrical World Championships. The BAF have never entered a team before, but now that you are a member, we, the committee, would like to enter a team. I am asking you to form a team, coach it and win the championship for Great Britain and the BAF. You interested?"

I really didn't understand what it all entailed, but if you know me, you'll know I find it difficult to say no. I love challenges.

"It would be a pleasure for me to enter the championships, David."

"Great," he said. "This year, it is being held in Vichy, France. Don't come back if you lose, meeting closed."

How the heck am I going to do this? I may have said this phrase once or twice before.

I was coaching at my club, Highgate, in schools and now at the Dome. The Dome! Hang on, I have access to professional performers, all learning fencing, most are acrobats too, and if I can't choreograph a sequence using these talented people, I should become a male stripper. Doors, skirting boards, gloss or matt, you name it, I could strip the lot!

I received the competition rules and categories the following week. David was right; the event was to be held in Vichy, in the opera house.

The choreography I thought up at home. To win this thing I needed something to stand out from the rest – something new, something skilled, with a nod to all of our history but not stodgy or familiar.

I selected the categories. I entered three teams who I felt had the skill to execute my complex routines. We trained at the Dome. Once the teams were up and running to my specifications, with time to spare before the competition date, I asked Roy and Angela Goodall, my old masters, to come in to the Dome and have a look at the show I had staged. With great relief, they liked it and we were ready to go.

Regardless of Vichy's odd history, it was a pretty location for the championship to be held in. Professor Mike Joseph came with us. He was the BAF Secretary and was the UK's FIE/AAI delegate for the conference to be held during the early rounds of the competition. On the flight we talked about what we were to expect from the other teams. I had already thought about this when designing my choreography and, with my tongue firmly inside my cheek, I said, "I suspect a lot of leather, broadswords and Wagner."

Our routine was the exact opposite – light, fast and fun.

On arrival, funnily enough, there were a lot of beards, leather and broadswords to be seen… the men didn't look too bad either!

We had to qualify first. Lots of countries had several teams in each category. I had three teams entered into this competition – the Troupe Fantastique, the duo and solo categories. All three groups qualified and, to be honest, I didn't expect anything less. The evening of the competition was a long one. All three teams gave it their all and turned in perfect routines. Mike and I had secured a box at the back of the opera house to await the results. I have to say, looking back, the audience was getting used to heavy Wagner and Mussorgsky 'Night on Bald (or Bare!) Mountain' music. You could tell the audience's shoulders were dropping when they heard the start of yet another sequence.

When the GB troupe team burst onto the stage with loads of energy and smiling faces, the audience sat up a little. Then the music for our troupe performance started and 'Let Me Entertain You' by Robbie Williams blasted out, loud, brash and wonderful. The entire audience jumped up as if it were a concert. They started to clap and cheer with all the actions on stage. Mike and I sneaked a glance at each other with big grins on our faces – it was working!

The routine was set on a French railway station where there were people waiting for a train – a pretty young lady, gentlemen in suits, mechanics, and working painters and decorators, all on the platform. Then one little accident triggered a snowball effect and a fight ensued amongst everyone on the platform. Why would you have a sword with you when waiting for a train on a platform? Well, you wouldn't, so I had choreographed 'swordplay' with paint rollers, umbrellas, sticks, portable radio aerials, brooms, a riding crop and buckets. Basically, everything but a sword, and I even included hand fencing, as if it were a kung-fu fight – my own direct tribute to a style of teaching fencing which had gone out of fashion or favour. A historical doffing of my hat to the masters judging!

The entire sequence, with multiple different styles of fighting, plus acrobatics, left the beautiful young lady as the last one standing. She won her fight with her riding crop against the paint roller attacker. Looking around at the carnage on stage at the end, she turned and calmly walked off stage, to tremendous applause. This type of routine had never been seen before at this competition. We had no idea how the judges would view the sequence, but it absolutely got the audience's vote.

Two long hours passed before the results came in from the judges.

Solo candidates were the first results, given in reverse order – Angleterre, La France, La France.

Well done, BAF – we could go home with our heads held high, a third in the solo routine. My solo performer was thrilled to bits. I went up to congratulate him, hugs all round. I asked him what he wanted to do after finishing at the Dome, now he had come third in a world championship? He looked at me and smiled. "I want to become an action figure."

We both laughed. It broke the tension of the results yet to come.

The duo team was next, again, in reverse order – La France, Angleterre, Deutschland.

Hey, we're rocking and rolling! Second! My duo team were understandably disappointed, so close, yet so far. They were new to this skill and surely if they kept up the good work, they would win it next time.

The Troupe Fantastique was the last result to be announced, again in reverse order – La France, La France, Angleterre!

After all the Wagner, our soundtrack of Robbie Williams singing 'Let Me Entertain You' rang out to accompany the result!

Mike Joseph and I hugged each other and jumped up and down in our box. The audience, all of whom stayed behind to hear the last results, screamed congratulations into the box. I was a World Champion! Technically I was the best fight director in the world and I would hold that title for four years until the next event. I have the large gold medal in my office to this day and two certificates on my office wall, one from the FIE/AAI and the other from the BAF, both:

Championnats Du Monde
Artistique 2000

This was the very first time Great Britain had won a world title for theatrical fencing! The BAF has recognised me over the years for all my work in swordplay and fencing, with a BAF honorary diploma for my contribution to the art of fencing for stage and screen. These are rare honours indeed. Prof Bob Anderson, sword master on *By the Sword* (1991) and *The Legend of Zorro* (1995), arranged via the BAF to honour the actors Eric Roberts and F. Murray Abrahams for *By the Sword* and Sir Anthony Hopkins for *The Legend of Zorro*. I am the only other recipient of this award to date. I also hold a number of Awards of Merit from the Academy of which I am very proud.

I came home from Vichy as proud as any other world title holder. Yet you may be as surprised as I was, or maybe not, that, apart from my Academy, no one else in government, politics, sport or in the film world was the slightest bit interested in what I, we, had achieved. I couldn't even get a pint in the pub for winning a world title. The Academy contacted the Minister for Sport at the time, Labour MP Kate Hoey, and she did reply with a format letter, suggesting, "Please contact the Amateur Fencing Association," not even a congratulations or well done, Andy, or BAF.

Remember, the Amateur Fencing Association does not cover theatrical fencing at all and the BAF was and still is the only professional organisation for fencing that does, in conjunction with international bodies such as the AAI and FIE. It was a bit of an anti-climax, to say the least. Once again, my efforts with sword in hand were not acknowledged outside of my small, eclectic circle.

Was I bitter?

Disappointed, perhaps, but sadly not in the slightest bit surprised. I had won a world title and to this date I am still the only UK sword master to do so.

To answer the question, "What do you do now?" I kept calm and carried on. I wrote more screenplays!

⁄

Scott, by this time, was working in America, so having his valuable input became rare and Skype was still three years away. Although the internet was available from 1990, it was only available to some areas, so letters and phone calls were all we had. Scott, to this day, is a great sounding board for my ideas and I am told he has his eye-rolling down to a fine art now.

Garry was working full time as Music Master at Sherborne School, Dorset, and he was, and still is, a great fact checker for all my projects. In fact, I had a fact checker even before Donald J. Trump! Garry is especially great for the science I was writing about. Not only a senior music master and composer, Garry is also a Fellow of the Royal Astronomical Society.

On the 14th January 2004, President George W. Bush announced *his new vision for* space: "Our third goal, is to return to the moon by 2020, as the launching point for missions beyond. We choose to explore space because doing so improves our lives and lifts our national spirit, so let us continue the journey."

I am a great advocate of the manned spaceflight programmes – Mercury, Gemini, Apollo, Space Lab and then the Shuttle – so I listened with eagerness. The State of the Union Address was a speech given by the President on Tuesday, January 20th, 2004, just six days after the Visions in Space speech and yet the President never even mentioned it. Was the space programme going to be a political football again, like it was during the Cold War decades before? Had we not learnt anything in that time; was this another false dawn?

NASA has not been back to the moon since Apollo 17, in 1972, forty-seven years ago, as I write. There are only four Apollo astronauts left out of the twelve who walked on the moon still alive – Duke, Aldrin, Schmitt and Scott. It made me angry and frustrated. What do I do when I am angry and frustrated? I tell my pupils to kit up and I give them a sabre lesson, or a beat flèche épée lesson or I put pen to paper and I write. This time I wrote a documentary called *False Dawn: The Promise of Apollo* ©.

It took me a year to put the project together. I contacted NASA and spoke to their video catalogue department and managed to get all the raw film footage I needed. Once I had the footage, I had it digitalised so that I could now edit it on the brand-new equipment I had bought for this production, some Apple G-5 computers.

I am very proud of the script. It does ask the questions that manned spaceflight enthusiasts have asked – where's the moon base? Where's my jet pack? Where are the science benefits of a moon base? Where are our lunar solar panels for free energy?

False Dawn needed a narrator and having worked with David Morley on *Golden Swords* at the Globe Theatre, he was the natural person to go to as narrator on *False Dawn*. I sent him the script and arranged with an ex-fencing student called Rupert Coughlan, a Huddersfield University audio graduate, to record the narration. He also offered to edit the film too and I was delighted to accept. David and I travelled up to the audio studios in Huddersfield to record the narration, which Rupert then edited with the footage I had obtained from NASA. It is hard to believe, but all my in-house composers were engaged so the music for *False Dawn* was also composed by Rupert.

The final film documentary was picked up for release by US National Film Archives. If you are lucky you might still be able to find a copy. I am very proud of it and it got all this 'Politics v Science' hogwash off my chest, a little, anyway, for now. Climate change and what we are doing to the planet is currently on my agenda too.

After *False Dawn: The Promise of Apollo* © I launched into two film scripts, each with a scientific base. *Ground Zero* © was the first (named a decade before the tragic events of 9/11).

I played around with my idea for this screenplay for a while, wondering how the science community would respond to first contact and what they would do with the discovery of intelligent life outside of our solar system. There have been many films on that subject; *Close Encounters of the Third Kind* (1977) is one of the best examples. I eventually settled on a thriller based on a first contact scenario, where a team of scientists looking for evidence of cold dark matter (CDM) within the universe accidently discover a message that is more than 'Hello, Earth'. It is a warning that the fact you have detected the message means that the catastrophic event that happened to their civilisation is about to happen to Earth. I wanted to explore the reactions to this – what would the scientists do and would they be allowed to choose? In the story, someone takes it upon themselves to silence the scientific team from speaking of the warning by killing them off, one at a time. This is the story of their deaths and the investigation to reveal the truth. I think it has legs.

My office has been described as what it is like being inside my head. I have collected a lot of 'stuff' on my journey, from clapperboards to swords, posters, photographs, masks, helmets, hats and a lot of books. Katy calls it my 'man cave'. If my office is anything to go by, I have a fruitful imagination and my next story idea was another thriller.

In *Under the Cover of Darkness* ©, I was exploring how would a scientist go about assassination? When I came up with this crazy idea, in April 2003, the Human Genome Project was completed, so biology was the obvious weapon to consider. A scientist designed the perfect assassin – a genetically engineered lethal virus which was specific, tailored to an individual only and could be released in a room full of innocent targets, yet would only hunt down and kill the one person it was designed for. Of course, it is more complex than that and the story has more levels, including nature versus nurture, genetically modified crops, the political price of keeping lethal technology and more. I think this has legs too, and I enjoyed researching and writing both.

As I wrote these scripts, my writing evolved and became more refined. My study introduced me to the pioneers of Hollywood, in particular the swordsmen of the silver screen, and I would have to have been blinkered not to have read the fascinating stories of early film-makers.

Barnstormers were the pilots who took the newly invented aircraft to the limits of aeronautics and bravery. The silent film producers of the time were captivated by these pilots and wing-walkers – pilots who would get out of their cockpits at altitude and walk on the wings of their Curtiss Jenny biplanes. I read the biography of Lt Ormer Locklear. Very few people will have heard of him today and indeed his was new to me too. Locklear's story, however, is a very human tale of a heartfelt *ménage à trois,* a pioneering aviator, stunt pilot, wing-walker extraordinaire, actor and Hollywood star. This is a true story of the very early days of Hollywood and harked back to my action performing on film. I was intrigued by Locklear and his story set in 1917, just as World War I was closing. My screenplay called *Locklear* © is his true story and covers his first introduction to entertainment by the great Houdini, through his first starring role in a Hollywood silent, *The Great Air Robbery* (1919), Jacques Jaccard directing, to his last film, *The Skywayman* (1920), James P. Hogan directing.

Locklear was tragically killed on *The Skywayman* through no fault of his own, aged just twenty-nine. More people attended his funeral than Rudolph Valentino's and yet no one knows his name. This film, if I can get it off my desk to the screen, is one I would like to direct.

My active life allows me the opportunity to meet and talk with a huge cast of characters from all walks of life. The daily news is so graphic these days. I am not sure the planet is any worse today than it was when I started my journey, yet I am perhaps more aware of the predicament of everyday life now that I have a wife and children.

I have been aware for a decade or so now of the effects of the mental stress of life on people. Some have walked across the threshold of my fencing classes. Many of the people I was talking to were first attenders to incidents – police, fire and ambulance service people with stories to tell. Not all of them were in the services, but they were sufferers. The effects of what I discovered after reading up on the matter had a name: post-traumatic stress disorder (PTSD). This was technically a new classification of what had been observed since World War I, although back then they called it shellshock. Treatment since those dark days has come a long way. There is no cure. It is a matter of control by therapy, with strong support and understanding from family and friends if available. It is very common for PTSD sufferers to have their episodes triggered by a number of stimuli: smell, sight, sound and feelings. Adrenaline in the mouth is also a trigger. I felt I would like to help, if I could, especially since I had personally heard these stories from people I know. The only thing I knew I could do was put pen to paper. I came up with a fictional story about a soldier, home from Afghanistan with PTSD, managing his problem by escaping to a fantasy world when memories of his moment of trauma occurred. His fantasy world was his safe place, fenced off in his mind and unreachable by the PTSD he carried with him. It was a Wild West fantasy, with open plains, Native Americans and a ranch where he lived which, in the real world, he was working towards.

The film screenplay is called *Moments* ©, as life is made up of a series of moments, some loving, warm and soul-enriching, while others are horrific and sad. It tells the story of how people deal with these moments. *Moments* © is very close to my heart and inspired by one of the stuntmen cast in Sweden, when I directed *Birth of a Legend: Billy the Kid and the Lincoln County War* ©. His escape from PTSD was to be a cowboy at weekends. *Moments* was the last of the big four films I penned when I had my office at Pinewood Studios.

In the summer of 2014, I was appointed GB Team Captain for the Fencing Masters World Championships in Italy. One of my épée fencers and I, along with his lovely wife, went out for an evening meal. He asked me what I was working on. I told him that I was polishing a screenplay called *Moments* © and I told him a little about the story. This was an experienced épéeist, a fit, muscular man, and he was crying in front of me. His wife was telling him to come away, that it was okay to come away. I was upset too that I had said something that had disturbed him and triggered a moment. After a short while he told me he was a policeman and had attended a knife attack on a colleague. He had suffered with PTSD ever since. He told me my story needed to be made into a film, so that people will understand a little better about the problem. On my return to my office, a letter arrived from my friend, telling me a little more about the incident. I now know a little more about what he is suffering. *Moments* is very personal to me, as I interviewed so many people who suffer with PTSD. I feel I owe it to them all to bring them this script, as they all approved it. My journey continues on this story.

Meanwhile, I had not forsaken writing and producing for the theatre and reintroduce you now to my older brother, Garry Wilkinson. You know quite a bit about him already, but he won't mind me reminding you, dear reader. Garry is a true Renaissance man. Not only is he a Fellow of Trinity College of Music, London, he is also a Fellow of the Royal Astronomical Society and in 2000 he was a music master at Sherborne School in Dorset (a public school). Garry was asked to put on a celebration concert for the 450th anniversary of its foundation. However, knowing me as a young, inspiring writer, he suggested that we put on a musical stage play. We had lots of creative meetings and finally we came up with a new story that had never been told before. The iconic figure, Alan Turing, the Enigma code breaker, was an old boy of the school and we thought he might be the keystone to this new musical comedy; Garry would write all the music and songs and I would work on the story.

Code Crackers © was born. Set during WWII, this was an original play with all the elements you could think of – a famous old boy returning to school to present prizes, a dastardly plot by the Nazis to kidnap him, a local black-market racketeer and gangster called Jumbo, and our heroes and heroines from the Sherborne School Band – Sticks, Bones and Kitty Katz – who save the day. On the turn of a single playing card in a game of poker, our harmonious trio are cheated out of everything they own, and some things they don't own, by Jumbo! With the hoodlums in hot pursuit, our friends run straight into the arms of the Nazi spymasters! Only their fast talking can save them! *Code Crackers* © was performed in the summer of 2000, to packed houses. It was a huge success. The score was recorded by the outstanding Bournemouth Symphony Orchestra and a nice footnote is that the cast included a young Charlie Cox, now a Hollywood star.

I am sure you all know about or at least have heard of a BBC Radio 4 programme called *Desert Island Discs*, where guests imagine themselves stranded with only eight musical tracks they cherish. Only eight. Well, if I am ever asked to pop on to the island, there is one track in particular I would take with me from *Code Crackers* ©. 'Steal Away' is absolutely beautiful.

SCENE 8

YOUR LIFE IS A MOVIE, DIRECT IT WELL

How do you actually make a film?

There are, of course, numerous styles offered by numerous directors. Some are masters of the craft, others are jobbing directors, but I honestly couldn't say there is an A–Z method of directing a film.

There are so many variants to a film, so many 'X' factors that you cannot foresee, that even just one could change your whole production and create difficulties. Even if you have directed a few times before, your next one may be full of 'X' factors. To have a smooth production run is a real bonus, the same as it is for so many other things. Look at NASA's Apollo 1 fire and Apollo 13 mission, both with 'X' factors which were just not foreseen.

For example, take *Dr No* (1962), Sean Connery, Terence Young directing. By all accounts, this was an exceptionally smooth-running production, across worldwide locations, with an international cast and high production values. Yet *From Russia with Love* (1963), Sean Connery and Terence Young directing again just a year later, had a number of 'X' factor moments and problems that had to be solved. It is worth asking what those factors were so you could avoid them. Yet they were largely unforeseeable. It was basically the same crew and all the key elements to reprise the smooth running were there, but somehow the gremlins in the machine prevented it from materialising. Not that you would notice, though; it turned out to be another smash hit.

The film-making 'gods' are very fickle. *Cleopatra* (1963), Elizabeth Taylor, Joseph L. Mankiewicz directing, almost destroyed Twentieth Century Fox. There were cast changes during production, Elizabeth Taylor was very ill, other leading actors were signed on but as the production fell behind, they had to go to other commitments and were recast, fully built exterior sets were scrapped, taken down and moved to another country, shooting overran regularly, etc., etc. The list of 'X' factor problems went on and on.

There were benefits, however. If they hadn't moved the set to Pinewood then *Carry on Cleo* (1964), Sidney James, Gerald Thomas directing, would not have had the use of the sets at Pinewood Studios and some of the costumes to make their comedy – one of their best, in my opinion.

There is, however, a general outline plan for directing a movie, of course, and I have formulated my own plan and rules after watching, listening and learning from all the people I have known over my thirty-five years in the business. Of course, I am not in Mr Steven Spielberg's league and you would be silly not to pay attention to the masters of film when you get to see them work. I was fortunate. I did a few days on *Indiana Jones and the Last Crusade* (1989), Harrison Ford, directed by Steven Spielberg. A big production or project for me is probably a short five-minute commercial in Mr Spielberg's diary and the quality would be the same high standard.

Scale is the key perspective to consider when you have the opportunity to direct. Your work must be of equal quality, large or small. A useful thought to hold on to in your mind's eye when given a project like directing a film or writing a memoir, is the answer to this question: how do you eat an elephant? (Apologies to my vegetarian and vegan readers; this is just a metaphor.)

The answer is one bite at a time.

*

There were two million working parts on the Saturn V rocket that took Neil Armstrong, Buzz Aldrin and Michael Collins to the moon in 1969. Michael Collins drove around the moon for a bit, while Neil and Buzz finished having a stroll about. If 99.9 per cent of the Saturn V worked perfectly that would mean 2,000 parts would have failed, which led to a high risk that they wouldn't get to the moon or get back home afterwards. Gulp! In comparison shooting a film is relatively easy, a piece of cake.

Just a note of caution and a spoiler alert… once you know how a film should be made, films will never be the same again because you see and understand the process. Watching films soon becomes akin to going through a ghost train ride with the lights on. You see how the scares are engineered because you see all the wires and pulleys. You may be along for the ride, but you just don't react in the same way and get surprised or scared anymore. That's why Hitchcock only did things once, because once you know it, you can predict it.

The late director Stanley Donen, when collecting his Honorary Academy Award in 1998, said this:

"I'm going to let you in on the secret of being a good director. For the script you get Larry Gelbart, or Peter

Stone, or Huyck and Katz, or Frederic Raphael – like
that. If it's a musical, for the songs you get George and Ira
Gershwin, or Arthur Freed and Herb Brown, or Leonard
Bernstein and Comden and Green, or Alan Lerner and
Fritz Loewe – like that. Then you cast Cary Grant, or
Audrey Hepburn, Fred Astaire, Gene Kelly, Sophia Loren,
Richard Burton, Rex Harrison, Gregory Peck, Elizabeth
Taylor, Burt Reynolds, Gene Hackman or Frank Sinatra –
like that," he said. *"When filming starts you show up and*
you stay the hell out of the way. But you've got to show up,
you've got to show up. Otherwise you can't take the credit."

With all this good advice to choose from, which should I pick
to pass on to you and assist you with the craft of directing and
getting your film made? This memoir is not, nor ever has been,
intended to portray the only way to direct a film; it is just a
reflection of my evening memories on what I did to get myself
into this mess in the first place (a grateful nod to the wonderful
Mr Oliver Hardy).

I think the best thing I can do, dear reader, is to tell you how
I directed one of my own films, *Birth of a Legend: Billy the Kid &*
The Lincoln County War © (2012).

It is not a film title you want to get in the game charades, but it
was the right title. For ease of the typing and my sanity in repeating
it as we go along, I will reduce it to simply *BTK* – Billy the Kid.

The story of *BTK* came to me in the summer of 2011. I had
just watched on television one of my favourite films, *Chisum*
(1970), John Wayne, Andrew V McLaglen (one of my favourite
directors) at the helm. What piqued my interest most was the
story of the Englishman, John Henry Tunstall, played by Patric
Knowles, who was fifty-nine years of age at the time.

I remembered *Young Guns* (1988) when Terence Stamp
played Tunstall and he was fifty years old at that time. I then

asked myself whether the real John Tunstall, an elderly man in the Wild West, was really a friend of BTK?

I did a little research and found a couple of sources that placed Tunstall's age at the time of the Lincoln County War at twenty-five. Tunstall was born in Dalston, London in 1853 and was killed in the Lincoln County War in 1878.

This age difference immediately piqued my curiosity since, contrary to the films, Tunstall was really a contemporary of Billy the Kid, who was born in New York in 1859 and was killed by Pat Garrett in 1881. In 1878, when Tunstall and the Kid were friends, Tunstall was twenty-five and the Kid twenty-two – just a three-year difference. *There was the kernel of a story here that Hollywood has missed*, I said to myself. Yes, to myself. No one else was listening at this stage. The other missing part of this story was that of Tunstall's first twenty-one years in England, before he emigrated to Canada, then the United States.

Once again, with a little digging I found out that he enjoyed walking on Hampstead Heath in North London. As a young man, I knew Hampstead and the Heath, its bank holiday fun fairs, very well. Tunstall called Hampstead Heath his 'little Switzerland'.

I felt I had enough to write a treatment of the story idea I had, the story of BTK as seen through the eyes of the Englishman John Tunstall. I contacted a US-based historical magazine for further research purposes; the editor said if I was going to do anything on Billy the Kid, I had best talk with Frederick Nolan first.

"He is the acknowledged authority on the subject of the Lincoln County War and on Billy the Kid."

Okay then, Frederick Nolan, I will contact him. The magazine editor was reluctant to give me Mr Nolan's address, so I had to find it out for myself. It was rather mysterious.

Who was Frederick Nolan?

What part of the US did he live in?

Would I have to travel to the US to interview him for my script? As it turned out, to my delight, Frederick Nolan lived in England and not too far from where I lived. What a piece of good fortune, although I have to admit I was a little disappointed I wasn't off to the US to track him down.

After a period of correspondence, a meeting was arranged and I travelled to his home to chat about my ideas.

Fred and I got on together, famously. From the outset I was so impressed, not only with his encyclopaedic knowledge of the Lincoln County War, but also when I discovered that he was a prolific, published thriller writer.

One of his many, many books was *The Algonquin Project*, which was turned into the Hollywood film *Brass Target* (1978), Sophia Loren and directed by John Hough.

You may not believe this, but as time would pass, John Hough became a good friend of mine.

'Signs', anyone?

Fred and I would talk for hours and hours about the Lincoln County War. Fred would correct all my Hollywood errors and confirmed my age comparisons between BTK and Tunstall. Fred is still close with the surviving Tunstall family, and they meet for lunch every February 18th to mark the date Tunstall was killed back in 1878. Fred convinced me that the person who was the key witness to the events of the Lincoln County War was John Simpson Chisum, a cattle baron based in Roswell, New Mexico, a location now made more famous for the 'alleged' UFO crashing there in 1947. Our meetings produced a treatment for the forthcoming film I had in mind, although the title was all mine. Billy the Kid was a nobody cattle bum until the events of the Lincoln County War made him a legendary hero of the Wild West historical machine. Fred, with his huge experience, agreed to write the film I was to make into two docudramas. Part one was *BTK and the Lincoln County War* and part two was *The Betrayal*.

With a very limited budget and just one Wild West town in Kent, England, available to film in, I decided to make the north side of the town Silver Springs, with the saloon doubling as John Chisum's hotel, and Lincoln became the south side and included the livery stable, as it was the sparser side of the town. It was beginning to take shape and we had already filmed some scenes.

Fred had convinced me to actually go to New Mexico, before filming to have a look at the real Lincoln, so I might get a feel of where our story was to be set. Actually, filming in Lincoln and the surrounding area was impossible in any event. The locals, frankly, have had enough of film-makers and Wild West enthusiasts.

I booked a flight to see Lincoln in the 'flesh', so to speak. Before I left Fred gave me some advice by way of a story of his own experience. He said when I arrived in Lincoln and started investigating Billy, the locals would hear my English voice and would ask me which side I was on – Billy the Kid and Tunstall or Murphy and Dolan.

I was astounded and said, "You're kidding me? They are not still like that, are they?"

Fred replied, "Oh yes, you will be asked to walk down a certain side of the street, depending which side you support."

He then added, "The last time I gave an invited lecture on Billy the Kid in Lincoln, my wife and I, Heidi, booked into a small hotel and I went out to buy some supplies in the local store. I went in and picked up some items and went to pay with my credit card. The shopkeeper took the card, looked at the name Frederick Nolan and asked me, 'Are you that Englishman who wrote about Billy the Kid?' I naturally smiled and proudly said, yes, I was him. The shopkeeper's face turned to stone and he said, 'Sheriff Brady was a relative of mine and that no-good outlaw shot him dead in the street. Get out of my store.'"

Fred left quickly, without his items.

I arrived in Lincoln County on July 5th, the day after the Independence Day celebrations. To my astonishment, just where the Tunstall store once stood (if you know the story, it was burnt down with Billy held up inside before a dramatic escape), there, flying high, was a Union Jack. Now remember this was the day after the July 4th celebrations and there were still American flags flying everywhere. Fred had given me wise advice as the BTK story still awakened hot-blooded passions and was a major industry within the US.

I felt the true story of BTK needed to be told and Hollywood would have to play catch-up for once.

At about this time, I moved office to Pinewood Studios, Room 60, which was a spectacular office looking out over the gardens and I loved it very much. I was not so keen on the journey there from North London (nor later from Hertfordshire), which involved the notorious M25, London orbital road. The studios were the hub of the UK film business and I enjoyed being at the centre of it very much.

I put together my crew, cast and stunt team. My stunt team was going to be made up of the Swedish-based unit called Stuntmakers. Peter Lundberg worked in live Wild West action too, when not working on film, to keep his team active, tuned in and always ready at their peak. All his team rode horses expertly and all could shoot guns, including period weapons. Stuntmakers, with Janne Lindquist as my stunt coordinator, became the backbone of the stunt team for *Birth of a Legend: Billy the Kid & the Lincoln County War*.

I spoke to Mr David Morley, my King Henry VIII at the Globe, to play Chisum, who was narrating the story from his sick bed, as he was dying of throat cancer at the time of the Lincoln County War.

The cast and stunt team were now engaged and enthusiastic. I always ensure that the read-through of the script for the cast and, for that matter, the technical read through by the crew, is in a comfortable location. You will get very little enthusiasm in a tent on a cold day with no hot drinks, for example.

While teaching at the stunt school in Ystad one weekend, with the help of Janne Lindquist and Peter Lundberg, I was taken north to Hässleholm. There was the cowboy stunt show and I was introduced to my future stunt team for Billy.

They were all very keen, as was the Mayor of Hässleholm, to have a film being made in his area by a British film crew. I was so impressed and felt that the stunt team and the location would be perfect for *Billy*, as I wanted it to be as authentic as possible.

I scouted the locations with the mayor; in particular I was looking for a location in the script called Tunstall Canyon, where John Tunstall was actually murdered.

This time a good friend and businessman joined the production team and advised us on various matters – Prof David Austin, who was President of the British Academy of Fencing and had sent me to win the world title in Vichy in 2000.

We did a thorough location scout of the area. I knew I was on to a winning ticket when I took some photos of what I wanted to use as a location for Tunstall Canyon. It looked to me similar to the actual location in Fred Nolan's documentary book, *The Lincoln County War*. In fact, I sent the photographs to him via my mobile and in his immediate reply he asked me when I had visited Lincoln! I had found it! With the castle able to provide stabling for the horses and food and accommodation for the crew, we were all set.

A few of my actors needed to ride horses, for short scenes, so I had one of the horse masters from Stuntmakers work with them before a take, just to make sure they were happy and that the horses were all fit and able to do the action required.

I have a strong connection with horses. I was trained by my sister Maureen Wilkinson-Till, who taught me from a very young age how to ride – I still have the scars to prove it.

For film work, as an actor, you won't be stunting and will have grooms to put on bridles and saddles, so you don't really need to know all that, and they will be trained horses so won't be skittish around clashing swords or the explosion of gunfire. The skill of the rider is to stay in the saddle and stirrups (if available), to be seated, look like you belong there and in control. Most importantly, you must be able to ride to camera. No point giving a line or doing an action as your horse is running away with you and you exit out of shot left or right. No one will hear your lines or see your action.

Whether you are stationary, riding towards the camera, or riding beside or parallel to the camera (which is also moving – that is the definition of a tracking shot), it is important that you know your edge of frame. If the director doesn't tell you, then ask them. If you go out of frame, you'll get the blame even if no one told you where it is. They will blame the actor riding the horse and it will delay the set-up for the next scene while you do it again.

Your horse master will tell you which side of the horse is their good side. No, that is not a joke about good-looking horses. They may have better sight or hearing one side or the other or have been trained to fall one way. You won't take the fall unless you are the stuntman as well. Trust what they say.

When you arrive on a horse picture as a rider actor, it will be like entering a pentathlete competition with fencing, shooting, riding, swimming and running. The horses come from a pool which are assigned on the morning and you won't know them. That's why lots of pentathletes become stunt people, because they can do all these things.

When you arrive on a picture as the director, beware! When you cast an action sequence, everyone you ask can ride a horse like Lester Piggott, swim like Johnny Weissmuller and fence like Errol Flynn! I have said this before but it is worth mentioning again, so, beware!

No matter how careful you are, accidents do happen with actors on horses, as sadly was the case with the late, great Roy Kinnear.

Much to the British Horse Society's (BHS) chagrin and annoyance, you cannot ride with lance, sword or gun while holding the reins in a BHS two-handed way. Sorry BHS, we need one hand free. The horses you use will all be neck-trained and it will respond to one hand on the reins – left, right, forward or back, leaving the other hand free for your lariat, six shooter, lance or sword. When jousting, of course, your shield will also be on the rein arm and your lance will be in your free hand.

The rising trot is also very cavalry in style and was first used by them, rising on the right lead leg of the horse, which made long rides easy on both rider and horse. The Western gait of the 'jog' is most commonly used with trained action horses.

N

As you may recall, my offices were at Pinewood Studios and I needed a sound stage to complete all the interior work, which I had started in Kent. We needed to recreate the upstairs of the saloon and Chisum's bedroom where he tells the reporter his true account of Billy's story. We thought about going back to the Wild West town, but the rooms in their hotel were not big enough to film in easily. All of the team I needed for the interiors, including a production designer and the property acquisition team, were in place.

There was a problem at Pinewood, however; the wonderful director Mr Tim Burton had booked all of the sound stages except the 007 stage, one of, if not the largest sound stage in Europe and that was being used by Mr Ridley Scott, for his *Prometheus* (2012) production.

Mr Tim Burton was working on his forthcoming film with Johnny Depp, *Dark Shadows*. Pinewood were unable to help me with space. I was very disappointed that the timing had fallen so poorly, but I had no control over it. I would have to wait at least six months to get my little film onto one of the sound stages. Mr Tim Burton heard that I needed a small sound stage and, being a true film-maker, knowing that getting films made is tough as it is, gave me approval and a blessing to take Sound Stage 'S'.

'S' was the perfect size for what I needed; just a week to recreate the bedroom and shoot was all I needed. I sent a big thank you back through channels. We moved into Sound Stage 'S'.

The construction of the set went exceedingly well. I had engaged Ella Chaitow as my assistant. Ella, a fencing student of mine from the City of London Girls School and one of the fencers who came up to the Cutting Edge for additional training, is now a senior production coordinator in the business, having worked on films such as *Mission Impossible: Rogue Trader*, *Star Wars: The Force Awakens*, *Kingsman: The Golden Circle* and *Solo: A Star Wars Story*.

I do recall Ella coming to my Pinewood office a few years previously to my hiring her for *BTK*, asking if I could help her break in. I simply introduced her to some of the people I know, and she did the rest. An extraordinarily talented and motivated individual, she is productive and so easy to work with. I am very proud of all of Ella's achievements. Nick White and his crew were my camera department. All top-drawer crew.

I cannot say enough in praise of David Morley as an actor. David portrayed Chisum, who was dying of throat cancer, brilliantly and everyone was applauding him when he finished a long scene.

I wanted to do one exterior shot for a graveside scene for John Tunstall's funeral. We had permission from Pinewood to pick a location on the backlot to do the scene. Tunstall was murdered on 18th February 1878. It was not in Fred's book, yet I figured the scene needed a little something extra to make it work. Between you and me, and please don't tell anyone else, the burial scene of John Tunstall is a scene I had to abandon.

The artists among you know will know what I mean. You work on a painting for weeks, months even, and when you stand back and look at it, there is something not right. You're not quite sure what, but somehow it is not what you had in mind. This was what I felt at the graveside scene. I was never quite happy with it. I filmed it twice in two different locations, but it just wasn't quite the vision I had and I didn't have the time to spend on it. A school friend of mine, another great film buff, Michael Smith, played the non-speaking part of the 'Padre' at the graveside and there was an extra female mourner. The scene still lacked austerity. I asked for some snow candles, used to create snow scenes without using elaborate foam snow. I sent Ella to find some. She came back and said a special effects team on the lot said they would be more than happy to give me some for my scene. This is the brotherhood of film-makers and if you shout 'help', people come to your assistance. I shot the film with my 'Padre', my extra and BTK, and it was about 98 per cent what I wanted; it was now in the can.

Phase one, Kent, phase two, Hässleholm, and now phase three, Pinewood Studios, were completed, and now all I needed was a great soundtrack and a great editor.

For the soundtrack I called Scott, my younger brother, who now lived in Austin, Texas. I sent him the temp track I had used. If you are not sure what a temp track is, may I cordially invite you to go to my website, www.wilkinsonproductions.com, and ask you to listen to the podcast of Garry's documentary *Lost Film Scores*, where he explains how music is added to films. Essentially it is recorded music that has the flavour of the piece of music that the director wants for the scene. George Lucas used the Holst 'Planets Suite', particularly 'Mars', to demonstrate the style of music he wanted for the final scene in *Star Wars*. John Williams did an excellent job for Mr Lucas.

Scott's music was so perfect that it was exactly what I had been looking for and, even better, Chisum's theme became one of Frederick Nolan's favourite pieces of music.

As far as editing goes, I had an edit suite in my office at Pinewood. There are two types of editor – the off-line editor indexes the footage and the on-line editor then chooses the film from the bundles to make the film. It's a bit like doing a jigsaw puzzle – the off-line editor puts all the pieces in piles for straight edges, different colours or objects, and the on-line editor then has the picture on the box – the director's vision – and he assembles the film by looking at the picture. Director's cuts generally come about not because of differences between the editor and the director, but between the director and the producers who want to change the vision – adding more sex scenes or stunts or a narrator to explain the story, as in *Blade Runner*. I hired an off-line editor to assemble the footage and then a top-flight on-line editor, Tom Sharp, now a good family friend, to put it together.

Tom added his magic and the completed work was ready for sale through Amazon in the autumn of 2012.

✕

I have heard, over the years, actors and crew sharing their film-making stories, especially when all the good intentions of a film project go south or sour because a film director says that a scene has to be done today, in a certain way. They explain the need to rush the production to get everything in place, within financial constraints or even poor light or double bookings of things or people. The set atmosphere changes due to the rush and speed required and something almost like panic strikes the project, especially at the end of a long day when everyone is tired anyway.

I have been fortunate on my own projects. Where I was in charge, I have marshalled my team and sets so that all the work needed on a particular day is done in a calm and creative fashion.

Golden Swords, a massively complex theatre show, using hundreds of costumes, weapons and props, actors, fight directors and fighters from all over the country, was executed without any panic and reprised twice, once at the Globe Theatre in London and again at Warwick Castle, with the same excellent results. My personal film projects have all got underway with planning in pre-production, carefully thinking through how we could do things in a way which respected the people, time and money available, and communicating in a way that meant that everyone knew what, when and how everything would be done and by whom. My team then executed the plan without sleepless nights. This is *not* an accidental approach to film-making, as long experience has shown films cannot be made any other way, and cast and crew need to be sure-footed. Hopefully all your gremlins will be under lock and key!

Pre-production planning is the key to success. I have never really read a story about or heard on the grapevine that Hitchcock, Ford, Spielberg, Blake Edwards, Martin Scorsese or other top directors ever had a panic day when rushing to get the last shot to the detriment of the cast and crew.

Yes, there are numerous tales of the 'front desk' of a studio applying pressure on a director, but they are not creatives; they are working in a different bubble.

Everyone has their 'X' factor moments within a project, but you can do a wet day programme when you can't shoot outside. You just have to give yourself the time and space just to plan, identify risks and mitigate them.

N

I was an unknown film director. In theatre I had a little reputation, but behind the camera, none. This business is just that, a business, and it is brutal. It gives few breaks to unknowns, especially directors. I had accumulated seventy-three productions in front of camera, but to the accountants who finance films that meant nothing.

I set up a new company called BTK Pictures Ltd and we started filming, in three phases, as we had to finance it ourselves, stage by stage.

Why did I bore you with all this information before I got on with my suggestions for putting a film together? The previous pages are a framework for the ten most useful things I did to get *Birth of a Legend* made. I do hope you find it interesting and useful.

I.   The Script

Number one on my list is to get the best script you possibly can first. This is going to be your *Genesis Scroll*. From this, everything else will follow because the script is the director's vision for the film that he or she wants to make, albeit only on paper at this stage.

From the script, everything else flows. To start, there is the cinematography. The director of photography (DoP) is the person in charge of lighting a set or location, who will direct the gaffer who deals with the physical necessities of a lighting rig.

As the director, you can have a vision of what you want to see on the screen, but the devil is in the detail. Your DoP will understand how to create the look of the film you are searching for by using different combinations of natural and manufactured lighting. Should it be dark or light, *Lawrence of Arabia* or *Blade Runner*?; what is the mood or ambiance of the scene – a smoky club or Wild West bar? Is it grainy or black and white, with sharp or soft-focus edges? Just as an example, have a look at how the shadows are created and used in *The Third Man* (1949), Joseph Cotten, directed by Carol Reed. DoPs know to use their palettes to produce colours and tone and to combine the natural and artificial light to best effect, such as the magic hours of daylight and sunset. Many directors and DoPs work together for many years, each understanding the way the other thinks and what makes them tick.

Stanley Kubrick and Ridley Scott are both experts in the lighting of their films and directing. As you know, I am not a champion of wearing too many hats. I wear quite a few hats for my production company as it is. My advice to you is to limit the number of hats you wear, don't spread yourself too thinly and leave the lighting to the expert DoP.

II.   Pre-Production

Next, flowing freely across your desk will be questions on who to cast and which crew to engage. It is a long shopping list – a production designer, producer(s), locations, studio, stunt coordinator, visual effects, special effects, costume, make-up, sound and finally, but perhaps most importantly, the music.

Do you remember Darth Vader because of his dialogue in the film or from John Williams' music?

From this list, you can then decide who you actually need for your particular production and plan the crew requirements.

In the language of the film business, you will commonly find the term 'above and below the line'. This is a term widely used; however, its exact meaning and connotations can vary. In a film, people who are considered above the line are the director, screenwriter, DoP, musical score, producer(s) and the main cast of actors. Below the line are the crew, camera department, lighting department, gaffer, riggers, dolly, make-up, costume and so on, depending on the production. There are standard union rates for almost all of these roles.

The script is also your accountant's friend and your enemy. From the script, the budget can be estimated to a greater or lesser degree, and it will show how much money your vision will cost the financiers. Now all you have to do is find someone to give you the money.

Once you have all your key personnel hired, you can move into the next phase. Pre-production. This is where you have the most fun, in my opinion, with low stress levels and full-on creativity.

Hire a brilliant artist to create the storyboards and concept art for your vision. My storyboard artist, the amazing lady I hired for *BTK*, was an ex-student of the Cutting Edge Fencing Club, Alex Moore. She was six years old when we first met and is now a full-time artist and teacher of art. My office is covered with the artwork which Alex has done for my productions. Framed scenes from my vision of the story are valuable tools when working on a production and wonderful to help you in the evenings of your memory.

Everything you do in pre-production will reduce the possibility of meeting loose gremlins later in the production. You cannot plan for the unforeseeable, that's why we have insurance, yet if your productions are well crafted and organised, you should be able to manage all the unforeseen hiccups and take them in your stride, especially if you have the right people on your team.

I have always been able to 'feel' if the pre-production phase is going well and when the pre-production is out of balance, it is usually due to a failure in communication between key people, perhaps not saying something for fear of rocking the boat. Creating that atmosphere is down to the executive producer or more likely, the director, the person where the buck stops. If you create an atmosphere on your production that doesn't allow creative, productive engagement, then silence will bring mishap and a gremlin will be waiting to pounce.

III.   Casting

There are many books written by worldly wise teachers and acting coaches on the skills and techniques of acting, as they all work in different ways. Ask yourself a few questions to start with…

How do my favourite directors work with actors?

Can I learn from them?

Do all Oscar- or BAFTA-winning actors have sublime directors at the helm of their films?

There are several methods which actors use to find a character, from making it up as they go along, to putting on a bit of wardrobe, a pair of glasses and a new haircut, to complete immersion in researching and living the role for months before the performance. If you get to know your cast, even after a casual chat you may discover their 'on' switch and then you will understand and appreciate the method your cast use.

Some directors totally ignore the acting process, taking the view that 'I cast them, they're actors, so get on with it', some want the actors to turn up with a vision already mapped out for their performance and a few directors do an in-depth analysis of what the actor's performance should be.

In my humble opinion when casting, you should try to establish rapport with your cast, getting to know a little about them, their history and the journey that brought them to your casting. You should share a lot about your project, your vision and why you want it to be a certain way.

An engaged cast is a wonderful bonus to any production. The cast is the shop window of your vision. They will be the ones talking to the audience on your behalf, so it is important to get this element right from the outset. If, however, they consider it is just a job for them, to pay the bills, they're more likely to have no more than a lightweight, shallow conversation with the audience. This gremlin might best be avoided and the smooth running of the project may be best suited if you keep looking.

There is an old parable, you may know it, perhaps, but it rings so true when I think about casting, even at the writing stage!

> "The rain came down, the floods came, and the winds blew, and beat on that house; and it didn't fall, for it was founded on the rock. Everyone who hears these words of mine, and doesn't do them will be like a foolish man, who built his house on the sand."

Drawn from my experience on both sides of the camera and from my study of all aspects of the role I am undertaking, whether it is sword master or director, I have evolved this approach. There is no correct or right way and everyone has their own preferences, but add this to your range of knowledge and take what works for you to develop your own style.

I like to communicate with my actors, in fact with everyone. The fear of the camera, the physical beast in the room, just by its very presence, is intimidating for a lot of people, especially if they come from the stage. They perform to the fourth wall which is to say, they look directly at the camera or the audience (if they come from theatre), when of course all you want them to do is to perform and act as if the camera is not actually there.

If you have the budget, you can get professional casting agents, but on a low budget it is likely to be a luxury you cannot afford and it will be down to you to cast the roles. If casting is professionally undertaken, your 'A' cast will be well known and will have a pedigree. The chemistry between your cast is very important and not to be underestimated. This is where the buck stops, with you as director having the final choice. The decisions are down to you.

Films where the casting is sublime are, in my view, easy to spot. Kathleen Turner and Michael Douglas, in *Romancing the Stone* (1984), Robert Zemeckis directing, is a great example. In fact, one cannot go wrong watching all of Mr Zemeckis' films for casting. All outstanding jobs.

Alternatively consider Katharine Hepburn and Spencer Tracy, in any of their nine films together; John Wayne and Maureen O'Hara, in any of their five films together; Errol Flynn and Olivia de Havilland, who did eight films together.

The director's vision of their film can clearly be seen in the chemistry between Herbert Lom and Peter Sellers, in the *Pink Panther* films directed by Blake Edwards. It's just perfect.

You clearly see the chemistry when it is there and I am sure you can all think of your own films where the chemistry in the casting didn't work. Sometimes, for reasons unknown, it just doesn't happen and then you need to be wary to prevent it becoming a poisoned apple in your barrel of other cast members. The only way to discover such a crinkle in a project is to cover as many bases in rehearsal as you can. The main cast should meet first, without contractual obligation, to see if they all gel together. That is the time for you, and your producers, to observe very closely. Some directors like to shoot rehearsals, where it's all much more relaxed, without telling the cast it is being filmed so they cannot see the beast in the room – the camera. Having a relaxed atmosphere and letting the scenes flow without the demands of the camera can often bring out exquisite performances for you, the director, and the other cast members in the scene.

These are, of course, professional actors and actresses who will deliver the role they have been cast for and if there are any problems, you must deal with them professionally too, in a calm, clear voice. A raised voice from the director is a sign of a loss of control of your set, and that will be felt by the rest of the cast and crew. So be firm but helpful and use humour to make it light if possible, though not of course if you are working on an emotional, violent or sad scene. It often helps, I find, to evoke something from them that you discovered during your casting interview and personal chat. Never get personal or hurtful, this is entertainment, after all, and you are all professionals. It may need only a reminder of a feeling that they may be searching for or a thought to make them remember a situation or feeling from the past that they can draw on. Always speak *to* them, not *at* them. If your actor needs more, or perhaps even less, from you and you are still not getting what you are after, then perhaps the casting was wrong.

I am often asked by fight directors and actors what is required to be employable on a film or theatre production: the answer is usability and whether you can be plugged into a position or role to help the production and are qualified to do so.

Over my years of experience, where I have been sword master on a film, I have been 'plugged in' and left to get on with the job, secure in the knowledge that I am qualified and capable of instructing novices and experienced fencers.

I have to say the knowledge and understanding of the language of swordplay, like 'circular parry of sixte', is quite poor by those who claim they can perform or even instruct swordplay. If you offer yourself as a qualified sword person, you must be fluent in the language of swordplay and proficient with sword in hand, and if it is revealed on set that you are not, the consequences will be significant for the production as the sword master will need more time to teach you. You may not be called back.

IV.   Pre-production Shot List

How do you eat an elephant?

Yes, I know you know, now. The pre-production shot list is essential so that you can make this manageable and sleep at night.

Working out each and every scene, including how, when and what is required from the cast and crew on a daily basis, will ease the pressure. This is the daily shot list and from this entire series of other important lists are created.

One of the first problems to resolve is how many film units you need – providing, of course, you have that luxury in your budget. The first unit deals with the main cast and all the dialogue in the scene. The second unit deals with all the action elements, the direction of the chase, all the external elements, obstacles encountered on the chase, involving various vehicles. The third unit will deal with the close-ups of items and over-the-shoulder shots or point-of-view shots of the chase. Unit three also picks up all the loose ends of the scene. You can break it down how you wish, but generally the second unit will not work with the main cast (unless they are the stunt unit), filming instead the incidental shots, such as an exterior shot of a train moving though countryside or an exterior shot of a ship at sea. Do not make the mistake of thinking the second or third units are less skilled or valuable. That is a big mistake. All are very highly skilled and professional; their work can make a film special. Some of the best second unit directors are either editors, such as John Glenn, who became a Bond director, or stunt coordinators such as Yakima Canutt and Vic Armstrong.

And speaking of action sequences, these may take as many as 100 to 200 bites to get the scene you want. If you watch an action sequence, you will see there are lots and lots of edits to show all the elements of the sequence and raise the tension of the scene, for example a motor car chase ending in a crash and the hero's escape. The reason you have different units on a film is to cover all the bases of the script, and if all the units can work together, this formula can cut down the shooting days and be very cost-effective.

The call sheet is a list of all those needed on that day and where, when and for how long they are needed. Notes can be added to the call sheet to refresh the memory of key personnel involved.

Now why have I said this should be in pre-production?

It is easier to fix anomalies in pre-production than when filming ,so talking to everyone required for the scene, I mean everyone with a title on the film, is essential. It will allow you to make specific notes of issues on the call sheet and reminds everyone to sing from the same song sheet on the day.

It is particularly important because, and sorry to disappoint those of you who didn't know, it is very rare to shoot an entire film in sequence, i.e. scene one, two, three, four, etc. *Saving Private Ryan* (1998), Tom Hanks and directed by Steven Spielberg, is perhaps the most well-known film shot in sequence on purpose. All designed and managed in pre-production. This was a directorial choice by Mr Spielberg. The story concerned the D-Day landings and a group of soldiers ordered to rescue the last surviving member of a family, who was somewhere in Northern France. Day one of the film and day one for the cast was the landing and then the subsequent days concerned the push into France to find Private Ryan. The cast looked like they had fought a battle, every day, which they did. Scene one was followed by scene two and so on. A very powerful masterclass on how to make a movie.

Another is Kenneth Branagh's *Henry V*, where the Battle of Harfleur was filmed before the Battle of Agincourt as it was in real life in 1415. The 'cut to' scenes included the weary English soldiers marching from battle to battle.

For other films, though, the sequencing of shots is much more likely to be based on which sets are ready or locations are available, whether cast members are free and able to work, and perhaps even the weather conditions. It is quite possible you may need to film the end before the beginning of the film.

When you are shooting a film, the easiest way to remember what you are doing at any one moment is to build a formula of shots you stick to, if at all possible.

There are essentially three different types of shot – a wide shot establishes *where* you are in the scene, a medium shot shows *who* is in the scene and finally a two shot as you get closer to those playing in the scene, for example a poker game with two to three people, is a two shot. Then you have to do pick-ups.

It's easy to get lost here, so imagine that you're having a conversation with a friend in the pub and someone is listening. They are the camera and may look at both of you to start with, then at one or other of you as you speak or respond to what has been said, back and forth during the conversation. That sequencing is achieved in the editing process and you need to provide the editor with the material to do that. All you do is film both sides, fully, without moving the camera, even when the dialogue goes out of shot of the camera. Don't worry, you will pick that up when you shoot in the other direction. If you make sure the cuts are whole and have a proper conversation, your editor can use a longer rather than an MTV or fast-edit style, which as a viewer I personally find uncomfortable. Film the lot!

Treat each scene as a little separate project. For example, shoot the horse-riding scene to include the master, tracking, close-ups, two shot, then all the angles of the characters riding and those characters watching the scene, the impact of hooves on the ground in puddles or dust thrown up. Always think about what else needs to be done to satisfy the script, while appeasing the writer and editor and staying within budget so everyone remains happy with the day's work.

As an example, film a conversation from a two-shot point of view (often shortened to POV), then film all of one person's dialogue, perhaps moving the camera around over their shoulder, then you reverse and do their dialogue. Remember the eyeline, that is where your actor should be lookin,g and remember that the shadow of the eyeline will also appear on a close-up in a confined area; for example in a submarine cabin, there will be shadows and that will be the eyeline for the cast member talking to camera. This is important because, if it is wrong, the audience will realise the actor is speaking to thin air when there should be someone opposite them.

You should be working this out in pre-production rather than wasting valuable time and resources on set thinking about what you are going to do next. The cast and crew want you to get on with it.

That's not to say that you shouldn't give yourself a moment to think when you need it. Rushing never looks or is professional. If you need a moment, pick up your director's eyepiece, stand away from everyone and look at something on set or location. This will give you a few moments of thinking time yet you still will look busy and professional.

Of course, when you're not shooting in sequence, the energy levels from your cast and crew need to be watched. If the scene is towards the end of the film, where the cast should be exhausted within the story, they cannot look or act like they have just come from a spa weekend. All of this can feature in your call sheets.

V.   Communication

I may have mentioned this before and I cannot emphasise enough how important communication is between you and your entire team. Delegate some of the cascading of your thinking and vision by all means, but communicating your aims and ambitions to everyone is key!

I am not asking the director to talk to everyone, every day, because you'll end up annoying people, although your key personnel should and they should report back to you, every day at one of the staff production meetings, normally first thing in the morning before everyone else arrives. Yes, there are long days on production.

The film is not only going to be your vision, it needs to be your cast and crew's vision too, so tell them that and get them engaged and involved! The director should engage with the main cast as soon as possible after casting. Senior members of the cast, those who have been in the business for a while, will respect you all the more if you share with them what you have in mind, how you see the vision and why they were cast in the first place. Obviously, they have something to offer and to bring to your film, so take them with you on this journey too. Trust me, if they are not interested in what you are saying about the film you are aiming for, you may have cast them poorly.

In 2005 I wrote and directed a full-length documentary of the manned spaceflight programme of NASA, called *False Dawn: The Promise of Apollo* ©. In the film, I talk about how the team at NASA pulled the entire nation in one direction, which was to put a man on the moon. Thousands of people would be needed, including engineers, technicians, tool builders, scientists and computer engineers, and they had to build the infrastructure to achieve President Kennedy's goal. They came from all over the USA, from different time zones, but they did it. Communication between all departments and sections of people across the world was achieved.

Film-making is exactly the same, perhaps not on the same scale as putting a man on the moon, although it sometimes feels like it.

Your project is not a memory test. It can take years to get a project off the ground and yet somehow you need to keep everyone fresh and active with the project. If you don't talk about it, it will die. If the read-through of your scripts is in January and the pre-production is not until March, then you can come off the boil. So, keep your cast fresh, invigorated, challenged, but don't be annoying. They are working on other things to pay their bills!

One short cut to creating great communication is for the director to surround themselves with a troupe of actors and crew, who follow them from project to project, rather like a theatre production company, and well-known examples include John Ford, John Wayne and Clint Eastwood. This breeds trust, familiarity and a family atmosphere for their continuing projects, and reduces and controls both budgets and the time it takes from conception to delivery of the production.

However, this approach has also often brought a level of criticism, a suggestion that it lacks innovation and fresh ideas and just produces slightly different versions of the first film. Sometimes that is reflected in the box office, sometimes not. Criticism is a thorny subject. People within the entertainment industry who make films generally treat good and bad reviews the same way and simply ignore them. Critics don't make films or write scripts. They sit in judgement on other people's work; work they cannot do themselves.

VI.   Time

You will be surprised how often time is forgotten when planning a film. How long is a filming day? No, that is not a daft question – a day is twenty-four hours, yes, we know that, but which time of the year will you be filming? If you want to film exterior shots in the autumn, your day will be much, much shorter in the UK.

You'll get a lot done from the read-through of the script, such as character developments, costumes and cast relationship-building. It will be the first time as a director you get to hear your script read by the actors and you'll be able to temper them to your vision. Raise those who are shy and temper those who are too much for the character or for a scene.

Post-production time is important too. You will need to remember that editors need quite a long time to review all the footage and that computer-generated imagery requires time for the rendering of the digital images so they can be used and manipulated.

Time is linked directly to the budget, so don't waste it and use your pre-production time efficiently and wisely.

VII. The Shoot

The day has finally arrived – enjoy it! Get that vision of yours made! Shoot as much as you can.

There will be choices to be made, some in pre-production and some as the shooting starts. You may choose one style and stick to it, or shift as the mood takes you. I was working as a sword master on an advert for a young director at Arundel Castle and he sent me a note asking me what I thought of his style of direction. As a young, enthusiastic director, he was obviously searching for his style, yet it was still in its formative stages. I hope he found it!

Every director would like to show off their talent, their style or imagination and leave a signature on their films. Alfred Hitchcock, a master of direction, once said he would never do a sequence that had been seen before. He created styles and images that others would copy; he would call all those who copied his work as lacking original thought. In the climax to *North by Northwest* (1959), you see Cary Grant, the main character, standing on a road surrounded by a field of crops, with a single onlooker on the opposite side of the road, waiting for a bus going in the other direction. Hitchcock shows the audience in a master shot, the entire scene – north, south, east and west. The audience is put in the same position as the lead character and knows they can be pre-warned of any peril coming. Yet Hitchcock, for the first time on film, used a crop duster plane as the protagonist and no one in the scene, especially the audience, thought of looking upwards for the peril to strike! Mr Hitchcock did!

You may not think this scene extraordinary today, yet this was the first time it had ever been seen. Of course, every other film since which uses aircraft or helicopters to chase characters on the ground is a reworking of Hitchcock's first time. Sometimes it is done well, for example in *Capricorn One* (1977) helicopters were used to hunt down the three astronauts in the desert.

The times change and so do styles. Three-time Oscar-winning director John Ford would keep the camera locked down, with no sweeping cranes or hand-held camera movements. In *The Quiet Man* (1952) it is said that an assistant director suggested to Ford that, to film the train coming into the station, they put the camera on a crane and pan down from above, as the train arrived. Apparently, Ford asked if the assistant saw his trains coming into the station in this way. The assistant said no and Ford said, "No, neither do I." Not surprisingly, the camera stayed on the platform as the train arrived.

One of best examples of a director's style that, I believe, was never used before (and let me know if you can prove me wrong) is in *Contact* (1997), directed by Robert Zemeckis. When Ellie's father dies, she runs up the stairs to get his medicine. The audience follow her up the stairs, along the landing corridor and, all of a sudden, you see her face in the cabinet mirror and she opens the door to get the medicine. It looks as though it was all one continuous shot, yet you are in front of her and then you see the mirror in the cabinet. It's a beautiful shot, but the audience will not necessarily appreciate its complexity, especially without understanding how it was done. A special piece of film, which made me smile on seeing it; it still does to this day. Well done, very nice.

Of course, *2001: A Space Odyssey* (1968), directed by Stanley Kubrick, is perhaps the epitome of film-making. It required the technology for his vision to be invented before the film could be made. The concept of filming in space had not really been seen on film yet as man had not landed on the moon, so camera use, set design, spaceflight – all had to be started from scratch, and of course there were no computer graphic images (CGI) back then. Mr Kubrick was in charge of production, from concept to delivery. The sets were on gimbals, which meant that the sets would move while the camera was stationary or vice versa. All planned and technically designed to a level that was unsurpassed.

Although other films had outstanding production values, just look at the epics *The Ten Commandments* (1956), *Ben-Hur* (1959), *The Fall of the Roman Empire* (1964), *2001* raised the benchmark, as it was the first film where someone like Charlie Chaplin from the silent movie era would have walked on set and not recognised all the equipment and changes in role of the director. Kubrick had changed all that and inspired future generations. *2001* is outstanding and way above the accepted level of films being produced at that time or even today, even with *Star Wars* and the Marvel adventures. I think *2001* is the standard against which future films will be measured.

Other directors use tricks of the camera to tell the story. Mr Spielberg is an expert on using the camera to invigorate a scene to the maximum. To name just one of his many examples, in *War of the Worlds* (2005), an extra was using a video camera to film the extra-terrestrial invasion. As they flee, they stumble and the camera falls to the ground. Despite the big action going on in the scene, the action is momentarily just viewed on the small video screen, which was very clever.

Cloverfield (2008), Lizzy Caplan, directed by Matt Reeves, was very innovative, perhaps taking the same theme to its natural conclusion, using a hand-held camera for the entire film. However, as an audience member, I found the shaky, unfocussed and jittery camera movement only acceptable for a few minutes at a time and as a consequence, I have not revisited it. I understand, though, that *Cloverfield* raises its hat to the modern age of social media, YouTube, the gamesters' generation and mobile phone technology.

It also demonstrates that the choice of aspect ratio (AR) is a key creative decision made by the director for the audience. It determines the relative proportions, width and height of the film frame. I could chat away for an entire chapter about the Golden Ratio, based on the Fibonacci Sequence (the sequence of numbers is as follows: 0, 1, 1, 2, 3, 5, 8, 13, 21, 34, so on). Not only is the sequence linked to the film aspect ratios and proportions in nature, it also converts miles to kilometres!

The aspect ratio is why, when you see some films on the television, they look squished or you don't see the entire picture. *Cloverfield* has an AR of 1.85.1 which has a slight letterbox look to it and is very close to 16.9 AR, which is used mainly for HD television broadcasting. The film will work well, therefore, on DVD on a small TV screen. For me, streaming and small screen is the home for this type of film-making, whilst cinema is the ultimate form of distribution of the film industry.

A director's style can also be observed in the choice of how their film is edited. Fast and furious cutting, what I call the MTV cut, where you see any single shot for just one or two seconds until it changes again, is an acquired taste when it comes to watchability.

Easily comparable to David Lean's scene in *Lawrence of Arabia* (1962) of Omar Sharif riding to camera on a camel through the shimmering heat of the desert, interspersed with a handful of close-up edits of Peter O'Toole. The entire scene, including the short build-up and the killing of the man at the water hole, is 3:03 minutes, and David Lean has said in interviews he thought he should have held it longer. Likewise, in Hitchcock's *Rope* (1948), scenes are very effectively filmed as if they were a stage play, performed at a theatre, with no cuts or editing for long periods, placing the camera as the fourth wall on a tracking dolly.

VIII. Wrap Party

This is standard fair these days on films with a budget, and even if you are making a low-budget film, a get-together with the cast and crew, to say thank you, is always, but always, most welcome. A T-shirt or something is a nice touch too. When everyone goes home with a pat on the back, people remember it and the good word of mouth, the buzz about you and your production, is free!

IX. Editing and Post-Production

You may think the hard work is all over and you have now made the film you wanted. Nope! Sorry!

Your film is actually yet to be put together and awaits the edit room. Post-production should be handled as if it were the shoot itself and a good post-production producer is worth every penny.

The editors are possibly the most valuable people you work with closely. You must establish a good working relationship with your editor and again clearly explain your vision. If budgets will allow you the extra time with the editor, sit with them as much as you can, since the editing room is where you win your awards!

However, it is not just a question of splicing the film together. Post-production has a whole range of different and complicated aspects to it, many of which can be neglected or overlooked altogether.

Foley is one aspect of post-production which is often forgotten by a director, as they have far too much else to think about and perhaps wear too many hats, and can be a character in the film, if used well. Foley (named after sound-effect artist Jack Foley) is the reproduction of everyday sound effects that are added to film. These reproduced sounds can be anything from the swishing of clothing and footsteps or sword-fighting blades clashing, to squeaky doors and breaking glass. It requires extensive creativity to produce new and imagined noises; for example Ben Burtt, the sound designer on *Star Wars*, used the sound of a spanner hitting a high-tension metal cable as part of the sound effect for a blaster in the film.

Now, I know you have already come to the conclusion that I am a sad film nut, that stands in the corner of parties on my own, but have you listened to a wet towel falling to the bathroom floor after your morning shower? To me it sounds like a conflagration, a burst of flames. It does! Try it!

Anyway, poor or obvious, foley is now more often utilised as a comedic tool in films. In *The Villain* (1979), Kirk Douglas, directed by ex-stuntman Hal Needham, the foley has the main character, the Villain, played by Mr Douglas, walking with spurs on, even when barefoot, with every single step taken, on every type of surface and at various speeds.

Foley in radio and audio production is one of the most important tools for a producer or director. The foley in audio creates an image in the mind of every listener to replace the visuals of film and becomes your very own personal cinema, in your head. Foley is immensely important and everyone who wants to embrace all media should study it closely, as I am learning to do now with Wilkinson Productions Audio.

X.   Musical Score

Another post-production thread is the musical score. I'm a fortunate man, as my two brothers, Garry and Scott, are both accomplished musicians. Film music is something I listen to daily; I kid you not. I'm writing this listening to John Williams' music from films. This afternoon it will be Swashbucklers, I think. I buzz along to most of the music, as I am the only one in the office today.

Scott and I had a lovely lunch one day a few years ago with a very well-known British film director, who has worked in Hollywood for Disney and directed a number of classic films there. We were talking about film music and he said he really paid it no mind and that there was very little music in his films. (He mentioned a title of one of his films which I saw many years ago, so I checked it out later and found it was packed full of great film music!)

I challenged his lack of interest in music and said that I couldn't believe that he hadn't left the cinema after watching *Indiana Jones: Raiders of the Lost Ark* whistling Indy's theme. He denied even being aware of it, and Scott and I were flabbergasted. I guess some directors just don't understand film music. It is just not on their radar, yet to me it is part of the film experience.

This is not uncommon or a rare observation and is true of other people. When I was courting Katy, she would often ask what I was humming and inevitably it was a film score, perhaps the *Great Escape* (1963) theme. Other music, like rock 'n' roll or country, just doesn't make me feel much at all when listening to it, yet put on a soundtrack from Korngold, Horner, Bernstein, or Williams and I'm there, smile across my face, riding into the movie or looking for a sword to join in the fight!

I appreciate film music; the score underlines the drama of your vision. I am not unique in putting this so high on my to-do list in post-production. The best directors know the value of a film score; just look at Stanley Kubrick, Alfred Hitchcock and certainly Steven Spielberg.

The composer will need to see the footage as soon as possible, but there is often no harm in giving the composer a temp track to get the juices flowing.

∧

Well, that is basically the ten items on my board; my ten important things to remember. Yet X never marks the spot (name the film?).

My apologies if this is more action film-orientated rather than based on the rom-com genre, yet the essential steps are the same. I'm sure directing a rom-com would be a challenge I'd welcome! I'd make a perfect Cary Grant type, wouldn't I? Nah!

You may look back at this last section of my memoir and say that I am naïve and that no film can be made like this. But I have a little experience, as I was elected to BAFTA in 2002 and still am a member. Is it unrealistic to get a great team together and all singing from the same song sheet, especially on a low budget? No, it works; it really does.

I was fortunate that Ivor Benjamin, a wonderfully talented man, knew of me and my reputation as a new director and swordsman. He was then the CEO of the Directors' Guild of Great Britain and I was invited to become a member at a time when it was the only guild for directors in the UK. After a short while, I was invited by Ivor and other members of the guild to become a member of the committee, and I gratefully accepted. This was an amazing opportunity to meet lots of interesting directors such as Herbert Wise (*I, Claudius*), John Hough (*Escape from Witch Mountain*, 1975) and Piers Haggard (*Pennies from Heaven*, 1978) to name just a few, and I learned a huge amount from them simply by keeping my ears open and my mouth shut! I learnt the practical side of creating the magic from these people and learnt from their experience.

So, believe me when I say that communication, sharing common goals and being surrounded by the most engaged team you can muster are the essential elements. However, I always remember, as my father would remind me, the fable of the Emperor's New Clothes. A story where people believe or pretend to believe in the worth or importance of something that is worthless or fear to point out an obvious truth that is counter to prevailing opinion. In other words, never get a big head, about anything; remember who you are and that you always have new things to learn.

Finally, if you want to know how much work goes into creating your vision, please try and find *The Making of Stanley Kubrick's 2001: A Space Odyssey*. It will put you in the picture, literally.

SCENE 9

WHERE VIOLENCE BEGINS...

…and reason and discourse ends.

This is an odd chapter title for you; however, I have actually given this as a lecture for the Directors' Guild of Great Britain (DGGB) a number of times, co-hosted by the chair of the DGGB Ivor Benjamin, another real aficionado of the film world, to an audience of directors, producers, writers, actors, stuntmen and fight directors. I have also given an abridged version to the fencing community, for coaches who have actors turning up to their classes wanting to learn fencing and a little bit more.

Before I talk about the how, when, what, why and who of stage and screen violence, I would like to talk briefly in general terms. Dramatic violence begins at the point where reason and discourse ends, whether that is a slap to the face or full-out war. The level of violence depicted in any sequence is determined by many factors, and I will explore some of the key factors in this chapter.

In my lecture, I would now show you some film clips, and of course that is not possible in these pages. I know you are all film buffs and will know of the films I talk about and the violent scenes in them. I will, though, just be summarising the scenes for those not so familiar with these works. These are all theatrically released films made by world-class directors and illustrate what a film-maker needs to consider when making a film.

There is nothing quite like diving into the deep end. Since the first time I gave this lecture, the world has rolled on somewhat and many people ask how they can depict realistic violence in the creative world when, in the real world, fanatics are executing people and posting the footage online. The simple answer is you cannot.

Gladiators in the Circus Maximus were once brutally killed for entertainment purposes. The world rolled on from that time in our history and now, we make films about gladiators, recreating the violence of those times to help tell the story. In 80AD, to celebrate the opening of the Colosseum in Rome, 100 days of games took place, and it is thought that some 2,000 people and 9,000 animals died during the celebrations. In Ridley Scott's film *Gladiator*, after the director shouted, "Cut," all the gladiators got up from the sand and went home for tea.

Now, graphic scenes of violence, or the threat of imminent violence, are almost a prerequisite for getting a project greenlit, especially when you are looking at the golden dollar demographic, that is, the upper teenage market who are over seventeen years of age, are not students and therefore have an income. In the USA an R rating requires an under-seventeen-year-old to have an accompanying parent or adult guardian.

How far should a writer push the boundaries of a story? Remember, it is the writer who presents the script to the producer and the producer engages the director. Who calls the shots on how much violence should be filmed and eventually screened?

American Sniper (2014), starring Bradley Cooper, directed by Clint Eastwood, had an R rating in the USA. It is based on actual events and shows the sniper's view, through his scope, of a prisoner about to be drilled through the head with an electric drill. Does the fact that it is a depiction of reality justify the violence depicted?

Another example, *Saving Private Ryan* (1998), Tom Hanks, Steven Spielberg directing, is a graphic telling of the D-Day landings, June 6th 1944. The re-creation of the landings themselves are violent, showing brutal injuries, as they were in real life. Yet on the same topic, *The Longest Day* (1962), John Wayne and directed by Ken Annakin, Andrew Marton, Bernhard Wicki, Gerd Oswald and Darryl F. Zanuck, provided a far less graphic telling of the story.

Look at the figures for these films. *American Sniper* cost just under $59 million and took around $550 million by 2019. *Saving Private Ryan* cost around $70 million and has taken about $482 million. *The Longest Day*, made in the 1960s, cost $10 million and has made around $50 million.

Make of those figures what you wish. Violence or the threat of violence is an integral part of the storytelling process and there is clearly a market for these films. The context of the violence defines its type but the level of that violence will be a choice by the production team, writer, director, producer or financier. The level of violence you write into your film can and should have a full spectrum from your creative palette, not just the one colour. But beware, it will also carry consequences, some more obvious than others.

To this day I remember when I first watched *In the Heat of the Night* (1967), Sidney Poitier, Rod Steiger and directed by Norman Jewison. In this film, the violence is delivered in the context of a racially fuelled environment, not a war zone. The writers and director used a simple slap to the face as the punctuation to one of the key scenes. It was so effective I still remember it all these years later. A marked difference, I am sure you will agree, to the D-Day landing scenes of *Saving Private Ryan*. It is all about context.

In one of my lectures, I asked two colleagues, both Equity fight directors, one male, one female, to arrive for the show as a couple and mix with the audience. They were an unremarkable couple and sat with the audience, where they listened and took notes and chatted away. As the day wore on, I asked them to have a small argument, overheard by others at coffee breaks. The argument gradually got louder and louder, and they both became more agitated with each other. This laid the groundwork and, just as I was explaining an example of creating violence with small-scale argument and slap rather than a long and involved car chase and scene, their argument broke into a domestic fight, punctuated with a slap to the face. The audience was not expecting it and was stunned and uncomfortable that the couple's fight had ended up on stage in the middle of a lecture. The fight ended up near my lectern where I had been standing watching. I stepped forward to rescue the young man as the lady was winning. I stepped between them and then turned to the audience and introduced them. To much relief and applause, they kissed and made up. As they left the stage and I continued with my talk, the male returned to the stage and broke a bottle over my head. Though the audience now knew who he was, they still gasped as it happened. That was the end of my lecture and I went to A&E – no, no, only kidding! It was a stage breakaway bottle.

N

This might be the place to talk more on my theatre experiences, considering I won the world title for artistic fencing and combat.

Swordplay is not the only form of violence for the stage, just as car crashes are not the only form of stunting in film. The sound of a fight on stage is unique to this media, as it is performed live, not added in post-production.

The sound of the blow landing in a fight on stage is called the knap, as in breaking or chipping stone. It is hard to describe, especially in a book, how you recreate the sound of a blow arriving in a fight scene. You need to slap a part of your body to simulate the sound of a punch or kick landing on different parts of the body, unseen, if at all possible, by the audience. It is difficult, especially if you are performing theatre in the round.

All fighting, whether on stage or in film, has to be acted to become believable and it is most often the reaction of the receiver of the blow that 'sells' it to the audience more than how it was delivered. Katy has taken great pleasure in the past in smashing my head off bar counters or slapping me across the face, without actually coming anywhere near me. I can honestly say, judging by the reaction of the audience, big or small, everyone was convinced that she had dealt me the blow I deserved. Meanwhile I have taught her how to pretend that I am dragging her around by her hair.

However, there is one move that is just too risky to teach her – a kick in the nether regions. Believe me or not, I can recreate this action, and the female 70 per cent of a class love to practise it on the not-so-keen male 30 per cent. Of course, if you miss where you're supposed to hit and actually land the blow, the choir gets a new soprano in the chorus. So, please don't try this without proper training by a qualified fight director, especially a fight director who has a voice with a normal pitch!

In contrast to theatre, in film the camera is used as your smoke and mirrors, and selecting the correct angles will conceal that the blow has not connected. The film punch was perfected by the stunt coordinator and stuntman Yakima Canutt and the huge star of Hollywood, John Wayne. Canutt and Wayne were good friends on and off camera, and they worked out a good system of big movements (hand coming around like a windmill), which made it look really hard. This came to be known as the 'pass blow punch', and with the camera placed at an angle to the performers to mask the blow, the reaction to the punch sells it to the audience.

When I was an action performer on the television series *The Paradise Club* (1989–1990), Don Henderson, playing the retired ex-priest Frank Kane, headbutted me in a scene where I smashed up the club with a baseball bat and my head bounced off the counter. The angle was such that it looked as if his forehead hit my nose, but in fact it was to the side, just like a pass blow punch.

Learning stage combat is important and requires some basic training to protect yourself before moving into unarmed combat. One important thing to learn before attempting supervised training in unarmed combat is to know how to fall. I learnt my skills in falling at my secondary school, in our judo club; however, there are other ways to learn: wrestling, gymnastics and other martial arts. In these classes you are taught how to roll, chin on chest, through your shoulder, and how to land and protect yourself, with palms open, fingers closed, hitting the ground as you go to stem your movement. Chin on chest is the key.

In armed combat and often in swordplay and with firearms, the fight will need to show impact from the type of weapon and blood will need to flow. The visual effects people will take over and put a squib, an electronically fired pouch of theatre blood, under your costume. When the blow arrives, the pouch is triggered.

Of course, although all the fighting looks impulsive, it is of course well prepared and protective padding is always a necessity, especially for the knees, elbows and spine, and the wardrobe departments of both film and theatre are magicians in concealing padding. Your fight director or stunt coordinator will always tell you where on the body you will need protection. Don't forget that you may need to repeat a movement a number of times for the camera, and the cumulative effect can be harmful, even from small things, like crawling on hard surfaces. Too many macho fight directors and stuntmen walk with a limp later in life because they failed to heed this basic rule. It is only entertainment, after all, and it is a controlled environment where there is time to plan, so minimise the risk to yourself and your team.

The often-quoted Hollywood saying that if you don't make the jump raw, without safety in place, you'll never work in this town again really is a myth and a cliché.

An interesting fact here: ninety-three million miles away in the heavens above us is the sun. It is important that when you are choreographing a fight outside, you remember that the sun will move! Not only will it cast shadows differently, low and long, east or west and none at all at midday, but it may also be in the actors' eyes. Take as an example a fight routine where the eighth blow is to your head, so you parry quinte and riposte afterwards. You might be taught this in the morning and as you rehearse the sun moves so by the time you film it, or perform it, the sun is in your face and eyes now. You would never look at or go to the attacking blade in real life and nor should you do it in a fight. The principle of defence is to bat the ball away. Too late and obviously you'll get hit and too early makes it look too staged. You would look with a peripheral glance for the blade; however, now with the sun in your eyes, you may not see it at all and the timing for the fight will be wrong. Equally, if you learnt the routine in the gym, studio or theatre, you might be taken by surprise outside. The choreography must consider all of these matters when you are performing outside, as well as the weather, which may make the ground slippery.

We are all human and can forget what we are supposed to do

next in our routine. In the heat of the moment it is easy to carry on and do what you thought was correct. It is always sensible to put a failsafe procedure in place to cover such moments – perhaps a movement of your body or blade or an easily recognisable word. No one should ever just drop their blade – it's a safety valve which can be used as a shield to enable you to step away when you have forgotten the movement or you think you are in danger or the sun is in your eyes or a horse has moved out of position.

It is the fight director's job to choreograph the best sequence and to ensure it is safe for all involved. That even includes warm-ups, which are just as important for those in fight routines as any athlete.

✐

Pick any of the Greek fables and myths and you will find violence. The Brothers Grimm knew that too, with stories such as *Hansel and Gretel*, where the threat of child cannibalism looms large. The stories we tell our children at bedtime – *The Three Little Pigs*, for example, has overtones of violence; after all, the big bad wolf is boiled alive as he climbs down the chimney of the brick-built house.

Dramatic violence is just one device, in the writer's box of tricks, to help tell a story. Violence without context rarely, if ever, contributes or takes forward a story or a character's story arc. Even a psychopath who kills randomly or a religious fanatic executing people does so in the context of *their* story. However, in the business we are in, storytelling, we must endeavour to bring the audience along with us for the ride.

Whether it is a soldier on a D-Day beach or a police officer slapped by an elderly, rich racist in a southern town in America or a Navy Seal sniper trying to shoot a man before he kills a child, how you tell your story, how you engage your audience and fail to repulse them with violence is what I hope to explore.

It is true to say, no matter what form of violence your story calls for, you will, eventually, encounter censorship of one form or another. Censorship is a living, breathing, wired-up, plugged-in, social media-fuelled beast. Word of mouth can make or break a production. The beast is not hard to find; just look at any theatre box office with a lack of ticket sales or outside a cinema, where a higher classification has meant your golden dollar has sunk lower than your IMDb rating. Whatever theatrical violence you depict, you will be judged, one way or another.

Censorship, within the rules of the industry, is largely an interpretation of your work, by independent organisations or groups with reference to a policy framework set by government or by private agenda. Censorship is often contradictory in execution and illogical in procedure and remains one of the hottest subjects when it is applied to the arts.

The Hays Code in Hollywood from the 1930s to 1968 had very clearly defined boundaries, which the film-maker could not cross. If they did, the film was simply not released. Today each country has an independent body to monitor the content of films. The most widely known are the Motion Picture Association of America and the British Board of Film Classification.

Theatre, I believe, has no such official censorship, although of course you must stay within the bounds of the law and action may be taken against your production by an individual, or group, through the courts if needs be, and a rewrite asked for with the threat 'lights out' if adjudication goes against you. Do any of you remember, a few years back, *The Jerry Springer Stage Show*? It was not a graphically violent scene which tipped the balance in this case; it was one considered to be blasphemous that caused the producers nightmares and threatened them with private prosecution, I believe.

For some years now, BAFTA has included computer game designers in its membership. Computer-generated images are appearing in more films than not these days, with films such as *The Day After Tomorrow* (2004), *300* (2006), *Beowulf* (2007), *2012* (made in 2009) and *Avatar* (2009), and of course all of the superhero films. You can see it was forward-thinking of BAFTA to embrace this technology and the experts who use it within its membership.

Yet, there is a potential quandary to violence depicted using CGI characters. My children are Xbox players. They won't allow me on to play as I am too slow with the controllers, so they say, but I am unbeatable at *Guitar Hero*, much to their shame and embarrassment, as I do tend to rock 'n' roll with the best of them, especially in the Sainsbury's car park when I have an ear worm. I know I will have therapy bills to pay for the kids in the future.

I digress. The Xbox game *Call of Duty* had a 15 rating when it came out a number of years ago. The similarities between this and *American Sniper* are obvious; both have a story set during a world war, the characters have objectives and it is violent.

However, there is a difference between the two. The Xbox game lets you, the player, kill people in a variety of nasty ways. You, the player, choose which baddies to kill and how. Even as they crawl away, as wounded participants, you as the player can shoot them. Should a game, which is just computer-animated characters, have a similar certificate to say *Saving Private Ryan*, or should it be rated lower because it's not 'real'? After all, in *Call of Duty* you as the gamer are creating the violence. Perhaps both certificates are actually too low?

The BBFC gave *Avatar* a rating of 12A. The MPAA gave it a PG13 (requiring under-thirteens to have a parent or guardian with them). Why the slight difference in certification? The MPAA state that *Avatar* has 'intense epic battle sequences and warfare, sensuality, language' and 'some smoking'. The MPAA censors decreed the act of seeing someone smoking in a film is more controversial, more harmful, than scenes of CGI warfare. Should we be re-categorising the classic DVD film market, as almost all of the films from the 1940s and '50s would need a revised certificate?

Whereas the criminal law describes violence against an individual with reference to degrees of severity of the physical damage, ranging from common assault to grievous bodily harm, does violence in an artistic form need to be justified any further than a recommended age for viewing?

As I have said, *Saving Private Ryan* follows a group of soldiers from the landing beaches on D-Day to a small French town some miles inland. Steven Spielberg, as the director, made a creative, artistic choice to depict graphic and realistic violence.

I had relatives who fought in WWII and have read many books by both historians and veterans on the subject. Many have said that Spielberg's film was as close as possible to what it was like without actually being there. The audience trusted Spielberg to make those choices.

Violence for violence's sake is harder to justify than violence in the context of a story with a beginning, middle and an end. Computer war games are often cited when the boundaries of certification are up for review.

The extreme violence in *Saving Private Ryan*, viewed in the context of World War II, specifically the D-Day landings, is a justified R rating. Smoking or not. However, times have changed and the beast keeps evolving. It is the wise creative genius who tracks the beast to keep an eye on the golden dollar.

I do apologise if my constant reference to money is grating on your ears. However, I am a strong advocate of Equity's campaign Professionally Made, Professionally Paid. The band 10cc wrote a song years ago – 'Art for Art's Sake' – and the lyric continues, if you get a chance, listen to it – yeah, man, I told you

I was an old rocker. We are all professionals and we are paid for our work.

Anyway, I have only scratched the surface so far, in terms of depicting violence in general terms. Let me up the ante a little by throwing these spanners in the works for your consideration.

Let us think about *The Passion of Christ* (R, 2004), Jim Caviezel directed by Mel Gibson, and *Zero Dark Thirty* (R, 2012) Jason Clarke, directed by Kathryn Bigelow.

Both films depict torture and are rated R – restricted viewing. The most severe classification there is. What should one do about torture in a scene?

I can actually tell you a personal story from when I was writing the screenplay for *Moments* ©, which I mentioned earlier. The story is fictional, but the theme is post-traumatic stress disorder (PTSD) and I have a torture scene in the script. It is the denouement of the film; it explains why my character is the way he is and, without hesitation, was one of the hardest scenes I have ever had to write. Let me explain further. You will recall that the screenplay is about PTSD and I personally know people with this problem and I have interviewed them for research purposes. I wanted to highlight the issues in an engaging way, not to wag my finger but to draw in an audience to the mental health issues facing so many front-line people today, not just soldiers, but first attenders, police, ambulance, fire services and so on.

My research was checked by those I met who are sufferers. My screenplay is dramatic, yet with many light touches. Self-deprecating humour is a common way sufferers cope with PTSD, as so many family members have told me.

I was fully aware that the torture scene I was writing might alter the demographic I was aiming at. After all, I want everyone to see this film to highlight this serious condition and to shine a torch into those dark areas, those problems that are faced by so many in the front-line of life. The scene might turn an otherwise emotional yet light-hearted story into a film only a few would see. An R certificate would say it was all about the torture, when in fact, the torture was the cause and I wanted to show the effects.

I made the creative decision to do the torture scene at the end of the film, as a flashback, and not at the beginning. In that way I ask the audience to follow my main character on his journey, to discover his problem and how he and his family were living with it. The audience, I hope, will fall in love with Tom, my main character, and his family, his life and his quest to find a mental sanctuary and a means to cope with the trauma. I hope that the BBFC will agree with me and give it an adolescent age rating.

Simon Weston, the soldier burned on the *Sir Galahad* during the Falklands War of 1982, entitled his autobiography *Moving On*. That is all you can hope and aim for, if you suffer with PTSD.

You may not believe this, but I swear it is true. I sent an early draft of *Moments* off to a professional script-reading service for comment. It is the last time I will ever do that. It came back with this note: "It doesn't work. He hasn't written a cure for his character at the end."

/

So far, we have glimpsed violence, talked about context, and hinted at moral issues facing writers and directors. How do we go about creating violence for stage and screen? What topics do you need to be aware of when adding this dynamic to your production?

It all begins with the writer. The most undervalued, overworked, yet vital, unsung hero of this entire sordid business we call entertainment. The writer has a story to tell and it includes elements of violence. They are free to write what they like, however, remembering what we have seen and the issues raised, the target audience for production must be a consideration for the writer. Censorship, either by recognised boards or by monitoring groups, could narrow your target audience. Even if a return of your investment, both in time and money, is the last thing on your mind, you will want people to come and see your production.

Those of you who specialise in theatre directing and stage fighting will appreciate that my examples have been drawn from recorded media. However, what we have been discussing today does apply across all forms of entertainment.

Let us for a moment assume, then, the first part of the creative process has been completed. The writing of the script is done and it is the best work of fiction since *Gone with the Wind*! Now what? Shakespeare, never one to help out a fight master, simply wrote 'They fight' whenever the scene called for action. I understand the stunt coordinators on *Saving Private Ryan* had the exact same problem. How do you take a page of violence and turn it into a reality?

Extracting scenes of violence from the written page and translating that into real performances is what I would like to turn to now. The script and the director's vision are the starting points when creating action. The script is the blueprint or map to guide you through the story and it will signpost:

- The genre/period you are working in – modern day, period, horror, comedy.
- The characters – who are they? Why are they fighting?
- The drama – seeing the characters at their best or worst or most vulnerable.
- The situation – why/where/when the action takes place.

This basic information will get the ball rolling and narrow down at least the context of the violence to be created. Further detailed reading of the script will provide the characterisation of the protagonists, the situation and setting and, perhaps, some clues to the intensity of the action from the preceding dialogue.

The key word for everyone to remember when designing a fight sequence is *energy*. The contrast between the build-up of a scene and the action that follows is crucial. If the energy levels are off, it can kill an entire sequence, even the whole *act* of a theatre play, as an audience sighs with disappointment. They feel cheated, perhaps. The extract from the dialogue does not match the visuals…

Macduff: "Turn around, you dog from hell, turn around!"

It certainly would not work if Macbeth turns and they fight with tickling sticks. To change or, even worse, ignore the scene's energy will, without doubt, break down the fourth wall and lose the audience for the rest of the play. Now, I may be teaching Granny how to suck eggs here, but this is where violence for the stage and violence for film clearly go their separate ways.

In a theatre production, the energy level has to be there throughout the whole live performance, matching the dialogue step for step. Once the violent scene is completed, the story moves on. In film, however, there is the added dynamic of the shots required to capture the action: master, mid-shot, close-up, pick-ups, over the shoulder (OTS), steady camera following the action, tracking… just to name a few from the tool box.

The energy for each take has to match the previous take. Calling 'Action' for take one has to have the same energy level for take six or take one hundred! If the energy is all over the place, the editor will strike you from their Christmas card list.

There is also another factor when considering the energy levels of an action sequence. Intensity – full-on, in-your-face violence, such as in *Saving Private Ryan* – can, once the initial shock has worn off, make the viewer desensitised and possibly switch off. The same can be said for too much light comedy; slapstick violence, especially if done poorly, soon becomes disregarded as amateurish. The old adage 'Dying is easy, comedy is hard' is never truer than when talking in terms of a comedy fight. After all, fights are supposed to begin at the point where reason and discourse end, and an audience may wonder if they are supposed to be laughing at the violence. Context, as always, is critical. It is not impossible to stage comedic fights; just look at the film *The Court Jester* (1955).

Your entry point into any violent scene has to be the preceding situation, dialogue, energy and intensity, as portrayed by your cast, prior to the point of action. "Once more unto the breach, dear friends," and all that.

The energy of the violence must complement the writer's storyline. I know that might sound obvious, but it is surprising how many times I have seen action that does not fit the dialogue or situation. Untrained fight directors with a sword fight to produce have, and I have seen it, just performed what we call the Scottish 8's swordplay fight. A clashing of the swords above your head, then below. That's all, folks! Boring, unconvincing and monotonous for the audience and viewed as lazy by those who know their stuff. In film there are far more checks and balances before your work is screened, so if a scene fails on screen then perhaps it is a bigger sin.

Once you have extracted all the information from the script, you can start to design your action accordingly. Easier said than done, I hear you cry.

A brief sidetrack here.

You know it is getting harder and harder to know what will shock people today. In 2004 during the American football Super Bowl, America went into apoplectic shock. Even the President, in a press conference later that evening, made a statement about what they had seen. What shocked America was not the 300lb, armour-clad players smashing several lumps off each other; oh no, it was a glimpse of Janet Jackson's right nipple – the controversial 'wardrobe malfunction'.

Go figure.

The imaginations of the two key people involved in any production have to establish a creative, symbiotic relationship, and they are the writer and director. Every script that comes across a desk, if it is a good script, will test and challenge these people, and there will be occasions when the writer has penned a scene that pushes the boundaries of violence. We have mentioned torture, and there are laws to protect children and the vulnerable in our society. However, they will ask themselves whether there are any boundaries they would not cross and what responsibilities they have to the audience not to cause them post-traumatic stress disorder, after watching a particularly violent or harrowing scene which they have devised. Hitchcock would have made a film, given the time, about a witness to a horrific crime suffering from PTSD – if it had that label back then.

A simple test might be to ask whether the audience sees all the violence in the scene, without any cutaway and, if so, whether it is justified in the context of the story.

I believe I am right in saying that *Deliverance* (R, 1972), Burt Reynolds, John Boorman directing, was the first time male rape was shown on film played fully by the two protagonists, Ned Beatty and Bill McKinney. I am sure you have heard all the rumours surrounding this one scene. It has become folklore in the film business and shocked the cinema-going world back in 1972. Google the stories if you are curious, but since I was not on the set I cannot say if any of the rumours are true. Just looking at the scene, however, the tension between the two actors prior to, during and after the scene is pretty evident. From the director's point of view, the scene was set, the characters were well defined and the energy level built up slowly. I doubt very much that the stunt coordinator, Bill Couch, was ever involved in any great detail in the scene. John Boorman directed brilliantly and to great effect using his professional actors. The impact of the scene on the audience has been well documented.

Extracting the violence from the page and putting it on the stage or screen boils down to the use of the script as a guide and collaboration between the writer and the director. The actors, normally and unfortunately, in my opinion, are the last to know 'what the hell is going on'. I cannot stress enough the need for communication between all departments to make the action something special. Compromise is often the result of not communicating, and 99.9 per cent of the time, the cause of all accidents on set.

Action scenes, if done well, punctuate a story and often mark the point in a character's journey where the call to adventure is first heard, a decision is made or a crossroads is encountered.

Casting the action sequences is, of course, critical. Directors will be offered a wide selection of actors and actresses to choose from and, despite what their agents say, very few will be expert fencers, horse riders, unarmed combat masters or Olympic swimmers. I know of one drama school in the UK that in fact offers all of that training to its students – E15 Drama School. I am sure there are others. As I have said before, after casting you may find out that your lead is not the cross between Johnny Weissmuller, Errol Flynn and Lester Piggott that you had hoped for. However, you do not have to despair.

I train actors of all ages who have never used a sword, thrown a punch or been in a stunt sequence. There are professionals in our business who can train a cast, if you have the luxury of time and the budget to match. The people you hire will be capable of advising you on the use of doubles and safety support.

The cast will not just be doing stunts or violent scenes, of course; there is another side to the coin. On average, the action/ violence in a script, unless it is a war film or a Bond movie, is usually less than a third of a production. Besides, in film, and yes, in theatre too, we have stunt doubles for the tricky stuff and professionals to decide what your actors can and should not attempt.

This leads me nicely on to the subject of working with sword masters, fight directors and stunt coordinators. It is quite usual to be required to engage specialists to secure completion and production insurance for a film. On stage, you will know when the script is presented whether you will need to give an expert like a fight director a call.

However, be aware of your cast's and your own limitations, and that your cast may feel uncomfortable with a scene and may need support and instruction. There is a lot of false bravado in this business, especially when you get involved with action sequences. Even experienced stuntmen can fall foul of their own bravado, to cover up an anxiety over a stunt. Inevitably, that is when accidents occur.

If you feel uncomfortable with a violent scene, then call on someone who might be able to offer advice – another director, a writer, an actor or an action specialist if you know one. Two heads are better than one.

However, if your action involves any of the following – sustained unarmed fighting, pyrotechnic effects, explosives, fire, car chases, vehicle knock-downs, crashes, gunfire, deep water or fast-flowing water, falls from any height, using animals or children in an action scene – then a qualified person or persons are required to supervise the scene. Insurance cover will demand it, and rightly so. This is only entertainment, after all.

Audiences are now familiar with CGI and green-screen action sequences in which the lead character flies a plane through a collapsing building and saves the dog at the same time. Entertaining, yes, but with no edge-of-the-seat thrill, in my opinion, and if done badly, completely unbelievable. There is a move back towards live action, yet still demanding impossible physical feats. People just cannot fly and are not bullet- and flame-proof. The audience cannot have real live action with CGI or green-screen outcomes. At the end of the day, either the audience's expectations will need to be managed or CGI/ green screen will have to produce more realistic effects. In the meantime, though, the people on film sets creating those scenes will need to have the strength of will to say, "No," to putting their crews in danger. I've done this myself on commercials.

Most, if not all, high-budget films now hire a health and safety representative to be on call. Sorry, there is no compromise when safety is concerned. On hearing this I guess some of you might have said to yourself, "Oh, do we really need all that? Look at all the expense it incurs." Again, *yes*. You will need to add the cost of staging the action into your budget, and the insurance and the risk assessment of the scene. It is much cheaper if you get the scene worked out in pre-production. As a director, it is also one less thing for you to worry about too; it will make your action look great when professionals are working with you.

Action comes at a cost, and on low-budget productions where violence is crucial to the story, you either make cuts elsewhere (no cakes at teatime) or re-think the issue. A well-timed slap to the face at a dramatic moment in the story, *In the Heat of the Night,* for example, is far more powerful than an unrealistic sword or fist fight.

The advice I would give is to keep looking at your script, know your limitations and work within them. It is better to do a simple set piece outstandingly well than a complicated one badly.

✗

There is of course a major difference between theatre and film violence. In theatre, the action will be repeated once a night, every night and twice on matinee days. In film, the action is repeated only for the camera, then you move on to the next set-up.

In theatre, the fight directors have done their work with the cast in the rehearsal room, training and blocking out the sequence. These daily rehearsals, carried out in a suitable and safe place, are essential.

In film, the specialist is standing on the set with everyone, coaching the actors while the director is waiting for the set-up to be completed.

In a troupe of actors, a fight captain is normally appointed who will schedule rehearsals and supervise the use of weapons, safety and storage of weapons after training and before a performance. Fight captains are actors or actresses who have passed their advanced proficiency award from one of the recognised dramatic combat academies that are now up and running worldwide. Academies are a good source for finding a fight director, as most of their instructors are fight directors too. Every actor in the scene should attend fight rehearsals and failure to turn up, especially while a show is running, is not only unprofessional but also potentially very dangerous. The stage management and even the director must be made aware of any abstainers, so action can be swiftly taken. A fight director will, from time to time, pop back and take a look to see nothing dangerous has crept into the fight.

Okay, here comes a little insider entertainment politics for you. This is unique, as far as I am aware, to the UK. There is an unwritten rule that theatre fight directors, with very few exceptions, rarely work on films and very few stuntmen or women work in theatre. A case of 'never the twain shall meet'.

Do not ask me why this happens in the UK, but it does. I've worked all over Europe and have not come across this. When the film business is quiet in say Sweden, film stuntmen often work in live theatre shows, for example Wild West theme parks, but in the UK, generally speaking, there is very little, if any, cross-working relationship. I think it all boils down to which list you qualify for or sign up to. We do love lists and bureaucracy in England.

My advice to those of you who wish to work in action across all media is to be on as few lists as possible, to be highly qualified in your field and to be the best at what you do. Keep your qualifications up to date and be dynamic and indispensable. At my own expense, I recently qualified, for fun and summer giggles, as a RYA Powerboat Rescue Cox. Who knows how many times will I use that.

Perhaps the best tool in the box to block out complex action sequences, sword fights, gunfights and battle scenes is the use of storyboards. Alex Moore is my storyboard artiste. She works closely with me when I am designing an action scene – drawing the action like stop/go animation in three-second bursts, extracting the scene from the page into a 2D picture for me then to transpose into real life. Storyboards can be used in theatre too. Do not think for one minute it is the sole preserve of the film director.

I also found storyboards useful working with stunt teams in Europe. They can see what I am trying to achieve with a scene, even if they do not understand a word I am saying, despite me speaking very loudly and slowly at them – a picture paints a thousand bruises.

Do actors do all their own stunts?

Roger Moore, when asked this question, said, "Yes, of course I do my own stunts. I also do all my own lying as well."

When it comes to risk assessment of an action sequence, the cast are too valuable to risk, and that is why you have stunt performers. The stunt coordinator will work with the cast and make them look good for the camera, then when it gets risky the stunt doubles take over and the action director will film the scene so the audience never knows. I like to keep up to date on any changes in the industry and I attend seminars as often as I can, so I am aware of the latest thinking. One in particular I recall was a 'Weapons on Set' seminar at Pinewood Studios, hosted by the Production Guild. Nick Jeffries (an armourer), Jeremy Johns (production manager on Pierce Brosnan's Bond films) and Mike Elliot (first AD on *Hot Fuzz*), were part of the panel. We also had police officers from CO 19 (the armed response unit) there too. The entertainment industry is finally realising that firearms on stage or for film is a major concern, and professional bodies within the industry have now produced a guideline for production companies. The accreditation for armourers is always high on the list and constantly reviewed. Just by way of example, under the Firearms Act 1968 it is a criminal offence for a person to provide any firearm (including blank firing prop guns) to a person who has served a jail sentence of more than three months. Doing background checks on your cast and extras is therefore essential.

More and more roles for actors for both stage and screen require a familiarity with firearms. Actors are generally very quick learners, and to make an actor or actress look more than competent with firearms is a relatively short learning process – handling weapons, loading them and firing them. Army, police and SWAT teams each have their own tactics and, for authenticity, qualified experts should guide the cast through the technical aspects.

This reminds me of a BAFTA Q&A that I attended on Joe Carnahan's film *Narc* (2002), which starred Jason Patric and Ray Liotta, both much under-used actors. They were taking questions when an earnest young actor stood and asked, "You must have studied police tactics on how to enter buildings and handle all those weapons. Can you tell us your thought process when you were training for these roles?" Both actors on stage looked at each other for a while, then Jason replied, "No thought process. We just watched a lot of *Starsky and Hutch.*"

✗

At the mention of the words health and safety, people generally switch off, glaze over or giggle, "Ah, the bonkers-conkers bit." However, the entertainment industry should be one where everyone goes home at the end of the day in one piece, no matter what their role. Saying 'no' to a director or senior production company official is very intimidating for an actor, especially if they want to work tomorrow, but that objective, unbiased view is essential.

The Health and Safety at Work Act 1974 applies to the creation of violence for stage and screen as much as any other employment. There must be a written health and safety policy that identifies the chain of responsibility at the venue and the arrangements for accident reporting, first aid, fire and safety. The law emphasises the control of risk in workplaces and the idea of risk assessment, which means an examination of what could cause harm and an evaluation of whether sufficient precautions have been taken and what more could be done in the event of an accident.

Of course, it is in everyone's interest to make sure people are protected and to ensure the production goes smoothly. Accidents are not acceptable anymore – the days when Cecil B DeMille would ask fifty extras to roll down the outside of a stone pyramid wearing nothing but a loincloth are over. Reputational damage can be extensive and stop filming in its tracks. You may recall the case of Michael Lush, who was a member of the public on *The Late, Late, Breakfast Show* with Noel Edmonds in 1986. Mr Lush won a prize to do a bungee jump on the show in a segment called 'Hang 'em High'. He was left unsupervised in a cradle, 120ft above the ground, and either his carabineer clip malfunctioned or it was not secured by the crew, and he jumped, on cue, falling to his death. It was almost the end of Noel Edmonds' career and it took years before he worked again. There have been similar issues following reality TV shows, where people give their all and then are seemingly left to get themselves back on track.

Violence as a form of entertainment has evolved from the gladiatorial combats for the masses in ancient Rome, through the crazy barnstorming wing-walkers of early Hollywood to the professional exponents of the action sequence as exemplified by action directors Yakima Canutt, Vic Armstrong and fight directors.

If done well, the action in a play or film will enhance, complement, punctuate, highlight and embellish the story. The best action will thrill and excite your audience and travel widely by word of mouth, far better than any poster or film review. The action needs as much attention to detail as the drama, love and laughter within your story, for there is no light without dark.

The three amigos –
my father, mother and my Uncle Bert.

RED ADAIR COMPANY, INC.
FIRE AND BLOWOUT SPECIALISTS

WILD WELL CONTROL

8705 KATY FREEWAY
SUITE 302
HOUSTON, TEXAS 77024
PHONE: 713/464-0230
TELEX: 762-125

February 27, 1985

Mr. Andrew A. Wilkinson
School House, New End
Heath Street
Hampstead N. W. 3
London I. H. U.
England

Dear Mr. Wilkinson,

Thank you for your recent letter wherein you inquired about employment opportunities within my firm.

We do very little hiring and do not have any immediate openings but, we will however, keep your letter on file and should a suitable opening occur in the near future, we will contact you.

Thanks again for your interest in our activities and best wishes to you in all your endeavors.

Very truly yours,
RED ADAIR COMPANY, INC.

Paul N. "Red" Adair

Paul N. "Red" Adair

PNA/srm

First, I wanted to be an oil well firefighter.

Professor Roy Goodall, my fencing master.

Continuity photograph from *The Fruit Machine* (1988).

Charlton Heston has nothing to fear.
Continuity Photograph around 1988

Dressed for banquet fights — note the right-hand injury. It's John Wayne time — I just got on with it. Still have the scar; it required eight stitches! (Opening a tin of cat food — I know, I know.)

Definition of Happiness – Battle of Agincourt for *Henry V* (1989) at Shepperton Studios.

Happy man on *Henry V*.

On set for *Henry V*.
Note the broadsword fighting stance.

I was cast as the bodyguard in many TV series in
the 1980s such as *The Paradise Club* (1989–90).

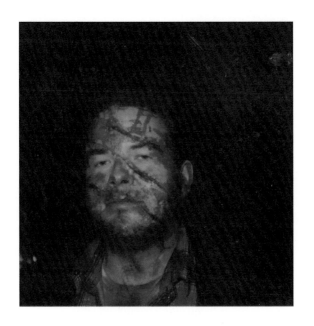

Photograph *Nightbreed* (1989)
having been killed by a berserker.

In action as The Rocket Man
in *Nightbreed* (1989).

Andy flying a helicopter —
onwards and upwards.

Giving Scott a fencing lesson at the
Cutting Edge Fencing Club.

Andy the coach at the
Cutting Edge Fencing Club.

World championship team,
Vichy, France, 2000.

World Title Troupe Fantastique Gold Medal.

Diamond Swords full dress rehearsal
at Warwick Castle (2009).

2014 Fencing Masters' World Championships, Florence, Italy,
with Professor Angela Goodall, Roy's wife.

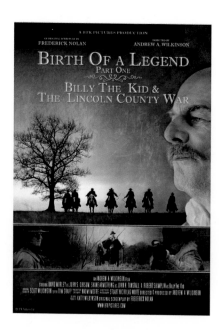

Billy the Kid film poster.

Billy the Kid — two future film stars,
Jake and Oscar.

Billy the Kid, on set in Kent with my first critics.

Cast and crew, *Billy the Kid*.

The posse having a break – the Magnificent Seven, Andy style!

Take One, Action!

Together with Ella Chaitow, my production manager,
at Stage S, Pinewood.

The filming starts on Stage S, Pinewood.

David Morely (playing John Chishum)
showing off the prosthetic on his neck.

Relaxing with Padre Michael Smith.

SCENE 10

WORKING IN YOUR MIND'S EYE

I am fairly new to audio, but I can say, I am the best sword master for radio drama in the world. Sorry, it had to be said. Of course, that is all achieved with foley and you know all about that now.

My introduction to radio had an inconspicuous start. I listen to radio at night, quite a lot. Music you know about, every day all day and also film scores and classical music. I am also a big fan of radio drama. *Journey into Space* (BBC, 1953) was the last radio series to get higher audience figures than television.

The masterpiece *War of the Worlds* (CBS 1938), by Orson Welles, was just groundbreaking radio drama. I recently attended the Audio Drama Festival 2019 at Goldsmiths, University of London; Professor Sean Street gave the opening lecture and mentioned Welles' *War of the Worlds*. It transpired that, at the same time as CBS broadcast *War of the Worlds*, on a rival station, scheduled in advance, they had a popsicle commercial. Orson Welles knew that many radio listeners, at that precise time, would channel hop while the commercial was on. He designed the drama so that when they tuned into CBS, they heard the scene of an army spokesperson talking about the destruction of Grover's Mill, New Jersey, by Martians, in the style of the reporter who had witnessed the Hindenburg crash just the year before. Was this the first use of fake news, I wonder? This Halloween broadcast of 1938 has now entered history as the radio programme that scared a nation. Welles became well known for such devices and in 1941, he interrupted his Sunday music show to announce the attack on Pearl Harbour, yet people did not believe him.

Radio still has that power today; however, we humans are overwhelmed with data, which surrounds us and penetrates our every waking moment on the planet. We wear headphones whilst walking around the streets or on public transport and are plugged into yet more media, including films, from our mobile phones, iTunes and 24/7 news cycles.

In all honesty, I did not think beyond those common, traditional listening traits when I first started in this business. I am not a plug-in, tune-out person. A good friend, one of my fencing students, Richard Shannon, is a prominent radio director and award-winning radio producer, and we would have casual chats about our work. I now understand how you can tap in to someone's internal cinema in their head and there is no aspect ratio for the mind!

My new adventure started on a cloudy day back in 2017. Katy and I, two lost souls on a Saturday morning, decided to explore a local aircraft museum. We had exhausted our boys over the years taking them to the Fleet Air Arm Museum, Yeovilton, and opted for a look around the de Havilland aircraft museum in Hertfordshire.

This museum is tucked away down a small, single-track road, behind some houses. An air museum is not what you would expect to find in rural Hertfordshire, yet the de Havilland is the home of the Mosquito, a WWII fighter bomber and wooden aircraft, made famous in the film *Mosquito Squadron* (1969), David McCallum, Boris Sagal directing.

We explored this fabulous find of a museum, looking round the many aircraft on display, both inside and outside the hangers, when I spotted, yes, I am going to show off now because I learned all about it, a DH110 Sea Vixen aircraft, with access to the cockpit. Up I went to the platform, transfixed by the controls of this jet fighter. Unbeknown to me, an RAF veteran stealthily followed me up to the entry platform and introduced himself. He invited me to take a seat in the cockpit, reluctantly (not really) I stepped in and sat down. I was trapped. I couldn't escape without knocking the veteran off the entry platform.

We started a conversation about the RAF and his lifelong service. I have to say, I was fascinated by his story. You may have noticed that I am attracted to stories, especially those I can turn into films, particularly about the military or action films. I pride myself on being a bit of a historian and was flabbergasted to hear tell of a branch of the service I had never come across before. They were fondly called the Radio Brats.

George Capel is a proud member of the Radio Brats, the affectionate nickname given to the young men who were the wireless and radio technicians of the RAF. On hearing his fascinating story, the adventures he and his buddies had and the period in which they served, which included the Korean and Cold Wars and the Cuban Missile Crisis in 1962, my production brain was switched on.

Obviously, George wanted to tell the Radio Brats story while the last few remaining members were still about to tell the tales. I agreed, especially since the 100th anniversary of the RAF in 2018 was coming up. The founder of the RAF, Hugh Trenchard, not only created the flying wing of the RAF with his right hand, at exactly the same time he also created the body of men who became the Radio Brats and the wings beneath the flyers' wings.

I said to George to leave it with me and I would think about what could be done. I did find *Secret Flight* (1946), Ralph Richardson, directed by Peter Ustinov, which was a film about early radar and therefore the birth of the Radio Brats. My problem with trying to get a film made about this story was a creative one. One where my head, for the first time, really, over-ruled my heart. I did not know about the Radio Brats and I prided myself on my historical knowledge. I found it difficult to see that 'Joe' financier would know what I was talking about and would see a return on his money. We did agree, reluctantly, on George's part, that the story could not be told on film. I decided to take the idea to Richard Shannon.

We agreed it would make a good radio documentary, Richard would produce it and I would be the Executive Producer. The project came together very quickly. With George's help, I arranged to meet as many surviving Radio Brats as I could in the time I had to produce the show. I liked the story so much I provided the budget out of my own pocket. The format of the programme I left to my award-winning producer, Richard. We decided on a montage radio show, which means no narrator – the interviewees tell the story. RAF Henlow, de Havilland's and my office were the locations for the recordings. I wrote forty-plus questions, which we asked each of the interviewees. This enabled the edit to be a little easier, as the retired RAF Radio Brats would answer in their own way and voice, and their answers would tell the story.

In post-production we added music, both recorded and original, written and composed specifically by Scott, with additional background sounds and old radio broadcasts of the worrying times often referred to as the 'thirteen days in October' 1962, when the world came so close to nuclear war.

Richard was very happy with the delivered radio show and said I did a grand job. We wanted to get a wider audience for the programme and Richard suggested I should contact the BBC and tell them Wilkinson Productions Ltd (WP) was now working in radio and audio production.

I did and the BBC sent me a detailed form on how WP could become an independent supplier. The company had to meet many criteria even before application. Don't bother, the BBC form said, if you are not A, B or C. You would be rejected at the first hurdle. I put together a small radio/audio production team, under the umbrella of WP. Richard of course would be my producer and director; Simon Morecroft, who had worked as a sound designer on radio drama, joined the team; and I had the great fortune of having both Garry and Scott willing to come on board as our in-house music department of composers. The BBC accepted our application in the autumn of 2017 and we have been an independent BBC Radio supplier since then.

I decided to have the WP website redesigned to just handle our radio and audio podcast side of the company. Wilkinson Productions Audio is available online now. Radio Brats and Garry's fabulous documentary entitled *Lost Film Scores* are currently available as I write. You will also find a selection of tracks from our past film, television and theatre scores, written by either Garry or Scott.

I may have mentioned that I am new to radio and audio, but WPA is a very exciting road to be on. I have not, nor could I, put film on the back burner. I have *Moments*, *Locklear* and *Billy the Kid Part II* to get off my desk, and I am still very much involved in swordplay and the Academy. Radio and audio at WPA is in addition to, not instead of.

Under Richard's supervision as producer, his post-graduates at Goldsmiths, University of London now have the opportunity to submit their radio/audio programmes to WPA. If Richard and I agree, we take them on and work to get them made, either via the BBC or as a podcast. WPA's broadcast footprint is science, crypto-science, history, drama and documentary.

Since embarking on this very exciting journey into the world of radio and audio, I have become aware of actually how much I listen, unknowingly, to radio and audio (podcasts), and not just to my film music.

I realise I am, in fact, an avid radio listener. My brain is always active, so I listen in at night when I need to relax and eventually fall asleep. Now, having a branch in radio, I am listening in much greater detail to the sound design produced. After all, radio is the cinema of the mind's eye. To my surprise, I have discovered that there are things that I, as an executive radio producer, would now remove from the broadcast if I were producing that show, especially when editing dramas.

I noticed something my children once had the annoying habit of doing, especially when I am in the middle of a conversation with them, which they may find stimulating, but more often than not annoying, but that's fine with me. I love that both our children have opinions and have no fear in expressing them. They are not sheep; they do not follow the flock. They stand on their own two feet and are not scared to do so. However, as they make their final statement to end our chat, they tend to do so while walking away from me and for them, the conversation is over. In their opinions! The trouble is, I never get to have my last say, perhaps for the better, and I cannot hear what they are telling me as they are walking away. I don't hear their final statement as they are out of the room, halfway up the stairs to their rooms!

I have noticed that on some radio drama, and more often than you'd suspect, a major character will make a key statement, like naming the murderer, and yet the editor is already fading out that statement for his next edit point. I never hear the answer clearly and for me the dramatic moment has been lost. The cut is always back to the previous volume setting too. It is very frustrating. Not all productions, just a few I have noticed recently, since becoming an executive producer. If you could only see me shake my head from side to side now. Okay, you can stop rolling your eyes.

Radio has that wonderful gift of putting you in your own cinema – what you hear, you see in your mind's eye. The challenge for the music producer and editor is to create those images without conflict in your mind, in your vision of the scene or atmosphere. Complementary editing and sounds for the production require deep, professional understanding and thought.

The ultimate exponent of this is, I think, Nelly Ben Hayoun, who has created the International Space Orchestra. A director and experienced sound designer, she works with scientists and engineers to devise events and experiences for public performance.

As I have said, I am the best fight director that there has ever been for radio, but it is all to do with the sound design, not the move or look but the sound of it. A *coulé*, an attack on the blade, where the blade slides continuously along the opponent's blade, sounds glorious on radio!

I see WPA as a ship on the ocean, with no fixed destination sailing uncharted waters. I very much enjoy navigating the ship through the many hidden rocks. I pick up passengers (writers), as I sail on by and they are helping me to navigate to harbours, where we can deliver projects. After all, people haven't rolled their eyes at me for a long while (wait till they read this memoir!); they have been quite restrained at my naïvety in this new voluminous medium.

The internet has opened up podcasting for audio as YouTube has for film. Quality will rise to the surface, in both media.

At the Audio Drama Festival 2019, I was blown away by the huge leap in technology for audio sound and recording,

3D recording, head tracking, and the very latest in personal fade in or out of a digital layered programme on your personal individual, listening device. Yes, that went over my head too until it was demonstrated for us.

Do you remember all the hoo-ha over *Jamaica Inn* (2014), BBC series, when viewers complained that they couldn't hear the mumbled dialogue? Well, with this new innovation, you will be able, at home, to control the volumes to suit your own needs. Watch this space, as it is coming soon! This is a short chapter, as I have only just started on this journey; there is so much more to come!

SCENE 11

MUSES ARE THE DAUGHTERS OF MEMORY

I hope my friends will tell you that I do not have a 'Remember when?' personality. Writing this memoir was not an easy task and I had to give it some considerable thought first, before my pen said 'Hello!' to the paper. I had to remember the events from the beginning, which is now a long time ago.

Memory is made up of a series of moments. Moments of your life that have had a meaning, of value to you, and that is why they remain in your memory, both the good and the bad ones. The Yin and Yang that is a balanced, happy mind.

The other synapses firing randomly in your brain, which make up the rest of your persona, are the overflowing boxes, packed full with what we can call curios or trivia; the details, considerations or pieces of information of little importance or value, which we all hold on to, without any effort.

Age takes these trivia-full boxes out, from time to time, to launder them. The odd sock goes missing and the box comes back a little lighter. Getting old is not for the young.

This next section is all about my odd socks. Perhaps in telling you all these trinkets of discovery I have come across on my journey, we will find a sock which matches one of yours and we can pair them up together. Never mind if we are both a tad colourblind; life is beautiful when full of colours, whatever they may be.

⚡

Over the thirty-five years, thus far, I have dabbled in this entertainment business, I have collected a brain full of trivia and knowledge, which is very difficult to incorporate into a memoir. For example, into which previous chapter do I put the trivia I have collected on the laugh track? Tricky, isn't it?

The laugh track is more commonly known as the 'canned laughter' on US comedy shows. When people find out I am in this wonderful, funny business, it is not long before I am asked, "What the **** is all that canned laughter about? It is so **** annoying!"

Some years ago, after being asked that very question, perhaps with less expletives, I decided to find out what I could about canned laughter. My starting point was something I had observed on one of my favourite shows. I am a big fan of M*A*S*H, both the film (1970) and the television show (1972 onwards). However, while the film did not have to endure the stigma of canned laughter, the television show did and still does in the repeats.

Watching the TV show, I noticed the canned laugher was used everywhere in the 4077 camp, except in the operating room. The scripts were just as good and funny in the OR but no canned laughter. Obviously, surgery was not a jokey matter to the studio. They didn't like the juxtaposition of the drama and humour, and they left the choice of laughing, or not, up to the viewer.

The origin of canned laughter comes from the heyday of radio in America from the 1920s until the 1950s, when television took over. In those years, the majority of radio comedy shows were performed before a live audience. In the 1950s, when television became the main driving force in entertainment, it was either filmed on location or on a closed studio set. There was no audience to react to the recordings, so they recreated it with a pre-recorded laughter audio track. The studio executives, keen to sell their new product, no doubt wanted to make the audiences, sitting at home alone or with their families, feel that they were part of the radio audience experience that they loved.

Larry Gelbart and Gene Reynolds, writers and co-creators of the TV show of *M*A*S*H*, tried to get the canned laughter taken off their shows from the outset. They finally succeeded in an episode called 'The Interview'. There was a real-life award-winning documentary of that year which they used as a template for 'The Interview' episode. It was agreed by the executives to give it a go, and it worked beautifully. *M*A*S*H* did not require canned laughter to be both funny and a hit!

I am sure you have noticed, however not made the connection, that in the opening credits of that super TV comedy *Cheers* (1982–1993), it has one of the cast members tell the viewing audience in a voiceover that '*Cheers* was filmed before a live studio audience'.

The great Bob Hope in *Ghost Breakers* (1940) says, "A good laugh would be worth a lot of money at this point," and this brings me nicely to my next piece of trivia, which is about a historical figure who during his conquests may have been responsible for the deaths of as many as forty million people. Genghis Khan, founder of the Mongol Empire in 1206, took over half the known world with an incredibly simple technological innovation: the stirrup.

The stirrup appeared in China and is credited to the Chinese Jin Dynasty in the first few centuries AD. Their use spread westward through the nomadic peoples of Central Eurasia (modern-day Mongolia) and they arrived in Europe during the Middle Ages. While generally speaking Hollywood (well, its horse masters) knows its history, I am hard pushed when watching Roman period films to find actors riding using stirrups. Saddles with high pommels or horns for grip, yes. Stirrups, no.

The early Hollywood Westerns of the 1920s and '30s – the 'two oaters', as they were called, as they used two reels of stock film – are perhaps the best historical record of Native American bare-back riding without stirrups or saddles.

⚡

Tell me, how many times have you tried to wiggle out of something you didn't want to do by finding a loophole in your partner's argument? Do you think of a loophole as an ambiguity in their argument or an inadequacy in the law or a set of rules? Or do you think of an arrow slit in a castle wall?

Sadly, the latter is the one I think of first. Castles and their design throughout history are a wonderful way to spend a weekend. Although it often means ending up on the M25 London orbital road in traffic, I have learnt so much about my surroundings and human nature.

For example, why do they have so many spiral staircases in castles? It is, of course, for defence, but had you realised that all spiral staircases in castles go up in a clockwise direction? That was by design, as it means the attacker climbing up the stairs has their sword hand (and most people, remember, are right-handed) by the column, which restricts their movement. The spiral also leaves them open for attack by the defender who is coming down the stairs, whose sword hand has more mobility and thrusting options.

Just think about the words used to describe a castle's construction and how they echo still in the twenty-first century – barbican, battlements, drawbridge, dungeon, gatehouse, keep and machicolations (which is an opening between the supporting corbels of a projecting parapet or the vault of a gate, through which stones or burning objects could be dropped on attackers).

Except for machicolations, over the years I think I have had a pint of the good stuff in a pub named after every one of those castle constructions!

✣

As the calm and gentle folk we all are, it is time to be honest. How many times have you wanted to give a work colleague, a gym membership administrator or a BT accounts operator a good pommelling?

The old French 'pommel' is from the twelfth century, meaning 'rounded knob', and is the diminutive of 'pom', meaning the hilt of a sword or the assembly. Seen in many films to dispatch a soldier or villain who is not worthy of killing but must be hastened to their exit from the scene, the sword is flipped in the hand and a blow using the pommel of the sword is used instead.

✣

My studies in castles and museums over the years have introduced me to weapons and history from all across the world, and fascinating it is too. It's also great for Scrabble games!

The *Kpinga* was a multi-bladed throwing knife of Central Africa. It was the long-range weapon of the Zande warrior. With three projecting blades and made from metal, it was so valued that it became a currency in its own right. You can see these in the Victoria and Albert Museum in London.

Bolas are a type of throwing weapon too, made of weights on the ends of interconnected cords made from local materials and used to capture animals by entangling their legs. *Bolas* were most famously used by the gauchos (South American cowboys). Yet, at the complete opposite end of the American continent, in the far north, the Inuit also use bolas, made from sinew and bones.

There is also a debate about the proper interpretation of engravings and artefacts that look remarkably like boomerangs in the Great Pyramid of Giza, Egypt!

N

Mesopotamia, the cradle of civilisation, sparked a flame of ingenuity for humanity to create practical uses of materials as both weapons for war and hunting, and currency. Throughout the Bronze and Iron Ages, the use of metallurgy for weapons for defence and for hunting became a universal goal. The trade routes were the earliest precursor of what we call 'the internet' today – a means of exchanging information or ideas, sharing knowledge about how best to achieve a goal and finding the best tools to replicate and take home. Trading the best of the best enhances civilisations.

All of these fascinating finds came to me in my research and led to an appreciation of the darker side of human nature – the weapons of battle, especially swords. All these stories and facts accompanied me on my journey to continue my training for my ultimate ambition, which was to recreate these stories and facts for the film business.

It also gave me a sound understanding that reinforced my skills base. This is still a major part of my life today. So much to learn, so much to understand.

∕

Laurel and Hardy, Buster Keaton, and Chaplin – who doesn't love the silent-era comics? All these stars are from the theatrical Vaudeville stage, top-billed, with crowd-pulling performances.

Vaudeville, originally a comedy without psychological or moral intentions and based on a comical situation: a kind of dramatic composition or light poetry, interspersed with songs. This was the birth of the visual stunt and therefore the stuntman. Many of the stuntmen of the early Hollywood era were from the Vaudeville stage. This is also where the term for a scene incorporating nothing but laughter was coined for the first time: 'slapstick'. Slapstick is comedy based on deliberately clumsy actions and humorously embarrassing events.

Yet the slapstick is an actual prop, often seen in circuses and pantomime. It is a device consisting of two flexible pieces of wood joined together at one end and is used off-stage to produce a loud slapping noise to give sound effects to the scene.

∕

I would like to be known as an honourable man, old-fashioned, perhaps, an old gent, maybe. This is a combination of upbringing, reading of history, watching films and just pure courtesy. The women I know, I hope, recall the times when I stood to greet them when they arrived or held doors open for them. For me, it is always ladies first. Am I a real throwback? A sad fantasist? How can I explain myself without sounding like a prig?

I am aware of this, as unthinkingly I wait and hold a door open for the person following me through. If it is a woman, I have, on more than one occasion, been given a look of disapproving hatred. This even happened to me yesterday. I opened a heavy door for Katy as we left a building and as we continued our conversation, I held the heavy door open for the next person. Unbeknown to me, it was for two women; one said, "Thank you." The other looked at me as if I were flotsam and said nothing. Not that I was expecting anything. Did I disrespect this person by holding the door open?

I cannot change my polite, honourable nature, but I do get knocked more than you would think in doing so, in today's society. I am a swordsman, in my heart, soul and head. This is my default setting after thirty-five years of behaving this way.

When a man escorts his partner, tradition has it that he offers his left arm. This tradition originates from medieval times when men escorted women around town and through the fields. Should a threat arise or the woman's honour require defending, the man's sword hand (his right hand) would be free, giving him quick and easy access to his sword, worn on his left side. To this day, the left arm rule still applies, especially to true swordsmen.

✎

We swordsmen are generally not known for screaming habdabs, except first thing in the morning when we first look at ourselves in the mirror before brushing our teeth. So, this is a fun bit of trivia from the film business, where the scream has a long and honourable pedigree and it even has its own credited name.

The Wilhelm scream is a stock sound effect. The scream is used when someone is shot, falls from a great height or just sees their face for the first time in the morning.

First used in the film *Distant Drums* (1951), Gary Cooper, Raoul Walsh directing. As of April 2019, the same scream has been used on film over 400 times. The actor and singer who created the scream sound effect is probably Mr Sheb Wooley (1921–2003), a prolific small part actor who appeared in many Westerns. Although never credited as the provider of the scream, he is credited as a voice artist in some 400 films and still counting! Boy, do I wish I had his agent, with a residual fee clause!

Why call it the Wilhelm scream then if Sheb Wooley performed it first for film? The debate goes on; however, the most likely and current favoured explanation is that it is named after a 'Private Wilhelm', a character in *The Charge at Feather River* (1953), Guy Madison, directed by Gordon Douglas. This was made two years after the original first scream was used. The actor playing Private Wilhelm in the film, who, having been shot in the leg with an arrow, screams out, was Ralph Brooks (1904–1991).

✗

I have a small but growing collection of film memorabilia in my office, including clapperboards I have used from the films I have directed in the past. Clapperboards have been essential to film-making since the talkies came to stand in the arc lights of the Hollywood film studio. The first talkie, *The Jazz Singer* (1927), Al Jolson, Alan Crosland directing, had to marry up the images and sound on film, since visual and audio tracks were recorded on separate media by separate equipment. To assist in synchronising of the picture and sound, the clapperboard was designed to designate and mark the various scenes and takes as they are filmed and audio-recorded. You'll find it's also often called clapper, clapboard, clacker, slate, slateboard, slapperboard, sync slate, time slate, sticks, board, smart slate, dumb slate and sound marker.

When a film's sound and picture are out of synchronisation, this is known as a 'lip flap', for the obvious reason that the actor's lips will be moving but no or unsynchronised sound will be coming out!

Other important information is also recorded on the clapperboard, so the editor can keep a track of the film they are editing, such as:

Production: **Take One, Action!**
Roll: **5** (the loaded film stock – four previously used)
Scene: **44**
Take: **1**
Director: **Andy Wilkinson**
Camera: **Alan Smithee**
Date: **25/12/2019**
Day / **Night** / Int. **Ext.**

✎

If this little memoir is your book at bedtime, then the eagle-eyed of you will have noticed the name Alan Smithee as my cameraman above. Alan Smithee is a name used in the film business if a creative, for example the director or writer, wishes to have their name removed from a production. This name has been agreed by all the professional guilds in the business, so it is an official pseudonym. The last film I believe to use the Alan Smithee name was *Women Wanted* (1999), Holly Hunter, Kiefer Sutherland, who also directed.

✎

If I said Sir Humphrey to you, what immediately springs to your mind? Yes, me too, it has to be *Yes, Minister* (1980), with Sir Nigel Hawthorne. Well, here is an interesting and colourful odd sock I would like to share with you.

I discovered after a little study, that Henry IV had four sons, namely Henry V and his brothers, Thomas, Duke of Clarence; John, Duke of Bedford; and the youngest, Humphrey, Duke of Gloucester (1391–1447).

Yes, your maths is correct, Humphrey was fifty-six when he died and, by all accounts, including the study of his few remaining bones, he was a tall man. He stood six feet tall. Rare, I think you would agree, by the standards of medieval England. Humphrey was a scholar (indeed, his library is still located in Oxford University and is part of the world-famous Bodleian) and a brave warrior who fought in the Battle of Agincourt – just like me!

He is buried in St Albans Abbey and is the only royal burial there. The underground vault is close to the shrine of Saint Alban and, situated on its south side, occupies a most prestigious burial place. Currently living as a local boy to St Albans and having only recently discovered an actual combatant of the Battle of Agincourt close by, I paid Humphrey, Duke of Gloucester, a visit in May 2019. In a wonderful booklet by Jane Kelsall, available in the Abbey, I learned that his grave lay unmolested until the great storm of 1703. The Abbey received quite a blow, excuse the pun, was damaged in the storm and the Duke's vault was forced open. The lead-lined coffin, with a body inside, became available for inspection by the monks of the Abbey and by the scientific community, mainly those based in universities. The body had been embalmed, possibly in alcohol, and was in excellent condition, preserved in a brown liquor which covered the body. This discovery soon became a national attraction and people from all over the country wanted to see the scholarly knight who fought at the side of Henry V at Agincourt.

However, as the preserved body was not protected or guarded, visitors would come and take vials of the brown liquor away with them as mementos. Some even took bones and teeth!

It was said that some local inns offered the parish clerk cheap brandy to keep the brown liquor topped up, keeping the attraction appealing and open and enabling future visitors to take vials of the 'blood' of the knight away with them. An iron grill sits over the vault today and what is left of Humphrey can rest in peace. I lit a candle at his resting place. I'm that type of guy.

N

My laundry is back and a few more odd socks have gone missing, oh well; however, before I go on the hunt for them, one last thing. Alan Smithee may be the name used by directors to have their name removed from a finished production, but there is an astonishing list of names, to me, anyway, of those directors who have never, or have yet to, reach the highest accolade in the film industry – an Oscar win. Below is a list of some of those great directors never to have won an Oscar. The list will surprise some of you:

- Stanley Kubrick
- Alfred Hitchcock
- Orson Welles
- Robert Altman
- Sidney Lumet
- Howard Hawks
- Charlie Chaplin
- Sergio Leone
- Ernst Lubitsch
- Cecil B. DeMille

- Akira Kurosawa
- Stanley Kramer
- Fritz Lang
- Federico Fellini
- Sam Peckinpah
- Jean-Luc Godard
- Otto Preminger
- Arthur Penn
- John Cassavetes
- And Ridley Scott (yes, I am totally surprised by that too, considering the volume of outstanding work he has created and directed).

I am in grand company without my Oscar and, like a few on the list, we are still working and we haven't given up yet!

SCENE 12

AND... CUT! ...PRINT!!!

Well, we made it!

It took a while to get here, but we are 'Halfway up the Hindu Kush'! (Katie Melua)

So, what I have learned, on my magical mystery tour of getting my foot into the film-business door?

I hope I have given you a flavour of the trials and tribulations I have endured. The bewildering, hard and often thankless moments, but also the tremendous joy of adding to my character, the skills I now cherish, the adventures I have had and the great people I have met.

You will find, as you explore this world, that you will become a social misfit. I don't know about you, but I find it hard to mix with people not in the creative bubble these days. Lawyers, doctors, academics, professionals will look at you and ask, "Really? How interesting, but what is your proper job?"

Normal folk will ask, "Who is the most famous person you know and can you get my daughter into your next film? Sally is a star."

I don't go to parties; life is far too short to justify my existence and choices to strangers. I do enjoy the Clint Eastwood Spaghetti Western handle *The Man with No Name*. Those of us who are not A-List cast, who are just doing a creative job they love, would fit nicely into a Charles Dickens novel. Never feel sorry for us, but understand that to fit in, once you have made that leap of faith into a world of celebrity and make-believe, is not necessarily an easy path.

The tabloids, across their front pages, in far more detail than I am comfortable with, tell the stories of young actors and actresses who cannot handle the limelight of fame and celebrity and lay bare whatever mental stress and anxiety they endure, even their choice to finally opt out of the game. True friends are rare. So very sad, as this is only entertainment, nothing more.

I always wanted to be a swordsman, a swashbuckler, and the only way I could achieve this, in the age I was born, was to get into films and be a swashbuckler on the screen. My tale is a complex one and one I could never tell a stranger at a party. The only way I can pass on what I have learned is by telling my story in this gentle conversation with you and hope that you have enjoyed our journey together.

One can get too fixated on a goal and I have, without question, as my journey was of my own making and no one else's. It would be the height of bad manners if I were not to mention my bedrock and my purpose for doing what I do. Over thirty years ago as I write, I found my other half: my wife Katy. I was her sabre coach. Yes, we met with swords in hand. Katy is not in the business, but she is my counsel and my guide. We have two fantastic additions to the family, Jake and Oscar, both loving and hard-working with great futures ahead of them, which they will achieve by their own making. I wonder where they learned that from?

Oh, Buster, our Labrador too. If I don't mention the dog, I'd get told off.

Both our families have suffered losses since my journey started, as all families do over time. There have been tough times, really tough ones, and good ones, and that is what makes up this wonderful tapestry we call life. All sunshine makes a desert, so they say.

I was a working-class boy, without the opportunity of a classical education, and I had multiple choices and responsibilities to consider as a young man. Looking back through my rose-tinted glasses and with hindsight, I think I made the best of the job that was handed to me.

Remember when I said, never ask an actor, "How are you?", as they always give you a résumé instead? Well, I'm not doing too badly, thanks for asking, but here is my résumé, since you did ask!

My memberships: British Academy of Fencing (world title-winning fight director/sword master), Equity, Equity Theatre Directors' Register, Writers' Guild of Great Britain, Directors UK, BAFTA, BBC Independent Radio Supplier.

I have directed both film and theatre and appeared in seventy-three film and television productions, in various capacities, mainly as a swordsman and action performer. I write, produce and direct and continue to do so, in film, theatre, television and radio productions.

I have arrived at a station, but this is not the end of my journey. Now this is where the work *really* begins! What's next?!

You have been great company on this journey; thank you for coming. See you on the red carpet!

WILKINSON PRODUCTIONS
MULTI MEDIA ENTERTAINMENT

EPILOGUE

I admire all those people in the entertainment and sporting arenas, from the prolific directors, writers and stunt coordinators to the club fencing coach, teaching all abilities and ages and the occasional actor how to use a sword.

It is tough to get into this business and to remain successful, as I'm sure you will appreciate having read this memoir. I especially admire anyone who can get a film made, not so much your standard YouTube fare, but one that gets distribution, a theatrical release or on to DVD.

For those of you who have had to work for their achievements, pass examinations, learnt how to do something exceptionally well, you deserve a pat on the back, a well done from me at least, if that means anything to you.

As I said, when people discover I am in the business, I am often told that they have a relative trying to break in and asked whether I have any advice. The next question is, "Can you give them a job?"

For a number of reasons, I can answer them honestly. I now know why I was turned down so many times when I asked for a helping hand. Mind you, I wasn't approaching production companies, but individuals further up the ladder than me. Nevertheless, much of the work in my office is sensitive in that, of what comes across my desk, 90 per cent is copyrighted to someone else, not me, and is confidential.

Speaking for myself and my companies, we are diverse film, theatre, television and radio production. I also train cast members in swordplay, which they or their future employers may wish to keep secret until the right moment arrives for the best publicity for their production. Training transient WP office candidates would be a full-time job for me. It is hard enough to keep up with what I do, let alone add more. Despite my workload, I am still a one-man band, even with an agent and the necessary associated people one needs to run a limited company and a list of professional freelance colleagues I can call upon.

Non-disclosure agreements are more common today than you would imagine. Intellectual property rights are very important to protect and it is a global concern.

My very own film, *Birth of a Legend: Billy the Kid and the Lincoln County War* ©, was pirated in Russia, with 50,000-plus copies made, resulting in zero return to me or my company that financed the film. The copyright was stolen after distribution, not while it was in our hands. Copyright theft is a major problem that affects all of us trying to make a living entertaining people.

The only advice I have for unskilled 'students' in the business is this. In summer break, from college, go about learning the etiquette of film-making. It cannot be taught in a classroom, or from a book, not even this one! You can do this in a number of ways.

Do what I did. Get familiar with the FAA, the Film Artistes Association (now within BECTU), to work as an extra. The more experienced professional extras will show you the ropes. The best will, anyway. Extras are more respected by other members of the crew these days too, because without them, your film cannot be made with any production value. Imagine, what would a battle scene look like without professional extras?

Another way is to become a runner, someone behind the camera and a person hired by the production company to fetch and carry and do all the menial tasks – collect post, make the coffee, keep everyone happy and hydrated, and do anything the production team requires – sometimes called a gofer, as in 'go for this and go for that'.

I don't have any suggestions as to getting work inside the production or post-production offices, other than it is easier if there is someone you know, personally. Use any connections you may have from your school, university, family friends or relatives. In my experience, though, family rarely take your advice about your business; to my boys, it's just 'something Dad does'.

There is no shame in asking for help, politely, when you need it. However, don't be taken for a fool or taken for granted, and do have a game plan. You have the right to try your hand and it is up to those further up the ladder to assist you. I have never understood those who pull up the drawbridge once they are in, stopping others of equal or higher value getting on.

Look what happened to Professor Goodall on *Young Sherlock Holmes*; those jealous of Roy pulled the drawbridge up.

Yet you will make it, if you keep knocking on that door.

The union for runners is BECTU as well and it is worth exploring their website. Being a runner will allow you to get to find out at grassroots level how to make a film and the etiquette of a film set, and if you're lucky, one day you may be able to watch a director at work. Certainly, you'll see the assistant directors working and you can 'work your ticket', as the industry calls it, to better and bigger employment opportunities.

The same ideas apply to the theatre. If you can get in by helping out with props, set painting and sweeping up, keep that broom busy, the opportunities may open for you.

Try provincial theatres before the West End, though most of this work is unpaid. Some theatres have a policy of employing for low or no wages, but this is all being reviewed by theatre unions.

You should, though, get something towards expenses. It is a foot in the door. You'll learn a lot, you'll get your name known, references and an entry on your CV. References mean a lot in this business, as much as the word of mouth.

The saddest journey in the world for me is the one that follows a precise itinerary. Please think outside the box.

For those of you who wish to enter the world of fight direction, sword master, stuntman or action director, my advice to you is to keep learning, have broad interests, watch as many plays and films as you can, and to keep your studies an ongoing adventure.

I do!

ANDY'S MEMORABLE FILMS

Have you ever, on a wet, cold evening, turned to your partner and asked, "What film are you in the mood to watch tonight?"

The choice of genre is a good starting point – should it be historical, epic, fantasy, thriller, rom-com or action-based? Then, think about the cast and your favourite actors and actresses, or a director, perhaps. Many of you will have been through this since the very first VHS film came on the market, though I guess in truth it has been like that since film was invented.

Here is a little bit of odd sock trivia for you. Do you know what the very first DVD film released was? Please post your answer to me on the back of a £20 note to… It was in fact *Twister* (1996).

For a bit of fun, I started listing my top 100 films – those which had won Oscars or received critical acclaim or which I thought had particular technical merit. However, there were so many films that I love which I just couldn't leave out and fail to share with you that the list grew and grew. So here are my favourite films (and I am sure I have omitted some – it became a game I played with the family – name a great movie which wasn't on the list!), not all BAFTA- or Oscar-winners, just the films I have no problem watching over and over again. And please forgive me for not including the current crop of Oscar- and BAFTA-winners – I had to save something for my second book.

Genre	Film	Year	Director	Notes
Drama	*12 Angry Men*	1957	Sidney Lumet	How to direct on a small set with twelve in the cast, a masterclass in filming the 'poker game conundrum'.
Sci-Fi	*2001: A Space Odyssey*	1968	Stanley Kubrick	Groundbreaking. The film that raised the technical bar, which is still the standard all films are held to.
Sci-Fi	*2010: The Year We Make Contact*	1984	Peter Hyams	A worthy sequel, with the use of computer technology to further the adventure.
Action Adventure	*300*	2006	Zack Snyder	The telling of the infamous Spartan conflicts.
Adventure Drama Mystery	*Abyss (The)*	1989	James Cameron	A major stepping stone in CGI.
Comedy Fantasy	*Addams Family (The)*	1991	Barry Sonnenfeld	Every home has a 'Thing'; mine has two.
Drama	*Admirable Crichton (Paradise Lagoon) (The)*	1957	Lewis Gilbert	A very English film, with charm and a little stoic message for us all.

Comedy	*Advance to the Rear*	1964	George Marshall	Anarchic comedy Western, worth tracking it down, if you can. It later became *F Troop* on TV.
Action Adventure Romance	*New Adventures of Don Juan (The)*	1948	Vincent Sherman	Errol Flynn at his light hearted best. The actress Sally Field's stepfather, Jock Mahoney, the stuntman who once played Tarzan, doubled Flynn in an unbelievable leap from a marble staircase at the end of the climatic duel. Watch out for that scene!
Action Adventure	*Adventures of Robin Hood (The)*	1938	Michael Curtiz	This film has everything. There is no other actor who is Robin Hood but Errol Flynn. The musical score, the costumes, the technicolor… the magic this film sprinkles on its audience makes it timeless.
CGI Action Animation	*Adventures of Tintin: Secrets of the Unicorn*	2011	Steven Spielberg	A masterclass in CGI film-making.
Sci-Fi Action	*Alien*	1979	Ridley Scott	"In space, no one can hear you scream."
Sci-Fi Action	*Aliens*	1986	James Cameron	Space marines are called in to take on some aliens.

Drama	*All the President's Men*	1976	Alan J. Pakula	A masterclass in direction. The best use of the 'god shot' in film.
Comedy Drama	*Always*	1989	Steven Spielberg	A charming remake of a classic film.
Sci-Fi Thriller	*Andromeda Strain (The)*	1971	Robert Wise	A science thriller, I am a big fan of this genre. I have three films written in this genre.
Comedy Drama Romance	*Apartment (The)*	1960	Billy Wilder	How does one fit in to society? This is perhaps the first film that takes you on that journey.
Drama War	*Apocalypse Now*	1979	Francis Ford Coppola	Based on the book *Heart of Darkness* by Joseph Conrad, this is a harrowing version is set in the Vietnam War.
Sci-Fi Drama	*Arrival*	2016	Denis Villeneuve	A film for the grown-up mind on first contact.
Action Adventure	*A-Team (The)*	2010	Joe Carnahan	A nod to my youth, which I loved. What great memories!
CGI Action Adventure Fantasy	*Avatar*	2009	James Cameron	As of 2019 – however, no longer now due to *Avengers: Endgame* – this was the highest-grossing box office film.
Action Crime Drama	*Back Draft*	1991	Ron Howard	Amazing fire scenes and stunts.
Adventure Comedy Sci-Fi	*Back to the Future* Trilogy	1985	Robert Zemeckis	This trilogy sums up the best of the 1980s film era.

Crime Drama Thriller	*Bad Day at Black Rock*	1955	John Sturges	The wonderful, great Spencer Tracy heads a fantastic cast, most of which reform to appear in another in my list. Now, which one?
Comedy Drama Musical	*Ballad of Buster Scruggs (The)*	2018	Ethan, Joel Coen	Really grows on you.
Comedy	*Bananas*	1971	Woody Allen	Warning: the theme is an ear worm off the scale!
Action Adventure	*Batman*	1989	Tim Burton	I had a few nights working on this film, so I like it a lot.
Action Crime Drama	*Batman: The Dark Knight*	2008	Christopher Nolan	If you have to pick one film from the now many, since the 1989 remastering of the original, this is the one I recommend you pick.
Action Drama History	*Battle of Britain (The)*	1969	Guy Hamilton	How do you eat an elephant? Don't panic! This is a huge film, so it can be done.
Comedy Drama	*Being There*	1979	Hal Ashby	This was my late father's favourite film, so every time I watch this Peter Sellers/Hal Ashby masterpiece I think of him.

Epic	*Ben-Hur*	1959	William Wyler	An epic. But there is something about this film that makes me think about the Wild West. It was written by the Governor of New Mexico, who signed the arrest warrant, dead or alive, on Billy the Kid; as you know, I directed *Birth of a Legend*, all about the Kid.
Comedy Drama Sci-Fi	*Bicentennial Man*	1999	Chris Columbus	A little-known gem of a film.
Comedy Drama	*Big Bus (The)*	1976	James Frawley	You have ships rolling over, buildings on fire, earthquakes, now the story of *The Big Bus*.
Western	*Big Jake*	1971	Andrew A. McLaglen	The John Wayne films of the 1970s never won awards, but to me they are some of his best films.
Action Adventure Comedy	*Big Trouble in Little China*	1986	John Carpenter	Really, a feel-good film with some clever, subtle humour that you need to watch out for.
Comedy	*Birdcage (The)*	1996	Mike Nichols	A remake of *La Cage Aux Folles* and a brilliant one. My family, to this day, quote from the script.
Comedy Drama	*Birdman*	2014	Alejandro G. Iñárritu	Ever wondered what happens to superheroes when they get to, well, my age?

Drama Horror	*Birds (The)*	1963	Alfred Hitchcock	Feeding the birds on a Sunday morning will never be quite the same again.
Action Sci-Fi	*Black Hole (The)*	1979	Gary Nelson	Before Touchstone Films (Disney's adult production arm) they made this serious sci-fi adventure.
Sci-Fi Thriller	*Blade Runner*	1982	Ridley Scott	Based on a Philip K. Dick short – *Do Androids Dream of Electric Sheep?* – the look of this film raised the bar.
Sci-Fi Thriller	*Blade Runner 2049*	2017	Denis Villeneuve	The quality continues. An outstanding follow-on.
Comedy Western	*Blazing Saddles*	1974	Mel Brooks	One of the best comedies ever written, directed by the king of comedy.
Crime Drama Thriller	*Blue Lamp (The)*	1950	Basil Dearden	A film that spawned a popular major TV series.
Action Crime Thriller	*Blue Thunder*	1983	John Badham	This is a great film about helicopters, military not rescue, however. What we see in this film actually exists in our world today. Scary.

Adventure Drama Romance	*Boom Town*	1940	Jack Conway	Spencer Tracy, Clark Gable, Claudette Colbert, Hedy Lamarr. The great Tracy and Gable are the oilmen roughnecks in this classic adventure, with Colbert and Lamarr leading their men to solid, safe ground.
Comedy	*Bowfinger*	1999	Frank Oz	Directed by 'Yoda' himself, this is a film that makes me laugh out loud, as I can relate to it in almost every scene, about how you struggle to get a film made. A must-see if you are a wannabe film-maker.
Drama War	*Bridge Too Far (A)*	1977	Richard Attenborough	A fascinating film-making process was involved here. Major scenes were shot and shown at fund-raising meetings to investors to show them how great the film would be with a little more money to complete.
Action Crime Thriller	*Bullitt*	1968	Peter Yates	A classic film, made famous by an amazingly well-filmed car chase.

Biography Crime Drama	*Butch Cassidy and the Sundance Kid*	1969	George Roy Hill	The film that made Robert Redford a star. A musical score that could only be used in the late 1960s, in my opinion. In what other decade could you have 'Raindrops Keep Fallin' on my Head' in a Western?
Comedy	*Cactus Jack (The Villain)*	1979	Hal Needham	An odd Kirk Douglas film, to be sure, especially when you consider Mr Douglas died in 2020 aged 103, making him sixty-three years old when he made *Cactus Jack*, a tribute to cartoon-type bad boys.
Comedy Drama Romance	*California Suit*	1978	Herbert Ross	A Neil Simon classic.
Action Thriller	*Capricorn One*	1977	Peter Hyams	A very good thriller, with spectacular aerobatic scenes.
Adventure Comedy History	*Carry On Cleo*	1964	Gerald Thomas	Okay, one of the best *Carry On* films, which used the sets from *Cleopatra* (1963).
Drama Romance War	*Casablanca*	1942	Michael Curtiz	Best movie of that era. 10/10 in my book.

Adventure Drama Romance	*Castaway*	2000	Robert Zemeckis	A lovely film, brilliantly thought out, as the first part of the film Tom Hanks wore lots of jumpers and warm clothing to make him look larger than he was, yet the latter half of the film Mr Hanks still lost a lot of weight to play the character stuck on a desert island. The production was a long one so that these scenes could be filmed.
Mystery Romance Thriller	*Catch a Thief (To)*	1955	Alfred Hitchcock	One of Hitch's best.
Comedy Mystery Romance	*Charade*	1963	Stanley Dolan	This is a director at ease with the film-making process and his cast. I learn a lot from watching this film.
Biography Western	*Chisum*	1970	Andrew V. McLaglen	Although I have directed a Billy the Kid Western film, I really like *Chisum* with the Duke!

Drama Mystery	*Citizen Kane*	1941	Orson Welles	This film is voted by critics as the number-one film of all time, every year. It is hard to comprehend that Mr Welles was just twenty-six when he made this film. What was I doing at twenty-six years of age? I was on my journey, that much we know.
Drama Sci-Fi	*Close Encounters of the Third Kind*	1977	Steven Spielberg	A blockbuster. The director's cut is a must.
Action Adventure Fantasy	*Conan: The Barbarian*	1982	John Milius	Muscles meet a great fantasy story.
Drama Mystery Sci-Fi	*Contact*	1997	Robert Zemeckis	Carl Sagan's story is beautifully filmed here.
Adventure Drama	*Convoy*	1978	Sam Peckinpah	A film conceived and based entirely on a song.
Crime Drama	*Cool Hand Luke*	1967	Stuart Rosenberg	Life on a chain gang in the southern states, none better.
Adventure Comedy Family	*Court Jester (The)*	1955	Melvin Frank, Norman Panama	Swordplay executed with comedic timing is very, very difficult to achieve; this is my example of how to do it brilliantly.
Adventure Drama Western	*Cowboys (The)*	1972	Mark Rydell	John Williams writes a cowboy score. Spoiler alert, one of a handful of films where the Duke doesn't make the last reel.

Drama History War	*Dam Busters (The)*	1955	Michael Anderson	I played the theme tune, as a double bass player, in my school orchestra. This film has always been a special film for me.
Sci-Fi	*Damnation Alley*	1977	Jack Smight	I read the book *Damnation Alley* by Roger Zelazny first. So, the film was a must for me when it came out. Due to the *Star Wars* phenomenon, it took a while from completion to release.
Comedy Sci-Fi	*Dark Star*	1974	John Carpenter	An early sci-fi hit. I can see where *Red Dwarf* may have gotten some inspiration from. A great song too. 'Benson Arizona' written by Carpenter and Bill Taylor.
Adventure Drama Sci-Fi	*Day After Tomorrow (The)*	2004	Roland Emmerich	BAFTA award-winning special effects.
Drama Sci-Fi	*Day the Earth Stood Still (The)*	1951	Robert Wise	"Klaatu Barada Nikto."
Comedy Drama	*Dead Poets Society*	1989	Peter Weir	Carpe diem.
Action Adventure Comedy	*Deadpool*	2016	Tim Miller	If you have had enough of the Marvel/ DC comic book superhero films, this is the best comedic swipe at the genre in style and vision.

Action Adventure Comedy	*Deadpool 2*	2018	David Leitch	A breath of fresh superhero air.
Comedy Crime Mystery	*Dead Men Don't Wear Plaid*	1982	Carl Reiner	"Cleaning woman!!" A brilliant, very clever comedy.
Adventure Drama Sci-Fi	*Destination Moon*	1950	Irving Pichel	I read a lot of Robert A. Heinlein as a youth; this film inspired my lifelong interest in science and human spaceflight.
Action Adventure	*Die Hard* Trilogy	1988 1990 1995	John McTiernan Renny Harlin John McTiernan	Some argue these films are Christmas holiday films, are they yours? "Yippee Ki Yay."
Action Adventure War	*Dirty Dozen (The)*	1967	Robert Aldrich	Pop back to a 1955 favourite for a connection. A classic.
Crime Thriller	*Dirty Harry* Trilogy	1971 1973 1976	Don Siegel Ted Post James Fargo	"Go ahead; make my day," and watch these films!
Comedy Drama History	*Dish (The)*	2000	Rob Stitch	An unfamiliar story of the 1969 moon landings. A charming, lovely film. I watch this at least once a year, as I love it!
Drama Romance War	*Doctor Zhivago*	1965	David Lean	Study as many David Lean films as you can.
Action Horror Thriller	*Dog Soldiers*	2002	Neil Marshall	Although a horror, my entire family love this film. It has intentional comedy moments too.

Adventure Comedy Drama	*Dogma*	1999	Kevin Smith	A young fencing student introduced me to this film – it is original and great fun!
Action Horror Thriller	*Duel*	1971	Steven Spielberg	This was an original TV movie for ABC, shot by Mr Spielberg on location in just twelve days. Carey Loftin (stuntman) is the mysterious devil truck driver!
Drama War	*Duellists (The)*	1977	Ridley Scott	A swordplay feast!
Action Drama History	*Dunkirk* (Original)	1958	Leslie Norman	Yes, Barry's father directed this great movie about the little boats that saved us from losing the British Army in WWII, on the beaches of Dunkirk.
Action Crime Thriller	*Eiger Sanction (The)*	1975	Clint Eastwood	A great John Williams score and a comfort movie thriller; we watch this at least once a year!
Adventure Biography Drama	*El Cid*	1961	Anthony Mann	Yakima Canutt staged all the action, swordplay by Enzo Musumeci Greco.
Drama Romance Western	*El Dorado*	1967	Howard Hawks	Written by Leigh Brackett, she also wrote the first screenplay for *Star Wars: The Empire Strikes Back*.

Crime Drama Mystery	*Electra Glide in Blue*	1973	James William Guercio	The soundtrack album has the most spectacular artwork posters. I have a copy, which I am very proud of.
Biography Drama	*Elephant Man*	1980	David Lynch	One of the uncredited executive producers is Mel Brooks. His name was kept out of all the publicity in case people thought this film was seen as a comedy, which it is not. Outstanding make-up and performances by all.
Action Adventure Fantasy	*Empire Strikes Back (The)*	1980	Irvin Kershner	As a swordsman I connected the dots on this film, from Jedi Knight to fencing master. Robert Anderson, whom I later knew, was Darth Vader's fencing double.
Action Adventure Drama	*Enemy Below (The)*	1957	Dick Powell	A story that has been turned into numerous other film and TV stories. Chess between two equals on opposite sides.
Biography Crime Drama	*Escape from Alcatraz*	1979	Don Siegel	Mr Eastwood stars; you can see his directing mentor, Mr Siegel, is so influential on his style. Smooth and no waste, two peas in a pod in directing terms.

Action Adventure Sci-Fi	*Escape from LA*	1996	John Carpenter	The name Snake Plissken enters the film lexicon for the second time.
Action Adventure Sci-Fi	*Escape from New York*	1981	John Carpenter	"The name's Snake Plissken."
Comedy Sci-Fi	*Evolution*	2001	Ivan Reitman	Will make you look at those slugs in the garden with new eyes.
Adventure Drama Fantasy	*Excalibur*	1981	John Boorman	I still await, eagerly, the sword to rise from the lake. I will stand shoulder to shoulder with the king.
Horror	*Exorcist (The)*	1973	William Friedkin	The only film, to date, to scare the *heebie-jeebies out of me!*
Adventure Comedy Romance	*Father Goose*	1964	Ralph Nelson	I aim to put my 'ten fine toes' in the sand at least once a year.
Drama Thriller	*Few Good Men (A)*	1992	Rob Reiner	A cracking good script, written by the master Aaron Sorkin.
Action Thriller	*Final Option (The) (Who Dares Wins)*	1982	Ian Sharp	The story of the SAS. Now, a little bit of trivia for you. The climax of the film has the SAS raiding an embassy building. This building is actually Pinewood Studios; the office the two SAS soldiers enter through, via helicopter, was my office for seven years!

Biography Drama History	*First Man*	2018	Damien Chazelle	*False Dawn: The Promise of Apollo* was my story of human spaceflight. This is a true telling of Neil Armstrong's journey from his home town to walking on the moon. What an emotional story.
Comedy Crime	*Fish Called Wanda (A)*	1988	Charles Crichton	A charming British comedy. I had a few days' work on it!
Western Drama	*Fist Full of Dollars (A)*	1964	Sergio Leone	The first Spaghetti Western to cross the Atlantic.
Action Adventure Sci-Fi	*Flash Gordon*	1980	Mike Hodges	I was blown away by the look of this film, still am. A must for all budding DoPs (Gilbert Taylor) and costume designers (Danilo Donati).
Adventure Drama	*Flight of the Phoenix (The)*	1965	Robert Aldrich	Dedicated to Paul Mantz, the stunt pilot who died during its making.
Western	*For a Few Dollars More*	1965	Sergio Leone	Equal to the first film.
Drama Romance	*Forrest Gump*	1994	Robert Zemeckis	An outstanding performance from Tom Hanks. A little sentimental for me as a film; however, it does work on all levels. A masterclass in storytelling.

Action Comedy Crime	*Freebie and the Bean*	1974	Richard Rush	The first of the buddy cop comedies I discovered. To me, still the best one.
Action Crime Drama	*French Connection*	1971	William Friedkin	Made a star of one of my favourite actors, Gene Hackman.
Comedy Drama Romance	*Front Page (The)*	1974	Billy Wilder	"Who reads the second paragraph?" Never a truer sentence ever written.
Action Crime Drama	*Fugitive (The)*	1993	Andrew Davis	The early TV series with David Janssen (1963) was a big hit. This is a great film in homage to the original feel of the TV series.
Drama War	*Full Metal Jacket*	1987	Stanley Kubrick	Vietnam recreated on the Isle of Dogs. Watch Kubrick at his most punchy.
Biography Drama History	*Gandhi*	1982	Richard Attenborough	An epic film.
Comedy Fantasy	*Ghostbusters*	1984	Ivan Reitman	Released the year my father passed. It is not on the list for any other reason than this film, along with *Back to the Future*, sums up the 1980s perfectly.

Comedy Crime Drama	*Gideon of Scotland Yard*	1958	John Ford	I admit, this film may have passed me by, until I noticed this very British story was directed by the master of the Western film genre, John Ford. Great cast, great story of the time. The baddies were all wearing dinner jackets.
Action Adventure Drama	*Gladiator*	2000	Ridley Scott	I was on my own when I first saw this film. It has all the elements of a classic epic, such as *Spartacus* or *Ben-Hur*. The score makes my swordsman blood rise. A modern classic.
Crime Drama	*Godfather Trilogy (The)*	1972 1974 1990	Francis Ford Coppola	A trilogy you must watch. A complex yet honest family saga set in the world of the mafia, held together with a love of the people in the film.
Action Adventure Thriller	*Goldfinger*	1964	Guy Hamilton	In my personal files this is ranked as the second best Bond film ever made.

Drama History Romance	*Gone with the Wind*	1939	Victor Fleming	Before blockbusters, there was *Gone with the Wind*. For all you eagle-eyed film warriors, Yakima Canutt has a small visible acting role in this film!
Biography Crime Drama	*Goodfellas*	1990	Martin Scorsese	A brutal film depicting the life of a hardened criminal and his supporters.
Western	*Good, the Bad and the Ugly (The)*	1966	Sergio Leone	This film is one of my top five of all time.
Drama Romance	*Good Will Hunting*	1997	Gus Van Sant	A wonderfully directed film.
Adventure Drama History	*Gray Lady Down*	1978	David Greene	Similar in terms of a claustrophobic set as to *12 Angry Men*, a good case study. Also, I discovered foley from this film (there is a spoiler alert coming here), a drowning man effect.
Comedy Drama War	*Great Dictator (The)*	1940	Charlie Chaplin	We could, of an evening, sit and talk all night about this film and why it is so important in the pantheon of film. If you haven't seen it yet, please do.
Adventure Drama History	*Great Escape (The)*	1963	John Sturges	I was introduced to Elmer Bernstein film music with this film. Also, actors doing their own stunts.

Adventure Drama Mystery	*Great Expectations*	1946	David Lean	Study all David Lean films!
Action Adventure Comedy	*Great Race (The)*	1965	Blake Edwards	I simply love this film. I watch it at least once a year. A comedy with huge class. And some really top-drawer fencing in it too!
Biography Drama Western	*Gunfight at the OK Corral*	1957	John Sturges	Watch how the director deals with an A-list cast with his camera.
Adventure Action Drama	*Guns of Navarone (The)*	1961	J. Lee Thompson	An Alistair Maclean story with a great cast!
Drama Western	*Hang 'Em High*	1968	Ted Post	You may have noticed, I like Westerns. Sorry, but I do. I can say I have directed one now too!
Drama Fantasy	*Harry Potter Series (8 films)*	2001 – 2011	Chris Columbus Alfonso Cuarón Mike Newell David Yates	A magical series of films. Raising the bar on production values.
Comedy Crime	*Hear No Evil, See No Evil*	1989	Arthur Hiller	However stressful my day, this film makes me laugh.
Drama War	*Heartbreak Ridge*	1986	Clint Eastwood	Some sparkling dialogue in this surprising 'Friday night' film. Mr Eastwood is the director I so admire and learn from.

Action Adventure Drama	*Hellfighters*	1968	Andrew V. McLaglen	Based on the life and times of Red Adair, a real oil well firefighter and a hero of mine. Did you spot Red's letter to me in this book?
Action Biography Drama	*Henry V*	1989	Kenneth Branagh	An in-your-face Shakespearian classic. The action is by Vic Armstrong (Indiana Jones) and the swordplay is not bad either (I had a hand in it).
Action Drama History	*Heroes of Telemark (The)*	1965	Anthony Mann	This is an underrated war film, in my opinion. A true story, worth your time watching it.
Comedy Mystery Thriller	*High Anxiety*	1977	Mel Brooks	A comedic tribute to works of Alfred Hitchcock, which I understood Hitch enjoyed and laughed at too.
Action Comedy	*Hooper*	1978	Hal Needham	A film about Hollywood stuntmen, directed by one of the best Hollywood stuntmen. A Friday-night cool drink and a pizza movie.
Comedy Musical Romance	*Horse Feathers*	1932	Norman Z. McLeod	Do you know the password?
Comedy	*How to Murder Your Wife*	1965	Richard Quine	A fantastically complete comedy with a great theme by Neal Hefti.

Action Adventure Thriller	*Hunt for Red October (The)*	1990	John McTiernan	A masterclass in how you film on a claustrophobic set. I know I have picked out a few films like this but to make a film look as good as this takes planning and skill. Learn from them.
Adventure Thriller	*Ice Station Zebra*	1968	John Sturges	See? We all stand on the shoulders of others.
Crime Drama Thriller	*In the Line of Fire*	1993	Clint Eastwood	Watch as many films as you can directed by Mr Eastwood.
Drama War	*In Which We Serve*	1942	Noel Coward/ David Lean	To this day I am fascinated by the language in the script for this film. Did people really talk like this in 1942?
Animation Action Adventure	*Incredibles (The)*	2004	Brad Bird	Not many animations on my list, but this is one of the best.
Action Comedy Crime	*Italian Job (The)*	1969	Peter Collinson	To mix my metaphors a little, this is the 'last night of the Proms' at any British film festival.

Action Adventure Comedy	*It's a Mad, Mad, Mad, Mad World*	1963	Stanley Kramer	The stuntmen, drivers, (the stunt driving is like a choreographed ballet – awesome Carey Loftin), fall guys (the fighters), aerial stunts (the flyers, Paul Mantz) all really earned their money on this film. A great comedy. Spencer Tracy is magnificent.
Drama Fantasy Family	*It's a Wonderful Life*	1946	Frank Capra	This film is screened in my house once every year – I wonder why?
Adventure Drama Thriller	*Jaws*	1975	Steven Spielberg	The first of the blockbusters. They're going to need a bigger cinema.
Drama Music Musical	*Jazz Singer (The)*	1927	Alan Crosland	The first of the talkies, signalling the end of the silent film era.
Action Adventure Comedy	*Jewel of the Nile*	1985	Lewis Teague	A grand sequel. Casting still magical.
Drama History Thriller	*JFK*	1991	Oliver Stone	A powerful film, with a wonderful film score.
Western	*Joe Kidd*	1972	John Sturges	The 1970s were the halcyon days of the Western.

Action Adventure Sci-Fi	*Jurassic Park*	1993	Steven Spielberg	Mr Spielberg won't like me saying this; however, I learnt about errors in continuity in scriptwriting and film from watching this film numerous times. What a great score by John Williams.
Adventure Comedy War	*Kelly's Heroes*	1970	Brian G. Hutton	My soft introduction to war films.
Adventure Horror Sci-Fi	*King Kong*	1933	Merian C. Cooper	The first monster film that really made me look again at the genre with respect and awe.
Action Adventure Drama	*King Kong*	2005	Peter Jackson	The film is a wonderful kaleidoscope of colour and images. I fell in love with the lighting of Naomi Watts.
Comedy Sport	*Kingpin*	1996	Bobby, Peter Farrelly	Sexy, stupid and funny. What a comedy should be.
Adventure Biographical History	*Lawrence of Arabia*	1962	David Lean	Study this film.
Drama Adventure (Swordplay)	*Le Bossu (On Guard)*	1997	Philippe de Broca	One of the best swordplay films to date. A *must*-see for any aspiring fight directors or sword masters.
Action Crime Thriller	*Lethal Weapon*	1987	Richard Donner	One of the best original 'buddy' movies.

Drama Romance War	*Life and Death of Colonel Blimp (The)*	1943	Michael Powell Emeric Pressburger	A military duel (late 1800s) is shown in detail. A charming film.
Comedy Drama	*Local Hero*	1983	Bill Forsyth	A charming film on all levels. As a family we watch this once a year, if we can.
Action Crime Drama	*Long Kiss Goodnight (The)*	1996	Renny Harlin	A cracking good script, some great one-liners from the main cast.
Comedy Crime Drama	*Longest Yard (The)* Also *Mean Machine (The)* in the UK	1974	Robert Altman	My introduction to Burt Reynolds.
Adventure Drama Fantasy	*Lord of the Rings Trilogy (The)*	2001 2002 2003	Peter Jackson	*Fellowship of the Ring* was the first film – technically very accurate – epic in scale: sword fights, riding heights of actors, visual effects become blended and thus invisible to the audience, no bleeding through in the images. Visual and special effects in harmony with real film.
Action Adventure Sci-Fi	*Mad Max*	1979	George Miller	My first apocalyptic film.
Action Adventure Western	*Magnificent Seven (The)*	1960	John Sturges	I could play the theme and most film buffs would know the film.
Film-Noir Mystery	*Maltese Falcon (The)*	1941	John Huston	Noir films became popular with the success of *Falcon*.

Comedy Drama Romance	*Man of the Year*	2006	Barry Levinson	Ten years too early, perhaps?
Drama Western	*Man Who Shot Liberty Valance (The)*	1962	John Ford	Although colour was available and the choice of film-makers, Ford chose black and white to shoot this film. A classic and one of my top Westerns.
Crime Thriller	*Marathon Man*	1976	John Schlesinger	"Is it safe?" You will never go to the dentist again!
Action Adventure Romance (Swordplay)	*Mark of Zorro (The)*	1940	Rouben Mamoulian	Rathbone and Power produce, to me, the best duel filmed to date.
Comedy Drama Romance	*Matter of Life and Death (A)*	1946	Michael Powell and Emeric Pressburger	Earth is in colour, heaven in black and white – many a debate with my film buff friends over this one!
Comedy Drama War	*M*A*S*H*	1970	Robert Altman	Can you laugh at war? No, not at war, but the situations war puts you in, yes.
Action Crime Drama	*McQ*	1974	John Sturges	John Wayne rivals Dirty Harry.
Action Comedy Crime	*Midnight Run*	1988	Martin Brest	A quirky buddy film.
Action Crime Mystery	*Minority Report*	2002	Steven Spielberg	The director's vision is clear with the use of CGI in key moments.
Thriller Drama	*Misery*	1990	Rob Reiner	Kathy Bates steals the show.

Action Adventure Thriller	*Mission Impossible: Fallout*	2018	Christopher McQuarrie	Keeps the Bond franchise nervous and on the ball, as this is so good!
Comedy Drama War	*Mister Roberts*	1955	John Ford	From stage to screen, I really like Fonda's underplaying of the main character 'Mister Roberts'.
Comedy	*Money Pit (The)*	1986	Richard Benjamin	A young Tom Hanks shows us what is yet to come in this sparkling comedy, my mum's favourite.
Animation Comedy Drama	*Monsters Inc.*	2001	Peter Docter	Makes me laugh.
Adventure Comedy Fantasy	*Monty Python and the Holy Grail*	1975	Terry Gilliam/ Terry Jones	You have a low budget and you want to make a film? This how you do it.
Comedy	*Monty Python's Life of Brian*	1979	Terry Jones	Enjoy this film as what it was intended for. A pure comedy, but you should really know your Latin before watching!
Action Crime Drama	*Mr Majestyk*	1974	Richard Fleischer	Charles Bronson stars as a melon grower, pushed by a small-time hood, but a mafia hit man gets involved. The silly people.
Crime Drama Mystery	*Murder on the Orient Express*	1974	Sidney Lumet	Tight filming, not on a submarine but a train. Outstanding.

Drama Family Musical	*My Fair Lady*	1964	George Cukor	Stage to screen. Bold re-casting of the major lead role, but I think it works. Great on a wet Sunday afternoon.
Comedy Drama	*My Favourite Year*	1982	Richard Benjamin	A little-known gem of a film.
Action Crime Thriller	*Narrow Margin*	1990	Peter Hyams	Hitchcock would have loved this, I think.
Action Fantasy Horror	*Nightbreed*	1990	Clive Barker	I have a small role in this film as the Rocket Man; I also had some action as a Berserker and posse member.
Adventure Mystery Drama	*North by Northwest*	1959	Alfred Hitchcock	You will not find any cliché shots in this film. You will, however, find similar shots in other films, as a tribute to Hitch and this film!
Adventure Comedy Crime	*O Brother, Where Art Thou?*	2000	Joel Coen	A modern telling of an ancient fable.
Comedy	*Odd Couple (The)*	1968	Gene Saks	"We're out of cornflakes. F.U." Need I say more?
Action Drama Sci-Fi	*Omega Man (The)*	1971	Boris Sagal	This is the best version in my book of a story told many times on film.
Horror	*Omen (The)*	1976	Richard Donner	A horror without the blood-soaking effects normally found in the 1970s. That makes for a scary film.

Comedy Musical Romance	*On the Town*	1949	Stanley Donen Gene Kelly	You can't help but smile when watching this film.
Comedy Romance War	*Operation Petticoat*	1959	Blake Edwards	An early screw-ball comedy by the master of same, Blake Edwards.
Action Crime Sci-Fi	*Outland*	1981	Peter Hyams	"Think it over" – watch the film and you will get that link!
Western	*Outlaw Josey Wales (The)*	1976	Clint Eastwood	One of my top five Westerns.
Comedy Drama Musical	*Paint Your Wagon*	1969	Joshua Logan	A big musical comedy/drama.
Drama Thriller	*Parallax View (The)*	1974	Alan J. Pakula	A great evening can be had watching these 1970s thrillers; most are listed here.
Comedy Crime	*Pink Panther Strikes Again*	1976	Blake Edwards	No matter how many times I watch this film, it makes me laugh.
Biography Drama History	*Post (The)*	2017	Steven Spielberg	The printed press is under attack in the twenty-first century. This film reminds us of the power of the press.
Action Adventure Sci-Fi	*Predator*	1987	John McTiernan	Arnold Schwarzenegger versus an alien predator, who would you put your hard-earned money on?

Adventure Family Fantasy	*Princess Bride (The)*	1987	Rob Reiner	Originally, William Goldman told this story to his children at bedtime, his wife made him write it down so he wouldn't forget it. This was the script for the film.
Adventure	*Prisoner of Zenda (The)*	1952	Richard Thorpe	Of all the versions, this 1952 one is my favourite.
Comedy Musical	*Producers (The)*	2005	Susan Stroman	I am a big fan of the 1967 version; however, I love the music and comedy of this 2005 version better.
Horror Mystery Thriller	*Psycho*	1960	Alfred Hitchcock	Horror, terror, left to your imagination, only the way Hitchcock can.
Comedy Drama Romance	*Quiet Man (The)*	1952	John Ford	My mother and father are John Wayne and Maureen O'Hara, in looks and temperament, in their youth.
Drama Horror Sci-Fi	*Quiet Place (A)*	2018	John Krasinski	A new take on the horror genre. Clever, very clever.
Action Adventure Drama	*Quigley Down Under*	1990	Simon Wincer	A Western set in Australia.
Action Adventure	*Raiders of the Lost Ark*	1981	Steven Spielberg	What a great adventure! There are a few continuity errors, but who cares? What a score!

Action Adventure Comedy	*Remo Williams: The Adventure Begins (Unarmed and Dangerous)*	1985	Guy Hamilton	Fred Ward and Joel Grey, perfect casting.
Comedy Crime Mystery	*Return of the Pink Panther (The)*	1975	Blake Edwards	You just have to laugh; perfect when you are feeling low.
Adventure Biography Drama	*Right Stuff (The)*	1983	Philip Kaufman	The true story of the Mercury Seven astronauts, based on Tom Wolfe's book.
Drama History War	*Rise and Fall of the Roman Empire (The)*	1964	Anthony Mann	One of the last of the big-budget epics.
Animation Adventure Comedy	*Road to El Dorado (The)*	2000	Bibo Bergeron Don Paul	One of the few animation films I have watched a few times. Great soundtrack by Elton John.
Adventure Comedy Family	*Road to Morocco*	1942	David Butler	The lyrics of the title song reflect the film making process
Adventure Biography Drama	*Rob Roy*	1995	Michael Caton-Jones	The two styles of fencing are shown here and it is performed brilliantly.
Adventure Comedy Musical	*Robin Hood: Men in Tights*	1993	Mel Brooks	"We're men, men in tights – tight, tights."
Action Adventure Drama	*Robin Hood: Prince of Thieves*	1991	Kevin Reynolds	As you have read, I had a number of weeks working on this film.
Action Crime Sci-Fi	*Robocop*	1987	Paul Verhoeven	There have been attempts to remake this film; however, I still prefer the '87 original.

Action Adventure Family	*Rocketeer*	1991	Joe Johnston	The Art Deco look of this film is a wonderful feast for the eyes.
Drama Sport	*Rocky* Trilogy	1976 1979 1982	John G. Avildsen Sylvester Stallone Sylvester Stallone	The best choreographed/ filmed boxing scenes I have ever seen.
Action Sci-Fi Sport	*Rollerball*	1975	Norman Jewison	This was the film that fuelled my passion for action on film, without swords!
Action Adventure Comedy	*Romancing the Stone*	1984	Robert Zemeckis	If you want to watch the cast gel, watch this film and smile!
Crime Drama Mystery	*Rope*	1948	Alfred Hitchcock	Very long shots – edits could be five minutes; a stage play filmed.
Comedy Romance	*Roxanne*	1987	Fred Schepisi	A beautiful retelling of the story of Cyrano de Bergerac.
Action Comedy Crime	*Running Scared*	1986	Peter Hyams	My first cinema-going experience in Los Angeles, USA.
Drama War	*Saving Private Ryan*	1998	Steven Spielberg	Filmed in sequence. Battle scenes very well created.
Action Adventure Comedy (Swordplay)	*Scaramouche*	1952	George Sidney	One of the longest duels ever filmed.
Drama	*Scent of a Woman*	1992	Martin Brest	This is one of my wife's favourite films.
Biography Drama History	*Schindler's List*	1993	Steven Spielberg	A harrowing true tale that needs to be told. Skilfully directed.

Adventure Drama Western	*Searchers (The)*	1956	John Ford	One of my top five Westerns.
Comedy Romance Sport	*Semi-Tough*	1977	Michael Ritchie	IT or pyramid power, which are you?
Action Crime Drama	*Sharkey's Machine*	1981	Burt Reynolds	A cop movie on the surface, but an emotional rollercoaster of a ride for the characters.
Drama	*Shawshank Redemption (The)*	1994	Frank Darabont	Voted since release as one of the top films yet made. Hard to dispute; it is a great film.
Drama Romance Western	*Shootist (The)*	1976	Don Siegel	John Wayne's last film.
Comedy Mystery	*Shot in the Dark (A)*	1964	Blake Edwards	Peter Sellers is brilliant.
Drama Mystery Sci-Fi	*Signs*	2002	M. Night Shyamalan	Since writing this memoir I find these signs, moments, everywhere.
Crime Drama Thriller	*Silence of the Lambs (The)*	1991	Jonathan Demme	Raised the bar for crime stories.
Comedy	*Silent Movie*	1976	Mel Brooks	"No" – the only word spoken in the film. Guess by whom?

Action Comedy Crime	*Silver Streak*	1976	Arthur Hiller	I met the second unit director, Max Kleven, on *Prince of Thieves*, and he gave me some sound advice. A really great man and a funny film. Fabulous soundtrack by Henry Mancini.
Comedy Musical Romance	*Singin' in the Rain*	1952	Stanley Donen Gene Kelly	Stanley Donen – *Singin' in the Rain* – died as I was writing this memoir, aged ninety-four years in 2019. "The secret of directing success is to get the best writers, songwriters and actors, and then when filming starts stay the hell out of the way. But you have to show up, otherwise you cannot take the credit."
Adventure Action Comedy	*Sky Captain and the World of Tomorrow*	2004	Kerry Conran	A little gem of a film. It is an original concept film, as if it was made by teenagers in the 1930s, with the innocence of early sci-fi with WWII looming. A great adventure story you may not know about.
Comedy Drama Sport	*Slap Shot*	1977	George Roy Hill	Made me laugh out loud in the cinema.

Action Comedy	*Smokey and the Bandit*	1977	Hal Needham	Not all films have to be satire, thought-provoking or political. They can be just for fun!
Comedy Drama Crime	*Sneakers*	1992	Phil Alden Robinson	Outstanding cast. Great script.
Comedy Music Romance	*Some Like It Hot*	1959	Billy Wilder	Outstanding casting. Directed by a master of the genre.
Western	*Sons of Katie Elder*	1965	Henry Hathaway	This is how you film the biggest star in Hollywood.
Comedy	*Sons of the Desert*	1933	William A. Seiter	Laurel and Hardy. Need I say more?
Comedy Music Drama	*Soul Men*	2008	Malcolm D. Lee	Again, casting is all about your film. This film is so funny with a great score.
Adventure Comedy Sci-Fi	*Space Balls*	1987	Mel Brooks	For a sci-fi comedy the special effects are outstanding!
Adventure Biography Drama	*Spartacus*	1960	Stanley Kubrick	Attention to detail from Mr Douglas and Kubrick can be seen on this film. Yakima Canutt as action director shines!
Adventure Comedy	*Spies Like Us*	1985	John Landis	I like this film. Although some argue that it was an attempt at bringing back the *Road to...* films with Bing Crosby and Bob Hope, it stands on its own feet.

Action Adventure Thriller	*Spy Who Loved Me (The)*	1977	Lewis Gilbert	The best Bond film by far, for so many reasons. Stanley Kubrick was one of the uncredited (by his own election) cinematographers on the huge 007 stage, the submarine set.
Biography Comedy Drama	*Stan & Ollie*	2018	Jon S. Baird	Outstanding!
Adventure Mystery Sci-Fi	*Star Trek: The Motion Picture*	1979	Robert Wise	From the small screen to the cinema. Will it work? Of course it did. Still going strong.
Action Adventure Fantasy	*Star Wars Episode IV: A New Hope*	1977	George Lucas	The film that started my journey.
Comedy Crime	*Stir Crazy*	1980	Sidney Poitier	An Oscar-winning actor directing laugh-out-loud films too! What a great talent!
Action Comedy Drama	*Stunt Man (The)*	1980	Richard Rush	Peter O'Toole is mesmerising as the director.
Action Adventure Drama	*Superman*	1979	Richard Donner	You will believe a man can fly.
Comedy Romance Western	*Support Your Local Gunfighter*	1971	Burt Kennedy	As a young film watcher with my family, this was a treat to watch.
Comedy Romance Western	*Support Your Local Sheriff*	1969	Burt Kennedy	Thanks for the memories!
Crime Drama	*Taxi Driver*	1976	Martin Scorsese	The break-through film for Robert De Niro.

Epic	*Ten Commandments (The)*	1956	Cecil B. DeMille	The break-through film for Charlton Heston. DeMille once said, "Give me any ten pages from the Bible and I'll make it into a movie."
Action Sci-Fi	*Terminator (The)* Trilogy	1984 1991 2003	James Cameron Jonathan Mostow	Franchise heaven! T2 is a break-through film in digital CGI film-making.
Horror	*Texas Chainsaw Massacre (The)*	1974	Tobe Hooper	My first viewing was at a senior citizen screening in what we would call a 'flea pit' cinema in North London. At the climax of the film, the chainsaw-wielding villain chasing his victim through a wood was spoilt a little by an elderly gentleman, speaking loudly to his wife next to him, "Well, how does *he* keep it going then?"
Horror Sci-Fi	*Them!*	1954	Gordon Douglas	A classic B movie, that is very hard to find on DVD!
Horror Sci-Fi	*Thing from Another World (The)*	1951	Christian Nyby	Again, a film that is screened once a year, at Halloween!
Drama	*Thirteen Days in October*	2000	Roger Donaldson	How close did we get to World War III? This film will tell you.
Comedy Drama	*This Happy Breed*	1944	David Lean	Noel Coward's script; once again the language is delicious.

Comedy Western	*Three Amigos (The)*	1986	John Landis	An 'infamous' cast.
Mystery Thriller	*Three Days of the Condor*	1975	Sydney Pollack	A classy political thriller; Redford at his best.
Action Adventure	*Three Musketeers (The)*	1948	George Sidney	Gene Kelly – a familiar story, with an inspirational casting of a song and dance star genius as D'Artagnan. The elegance of the sword fights is simply poetry in motion.
Action Adventure	*Three Musketeers (The)*	1973	Richard Lester	Oliver Reed – the sword fights, especially performed by Oliver Reed – are what sword fights really look like, with occasional beautiful comic scenes.
Adventure Romance Sci-Fi	*Time Machine (The)*	1969	George Pal	If you know the story my question is obvious. Which book would you take back? A little bit of trivia too: all George Pal directed or produced films have a tribute to Woody Woodpecker in the film; can you spot him?
Comedy	*To Be or Not to Be*	1983	Alan Johnson	"Excuse me, pardon me, excuse me…" I laughed while typing that line, knowing the scene.

Crime Drama Romance Western	*Tom Horn*	1980	William Wiard	Based on a true story. One of Steve McQueen's last films.
Action Biography Drama Western	*Tombstone*	1993	George P. Cosmatos	A Western that has a lot of style, a look that you wanted to find the fashion for and wear.
Comedy Drama Romance	*Tootsie*	1982	Sydney Pollack	Oscar-winning director and actor Sydney Pollack was nominated for directing this outstanding comedy about struggling actors. The entire cast is magical. See a film really come together, all due to Mr Pollack.
Action Drama History	*Tora! Tora! Tora!*	1970	Richard Fleischer Kinji Fukasaku (Japanese sequences) Toshio Masuda (Japanese sequences)	The huge budget to make the special effects and stunt sequences required the production to sell off the finished filmed action to other films in production to recover some of the costs. This film is worthy of your time.

Action Drama Thriller	*Towering Inferno (The)*	1974	John Guillermin	This will be hard to understand; however, *no* CGI was available when this film was made. The stellar cast had to be seen in all the set fires and explosions. Could this film be made in the same way again, today? A great film.
Action Adventure Sci-Fi	*Tron*	1982	Steven Lisberger	The first major CGI film.
Action Drama Western	*True Grit*	1969	Henry Hathaway	John Wayne starred in; his name appears above the film title, in approximately 142 films. This is the only one he won the Oscar for.
Western	*Undefeated (The)*	1969	Andrew V. McLaglen	Wayne helped to reboot Hudson's career with this film.
Drama Western	*Unforgiven*	1992	Clint Eastwood	Best Picture, Best Director Oscars for Mr Eastwood, who says this is the last Western he will make, as he doesn't want to repeat himself.
Crime Drama Thriller	*Untouchables (The)*	1987	Brian De Palma	Super production values, sets, costumes, guns, no detail missed. Sean Connery won an Oscar for his role too!

Mystery Romance Thriller	*Vertigo*	1958	Alfred Hitchcock	Study the camera movement in this film. Remember the camera was not a steady cam. Amazing.
Biography Comedy Drama	*Vice*	2018	Adam McKay	The story made me angry and mad as all this happened on my watch. The juxtaposition between anger and laughter makes this film a must watch.
Action Adventure History	*Vikings (The)*	1958	Richard Fleischer	A film from my childhood; I must have watched every time it was on television. Warning! The main theme is an ear worm. Even to this day, without any help, I can hum the main title music. Says something about the film, memorable.
Comedy Romance	*War of the Roses (The)*	1989	Danny Devito	From little acorns, the casting of *Romancing the Stone*, oaks grow.
Comedy Family Western	*Way Out West*	1937	James W. Horne	A very popular film with my entire family, as are 'The blue ridge mountains of Virginia'.
Action Adventure War	*Where Eagles Dare*	1968	Brian G. Hutton	A film I studied on my journey, as you have read in this book.
Action Adventure Drama	*Wild Geese (The)*	1978	Andrew V. McLaglen	Just a great film – great actors and script.

Fantasy Family Musical	*Willy Wonka & the Chocolate Factory*	1971	Mel Stuart	The Oompa Loompas have a strong union.
Comedy Fantasy Horror	*Witches of Eastwick (The)*	1987	George Miller	An unusual film mix of genres, but it works!
Adventure Family Fantasy	*Wizard of Oz (The)*	1939	Victor Fleming	Black and white to colour. Back in 1939 the audience was taken to Oz.
Comedy	*Young Frankenstein*	1974	Mel Brooks	Shooting this film in black and white was genius.
Adventure Fantasy Mystery	*Young Sherlock Holmes (The)*	1985	Barry Levinson	An important film on my journey, one I like very much.
Drama History War	*Zulu*	1964	Cy Endfield	A star-making film, Sir Michael Caine, plus a host of other cast members who went on to make a nice living after being in this film.

Fencing is a live sport. This guide was written in 1997, and the FIE have changed, altered and deleted the rules to keep the sport alive. Please check their website for the latest rules. For all you stage, film and historical choreographers – just enjoy!

ANDY WILKINSON'S

FENCING GUIDE

AN EASY-TO-USE REFERENCE GUIDE
FOR CLUB FENCERS

CONTENTS

Theory

INTRODUCTION

Dear Fencer,

There have been a number of excellent books on fencing over the years. Instruction and technique manuals are still being published today, some with a specific weapon in mind, while others deal with the art of fencing on a much grander scale.

However, when I was training, firstly as a fencer and then as a coach, I yearned for a book that I could carry with me in my kit bag to the salle. A book which had an easy-to-use reference section with clear definitions and notes made by an experienced coach to help me over the sometimes confusing terminology, complex physical movements and some of the more specific rules that related to my bouts with my fellow fencers. Since I have a number of students of various ages and abilities, I thought it would be a good idea if I were to sit down and write a fencing guide, drawing from my own notes and experience.

'Andy Wilkinson's Fencing Guide' is the result. An accumulation of all my personal notes coupled with practical experience. The fundamentals of stance, body positioning and grip have been excluded to a large extent since this fencing guide is intended for those fencers who are already working with a coach or who are about to commence their coaching training.

Within this guide I have included the practical and theory questions for the British Academy of Fencing Star Awards.

Finally, I would like to wish you every success with your chosen sport of fencing. Be safe, and have fun!

Andrew A. Wilkinson
Associate of The British Academy of Fencing
Highgate, London
June 1997

ANGULATED OFFENSIVE ACTIONS

Definition: Bending the wrist when placing a hit so as to present the point at right angles to the target.

Andy's Note:

Angulation is required when attempting to circumvent an opponent's parry, especially at foil and épée or, as in sabre, when performing a stop cut to the wrist on an opponent's attack to quarte.

However, angulation is best utilised in conjunction with the renewed attacks of the remise and reprise. We renew an attack by remise when an opponent parries incompletely and fails to riposte or parries and delays in riposting. By using a degree of angulation on the blade by bending the wrist you can circumvent the parry and score a valid hit.

If your opponent steps back while parrying on the rear foot and fails to riposte or delays in riposting, your reprise can incorporate a slight side step of the leading foot to aid the angulated renewed attack.

APPEL

Definition: An appel is a footwork action achieved by a crisp stamping on the piste of the ball of the front or rear foot.

Andy's Note:

The front foot appel is achieved by first raising the toes and lifting the foot approximately 15–20cm off the piste and crisply snapping it back down again, landing on the ball of the foot. A rear foot appel is achieved in the same way. The appel is used to provoke a response from your opponent, which you can then exploit immediately. The appel is incorporated in another footwork action, the balestra.

BALESTRA

Definition: A short jump forward during an attack.

Andy's Note:

The balestra is another footwork action achieved by simultaneously performing a front foot appel and a jump forward of approximately 30cm. The balestra should then be immediately followed by a lunge.

The balestra-lunge is used to gain distance and time on an observed error or a momentary weakness by your opponent.

BASIC POINT CONTROL

Definition: The controlled placement of the point onto the valid target area.

Andy's Note:

In foil and épée, point control is achieved by a combination of holding the weapon correctly and the use of the manipulators and aids of the sword hand. Wild movements of the sword during a fencing phrase, such as counter-ripostes, are usually caused by having too firm a hold on the grip of the sword, making the blade work heavy, and by the lack of doigté or finger play.

The firmness of the sword hand on the grip should be no more and no less than if you were shaking hands with a good friend. Finger play simply requires practice. The wide use of orthopaedic grips in modern fencing does reduce the necessity for learning finger play; nevertheless, the suppleness of the wrist and fingers required of the sword hand to achieve basic point control can be enhanced by the correct use and practice of finger play.

BROKEN TIME ACTIONS

Definition: A pause deliberately made between two movements that normally follow each other.

Andy's Note:

As the term 'broken time' implies it deals with periods of fencing time as required in compound attacks. Broken time is achieved during the execution of a compound attack by the withdrawal of the arm after the feint has been established. Instead of using finger play to deceive your opponent's parry of the feint, you withdraw your sword arm, momentarily losing priority of attack and as your opponent attempts to find your blade, you extend the sword arm once again, reclaiming priority and now being one period of fencing time ahead of your opponent's defence.

Broken time actions, in combination with an accelerated lunge or compound attacks done on the flèche, can be quite successful against an opponent who has wild defence or who attempts to parry while retreating.

Broken time actions are difficult to execute and require confidence in both your own blade control and timing. There is an inherent danger in attempting broken time actions against an opponent who is prone to stop-hit.

Remember, broken time actions can be used as a second intention action to draw a stop-hit from your opponent enabling you to parry the stop-hit and riposte from it – counter-time.

CEDING OR
OPPOSITION PARRIES

Definition: A ceding parry is formed by giving way to an opponent who is taking the blade.

Andy's Note:

Ceding and opposition parries are very similar in nature. Both are used as the defence against prise de fer (takings of the blade) actions and both require the defender to maintain contact with the attacker's blade.

In the case of the opposition parry it is important not to oppose your opponent's blade too early, but to bluff your opponent into thinking that the prise de fer has worked, only opposing your opponent's blade fully when their blade has reached the final line of the engagement. By maintaining contact with your opponent's blade throughout the prise de fer all you need to do is simply return to guard in the final line of the engagement.

Ceding parries require you to yield to the prise de fer until your opponent's blade has arrived in the final line of the thrust, when you pivot your sword hand and blade on the attacking blade and by bending your sword arm you terminate the attack in a covered position. For example, a prise de fer taking your blade from octave would result in a ceding parry of quarte.

COMPOUND ATTACKS

Definition: A compound attack is one that comprises one or more feints. A feint is a movement of the blade meant to resemble an attack and the purpose of which is to draw a parry.

Andy's Note:

I've found that the best way to fully understand the mechanics of compound attacks is to work out why we need to use them in the first place. We can reason that simple attacks, those requiring only one blade movement, can be unsuccessful against an adversary of equal speed and technique, whose judgement of distance is correct.

If we now break down the sequence of events which dictate whether a simple attack is successful or not, we can see why we use compound attacks. The key to understanding why is to analyse two crucial areas of fencing: distance and time.

From the attacker's point of view, the point of their sword must travel the greater distance to the target than the blade of the defender, who has only to move the forté across the target to defend it. Thus, in most cases, the attacker would have to be several times faster than the defender to reach the target before the parry was completed.

By using a feint to deceive the parry we would be gaining time by moving our blade ahead of the defence, but we would not necessarily be gaining any distance. Therefore, for a compound attack to have timing and distance, we must think of the attack as a progressive action.

The attacker must gain distance by starting the lunging movement while feinting and accelerating the lunge to gain full advantage once the parry or parries have been deceived. This is known as a progressive attack. The points to remember when executing a compound attack are that:

1. The feint(s) must be deep enough to convince your opponent that that is the path of your attack and that they must therefore defend themselves or be hit.
2. The golden rule which says 'Never pause on a feint'. In other words, a feint should always be followed up.
3. The timing for your deception of your opponent's parry is governed by the speed of your opponent's defence. To attempt to remove your blade too early would cause your attack to fail as surely as delaying too long. Practice makes perfect!
4. Your attack is progressive and your final acceleration places the hit on target decisively.
5. Your sword arm remains extended throughout the compound attack enabling you, as the attacker, to have priority of attack.

COUNTER-OFFENSIVE ACTIONS

I have decided to group all the counter-offensive actions together. The counter-offensive actions are: the stop-hit; the time-hit; counter-time and I have included second intention in this category for reasons that will be made clear later.

Definitions:

The stop-hit is a counter-offensive action that must, by hitting the attacker, arrest them in the development of their attack and fulfil the implication of its name.

The time-hit, which is more commonly known in modern fencing terminology as a stop-hit with opposition, anticipates and intercepts the final line of the attack and is delivered in such a way that the executant is covered.

Counter-time is the action of drawing the opponent's stop-hit or time-hit, parrying it and riposting from it.

Second intention is a premeditated action to provoke a response.

Andy's Note:

Counter-offensive actions are, by definition, counter-punches. An attack is in progress, and you select a counter-offensive action to arrest the attack or turn the attack to your advantage.

Stop-hits are very effective against badly executed compound attacks, i.e. your opponent has a bent arm on the feint or has wide and badly directed blade movements. Before the final thrust is made by your opponent, that is to say after the feint but before the hit in the final line, you can execute a stop-hit thrust, arresting the original attack immediately.

The legitimacy of the stroke is clearly defined in the FIE rules:

Rule 236 (d) – When compound attacks are made, the opponent has the right to stop-hit; but to be valid the stop-hit must precede the conclusion of the attack by an interval of fencing time; that is to say that the stop-hit must arrive before the attacker has begun the final movement of the attack.

Rule 9 – Fencing time is the time required to perform one simple fencing action.

As with the stop-hit, the time-hit to be valid must arrive before the attacker has begun the final movement of the attack. The time-hit is extensively used in épée fencing:

Rule 329 – At épée, when both competitors are hit, the question of priority of hits is raised only when there is an appreciable difference of time between the hits; if no such difference exists there is a 'double-hit', that is to say a hit is scored against each competitor.

Therefore, the time-hit helps to eliminate the prospect of a 'double-hit' while executing a stop-hit.

I am of the opinion that counter-time is by definition a second intention action.

Counter-time is obviously the answer to a fencer who is prone to stop-hit, or to a fencer who has the habit of attacking into your attack. In competitive terms, the latter example is the most dangerous type of fencer. The fencer who adopts the tactic of obstruction has done so in the hope of unsettling you and making you miss while they themselves land a valid hit.

To defeat this type of fencer you must draw their stop-hit or attack and use a counter-time action. Counter-time is not therefore an instinctive action. If it is not instinctive, it must be premeditated second intention.

Second intention, in itself, is not an offensive or defensive action. It is a means of provoking your opponent so that they make an error or alternatively, into an action which you are prepared for.

A beat, pressure or engagement on your opponent's blade will often provoke a response from your opponent; if you use second intention, you can be prepared for that response and act accordingly, either to hit by using a simple attack or compound attack, or to draw a stop-hit or time-hit as a counter-offensive action.

Second intention is often neglected by fencers when they are building a tactical plan on their opponent. It is to your benefit to find out what movements trigger a response from your opponent and to utilise that information to your advantage. Also remember certain footwork actions often provoke a reaction too, for example the appel.

COUNTER-RIPOSTES

Definition: A counter-riposte is the offensive movement that follows the successful parry of your opponent's riposte. The counter-riposte can be direct, indirect or compound.

Andy's Note:

After the first riposte all subsequent ones are called counter-ripostes. Counter-ripostes are numbered so that the phrasing can be clearly defined.

For example, if an attack is parried, the offensive movement made by the defender is called the riposte; if this riposte is parried by the original attacker, their next offensive movement is the first counter-riposte; should this counter-riposte be parried by the original defender, their next offensive movement is the second counter-riposte. Therefore, the original attacking fencer makes the odd number (1, 3, 5, etc.) while the original defender makes the even number (2, 4, 6, etc.).

A light hand and accurate blade/point control are essential when engaged in a series of counter-ripostes, otherwise it will rapidly develop into a series of wild, slashing movements.

If used tactically, counter-ripostes are useful second-intention actions against an opponent who has a very good defence. The first attack does not carry the full intent of a normal attack, but is intended to draw a parry and riposte from your opponent. Being prepared for this response, you execute a counter-riposte. For example, parrying your opponent's riposte while still on the lunge and executing the first counter-riposte from this position.

If you are the fencer who is being hit by the first counter-riposte you can use the second counter-riposte as a tactical response. For example, hitting your opponent on their recovery to guard after successfully parrying their first counter-riposte. Or a more advanced exercise would be to practise taking your body out of distance by either a half recovery, or shifting your body weight onto the rear foot while parrying, then execute the second counter-riposte with a half lunge or with a leaning forward of the body.

DÉROBEMENT

Definition: Evading an opponent's attempt to beat or take the blade while the sword arm is still extended.

Andy's Note:

The dérobement is achieved by first extending your sword arm and threatening your opponent's target. Your opponent is now faced with two immediate problems. A threatening blade and an opponent with an established priority. For them to proceed any further they must first deal with these problems.

You, on the other hand, have the all the immediate advantages. If your opponent attempts to attack your blade as a preparation, and take the priority of the attack away from you, you must avoid their attempt and carry out your threat of hitting them. This may be assisted by an over-enthusiastic opponent who may lunge on to your point assuming that their attack on your blade was successful when in fact it was avoided.

The same applies to any attempt by your opponent to take your blade in a prise de fer action. Dérobements are very effective against an opponent who attacks your blade while stepping forward.

If, however, your opponent finds your blade by either an attack on the blade or by prise de fer, the priority of the attack immediately reverts to your opponent and you must defend yourself.

ELEMENTARY DEFENCE

Definition: The principle of defence is forté to foible – strong against weak. There are three elementary defensive parries: lateral, circular and semi-circular.

Andy's Note:

Every fencer must strive to achieve a solid elementary defence, for without it, the fencer is left open and vulnerable to any number of attacks. Although we classify the lateral, circular and semi-circular parries as elementary, they require practice to achieve the almost instinctive nature of these defensive actions. An experienced fencer will be able to perform all elementary defensive actions as if they were second nature. All defensive actions must be controlled enabling the riposte to be accurate. As I have said earlier the 'principle of defence' is forté to foible – strong against weak.

    a. The lateral parry or simple instinctive party is the most natural parry of them all. It is the defensive action of carrying your sword arm and sword across your body in order to oppose the oncoming attack by the use of your blade's forté against the attacker's foible with the purpose of deflecting it.

It is achieved by moving the sword arm and blade from right to left if right-handed (left to right if left-handed), sufficiently far enough to close the line of the attack. The lateral parry can be used in both high and low lines:

Sixte to quarte; quarte to sixte; octave to septime; septime to octave.

There are a number of faults that arise if the simple parry is executed incorrectly. One fault is to move the sword arm too far across the body, locking the arm straight. Parrying in this extravagant way means that the fencer is protecting nothing but the air to the left (or right) of their target area. It is surprising how little the sword arm needs to move across the body before any attack is made 'safe'.

The second fault that can arise, especially in foil and épée fencing, is the pommel of the sword remaining in the wrist while parrying. This makes the point of your sword move away from your opponent's target area. In turn, this makes the riposte slow and it requires greater point control to achieve a clean hit. In foil and épée fencing, the pommel is released from the wrist by flexing the wrist and bending the arm at the elbow, this releases the pommel from the wrist so that the sword is transported to the new line in one simultaneous movement; point and forté forming the line of defence, from sixte to parry in quarte. The point of your sword remains in line for the riposte.

The lateral parry is truly an instinctive move. If you observe beginners, who have yet to be shown a defence movement, they will inevitably 'parry' laterally, with varying body contortions to accompany their wild blade movements.

From a coaching perspective, the lateral parry may well be the simplest of the elementary defensive strokes to teach, but to coach the correct blade position and timing of the parry is a more complex problem, as the natural instinct of the student fencer is to intercept and push away the oncoming attack.

In sabre fencing the lateral parry is achieved by first rolling the grip of the sword between the thumb and index finger while simultaneously rotating the wrist from a pronated position (fingernails down) to a supinated position (fingernails upward). The rolling of the grip in the sword hand is essential if the guard of the sword is to be used to protect the fingers from the cut. The thumb rolls from left to right (if right-handed) across the grip, as if you had a marble or a piece of pastry instead of a sword grip between your fingers.

With the finger guard now rotated 180 degrees from its starting position, it will protect the hand and fingers of the sword hand during the attack into quarte. Remember, apart from the guard protecting the hand, in sabre the hand is part of the target area and if it is hit will score a point for your opponent.

b. Circular parries (or counters) are those which, by describing a circular movement of the blade, bring back the attacker's blade to the line from which it started. There are as many circular parries as there are lateral parries.

For example, from an engaged position of sixte your opponent attempts to do a disengagement attack, but this time not into quarte but into sixte, just inside your guard. To take a lateral parry against such an attack would risk dragging the attack across the body before it is made 'safe' in quarte.

By describing a clockwise circle with the point of your sword, i.e. starting at twelve o'clock and moving through three, six, nine until you return back to twelve o'clock, you will gather the attacking blade and bring it back into the original line of the engagement. Forté to foible.

The circular parry of quarte is achieved in the same manner, but this time the blade must describe a circle in an anti-clockwise direction, twelve o'clock, nine, six, three, twelve, sweeping the attack back out, forté to foible.

The circular movement of the weapon is achieved by the use of finger play. Circular parries fail when the wrist stiffens in anticipation of the attack with the simultaneous raising of the sword hand in the attempt to collect your opponent's blade. Excessive use of the wrist when making a circular parry will result in wide and slow movements and loss of direction of the point.

c.   The semi-circular parry is a parry describing a half-circle from high to low line, or vice versa.

Semi-circular parries are those used to deflect attacks aimed at the low line: septime and octave. It is rare that fencers today engage blades in septime or octave; the advantage is negligible, unless it is part of a wider tactical plan. Compound attacks or attacks on the blade followed by an attack into the low line are the most common reason why a defending fencer selects a semi-circular parry.

From the high lines of tierce, quarte and sixte the blade describes a half-circle with the point of the sword coming into the centre of the body, starting at the top of the half-circle moving outwards on the last quarter. The pommel of the sword is allowed to release from the wrist to finish in a slight upward angle.

The point of your sword would now be pointing at the toe of your opponent. To defend against an attack in the high line while in the low line, reverse the above.

Semi-circular actions will always change the height of your guard, i.e. high line to low and vice versa. In fact, if you held a marker pen in your hand, instead of your sword, the image drawn on a sheet of paper held in front of you while executing a semi-circular parry from sixte and then a semi-circular parry from quarte would be that of an hour glass. Ripostes from the low line can be difficult to execute accurately and require practice.

ENGAGEMENTS

Definition: The crossing of the swords.

Andy's Note:

When a fencer crosses sword with their adversary they are deemed to be in a state of engagement. The engagement corresponds to the line in which the swords are crossed. For us to continue further we must quickly explore the theoretical lines which define the target area.

If we draw an imaginary vertical line from the base of our chin to the groin and then draw another imaginary horizontal line across our chest, level with the base of the rib cage, we have divided the target area into four. Each quarter has two guard positions within it. The position the sword hand has adopted, either pronation or supination, dictates what guard position you have arrived at. There are eight standard guard positions in all. Tradition has handed down their names from generation to generation and they are still used in modern terminology in nearly every fencing country. They are: prime, seconde, tierce, quarte, quinte, sixte, septime and octave.

Four in pronation – prime, seconde, tierce and quinte

(fingernails facing down) and four in supination – quarte, sixte, septime and octave (fingernails facing up).

We know that the standard on guard position is the sixte position. If you are right-handed it will be the top right quarter of your target with your fingers in a three-quarter supination position. If you rotate your sword hand into pronation while in this quarter you will now be in the guard position of tierce, the on guard position for sabre.

Moving your sword arm horizontally across the top of your torso, crossing the vertical line, you move into the next quarter; if right-handed it will be the quarter covering your heart. With your fingers in supination you will be in the guard position of quarte. If you rotate your sword hand into a slightly exaggerated pronation position, with the pommel of your sword outside your wrist and your thumb pointing directly down to the piste, you are now in the guard position of prime.

If you now rotate your sword hand back into supination, remaining on the left side of the body (if right-handed) and keeping the point of the sword low, i.e. pointing to the piste, you have now adopted the position of septime. The pronation guard in this quarter is called quinte. Quinte is very rarely used in foil and épée fencing, and sabre fencers have adopted a version of the quinte guard as the head parry.

Moving horizontally back to the right side of the body, with the blade of your sword still in a low line position, you will be entering the last of the theoretical quarters. With your sword hand in a supinated position, the point still low, you will be in the guard of octave. Rotating the sword hand into pronation, you will have adopted the guard of seconde. If you are a left-handed fencer, don't panic! Just simply reverse the above.

To engage your opponent's blade in any of the above guard positions you must remain covered. That is to say you engage the blade in such a way that the line in which the swords are crossed are closed to a direct thrust.

FLÈCHE

Definition: An attack made by a succession of running steps, instead of by the lunge or steps forward.

Andy's Note:

The flèche, as I write, is currently judged an illegal movement in sabre fencing by the FIE, therefore the use of the flèche as a means of delivering an attack only applies to foil and épée fencers.

A well-timed and executed simple attack by flèche is one of the hardest offensive actions to parry; however it should still be used selectively. Once you have decided to use a flèche, it must be successful. Failure to land leaves the attacker at their opponent's mercy, for the attacker cannot, as in a lunge, recover out of reach, but must fight on at close quarters or as they run past.

To execute a flèche correctly, the sword arm must first be fully extended while simultaneously throwing the body weight sharply forward and over the leading leg. The imbalance caused by the weight shift of the fencer lifts the rear foot from the piste; this foot must now be brought through to land in front of the leading leg as quickly as possible, thus beginning a series of short and rapid steps. The rules forbid the fencer attacking with flèche to make body contact with their opponent. They must run past their opponent rather than stopping short in front of them. The pass should always be made on the quarte side of the body regardless of whether their opponent is left or right-handed.

Some fencers make the error of thinking that the hit from a flèche is achieved after several steps, when in fact the hit should land at the very beginning of the flèche.

The speed of the attack is what makes the flèche hard to parry. The point of no return is when the fencer, with their sword arm fully extended, shifts their body weight forward. By using the muscles in the front of the thigh of the leading leg, the quadriceps, the flècheur can accelerate towards the target, ideally hitting your opponent before the rear foot has time to land in front of the leading leg.

GAINING AND BREAKING GROUND

Definition: Gaining and breaking ground is the action of stepping forward or backward. It is the footwork used in fencing to gain or maintain distance with your opponent, or to step out of reach.

Andy's Note:

Very few fencers think of the step back or step forward as being a form of preparation for attack. In their minds these two actions are simply the means of maintaining a correct distance. Nevertheless, both the step forward and the step back can be looked upon as preparing an attack.

It can be said that the attack, in whatever form it may take, is prepared by first stepping forward to within the fencing measure, thus taking up a correct and effective distance. The step forward, apart from helping maintain distance, is normally used against a fencer who has the habit of stepping back when attacked.

But be warned; by attacking with a step forward there is always a danger of being stop-hit. It is therefore safer to make your opponent commit the error of coming within your reach than to go after them.

The step back is not only used for putting yourself out of reach, but can be made to draw your opponent forward so that you can attack them while they advance. It is very useful against an adversary who has the advantage of reach.

GUARD POSITIONS

Definition: Prime, seconde, tierce, quarte, quinte, sixte, septime and octave.

Four in pronation – prime, seconde, tierce and quinte (fingernails facing down) and four in supination – quarte, sixte, septime and octave (fingernails facing up).

Andy's Note:

Mastering all eight guard positions is a fundamental requirement of any fencer. Being able to freely adopt a covered guard position quickly and effectively and being able to riposte from them is the key to successful fencing.

For further notes on guard positions, please refer to 'Engagements'.

HIT

Definition: The offensive action that lands with point or edge on the opponent.

Andy's Note:

Apart from the obvious observation that a valid hit gives you a point against your opponent, the method of executing a correct hit in foil, épée or sabre is perhaps not so obvious.

Whatever attack or counter-attack you use against your opponent, the final movement of the attack is the actual hit. Passé hits, or hits not showing to some degree the character of penetration (a bend in the blade of the sword when a hit is performed correctly) are considered failed attacks. Everything leading up to the hit may well have been performed correctly, but the hit fails to score.

It is therefore every fencer's responsibility to practise the techniques involved in the hit prior to every fencing session at a club, and without fail prior to any competition.

A successful hit requires a correctness of grip and the use of finger play. In foil and épée the hit is achieved from the on guard position by smoothly extending the sword arm to its maximum while simultaneously exerting a pressure of the thumb and a contraction of the index finger on the handle of your sword, lowering the point from its raised position of on guard, and therefore placing the point on the designated target. Once the hit has arrived the sword hand should be raised well above the level of your shoulder.

In sabre, the only cut and thrust competitive fencing sword, the hit can be made with either the point or with the whole of the front edge or with a third of the back edge. Hits with the point are placed exactly as with the foil; the hand position, however, is in a fully pronated position (fingernails down).

The Hungarian style of sabre fencing, which has been adopted by most sabreurs, clearly defines how a cut (hit) is to be performed.

To make a cut (hit) the sword arm is extended and the edge of the sabre presented at the target. At the moment when the arm reaches its full extension, a contraction of the last fingers of the sword hand, combined with a downward flexing of the wrist, delivers a light, crisp cut.

Heavy hitting is usually the result of excessive use of the forearm and neglect of the wrist and finger action.

Italo Santelli, the founder of the modern Hungarian school of sabre fencing, used to say to his pupils, "The sabre is your pen – write with it finely and with grace – write with it as you would your fiancée."

LUNGE

Definition: The extension of the arm, body and legs used to reach an opponent.

Andy's Note:

If you ask a fencer to do a lunge and recovery they will perform an extension of the sword arm, followed immediately by the raising of the front foot while driving from the rear foot towards your opponent as the rear arm falls in line with the now straight rear leg, palm uppermost – a perfect lunge – and the recovery begins with the bending of the rear leg, with the simultaneous raising of the rear arm and the raising of the front toes returning to the on guard position, the sword arm being the last to return in the recovery.

But not so many years ago the lunge and recovery were only one part of a combination of movements called the 'development' and 'return to guard'.

The extension of the sword arm, giving the fencer priority, was treated as the first part of the development. The footwork action of the lunge, following immediately after the extension, made up the final part of the development. The return to guard is as described above.

The reason I mention this change in terminology, from the earlier development and return to guard to the more accepted term encompassing all movements, the lunge, is to highlight the sometimes small and intricate movements required to successfully perform a smooth lunge and recovery.

The lunge is the means by which an attack is carried out when your opponent is within the fencing measure. The extension of the sword arm, which gives the attacker priority, draws the leading leg forward.

When I teach the lunge, I always like to describe these movements in the following way:

Imagine the little finger of the sword hand has an invisible piece of string attached to it. The other end is attached to the big toe of the leading foot. With the extension of the sword arm the string goes tight and begins to pull the leading foot forward with it.

The power and speed of the lunge comes from the rear foot and leg with the added boost of the rear arm thrown behind one's self with the palm uppermost. With the rear leg now straight, but not locked, and the rear foot flat on the piste, but not rolled on its side, the lunge has now been completed. The weight of the fencer remains evenly distributed between the front and rear leg.

The recovery is achieved as described above; the only thing a fencer must be aware of is that the return to guard must end in a covered guard position.

All of these movements combined together form the single smooth movement of the lunge. Point control gives the fencer a valid hit. Professor Léon Crosnier described the action of lunging and hitting an opponent in the following way: "Think of your point as being a fly, and try to catch it."

OFFENSIVE AND DEFENSIVE ACTIONS IN PRONATION

Definition: Offensive and defensive actions while the sword hand is in a pronated position, i.e. fingernails down.

Andy's Note:

The pronated guard positions of prime, seconde, tierce and quinte are all positions of defence, i.e. a parry of prime, a parry of seconde, etc. However, as launching points for offensive actions, tierce, the on guard position for sabre, is realistically the only viable option. Ripostes and counter-ripostes, however, can be achieved from all these pronated positions.

Preparations from these positions such as prise de fer require practice, but all prise de fer actions starting from a pronated position have the inherent danger of your opponent's blade slipping off, enabling them to score a hit against you.

But if we look at pronated hand positions being applied at the last instant prior to a hit, we can see the advantage of using pronation instead of supination. Attacks into the low line, especially those directly below your opponent's sword arm are eased considerably if the hit is applied with a pronated hand. The character of penetration (the bend in the blade) is now arching away from the obstructing sword arm of your opponent.

A riposte or counter-riposte from prime, which uses the thumb to place an 'inverted' hit on your opponent as in foil and épée, is a useful action against left-handed fencers.

In sabre, a riposte or counter-riposte from prime by molinello is a fast and very effective action.

OFFENSIVE AND DEFENSIVE ACTIONS IN SUPINATION

Definition: Offensive and defensive actions while the sword hand is in a supinated position, i.e. fingernails upward.

Andy's Note:

The supinated positions of quarte, sixte, septime and octave are all positions of defence, i.e. a parry of quarte, a parry of sixte etc., and unlike pronated positions, offensive actions can be launched from all these points. Naturally, ripostes and counter-ripostes can also be achieved from these supinated positions.

Septime and octave, being low-line guards, enable the confident attacking fencer to exploit a fencer who may shy away from low-line defence. Compound attacks starting and finishing in the low line are rare only because of the difficulty many fencers have with supinated hand positions while in the low line. Practice with good feints and a strong progressive attack will overcome this problem.

Preparations; attacks on the blade, prise de fer, can all be done with a supinated hand position in both the high and the low line.

By adopting a low-line guard, you may well invite your opponent to attack by means of a preparation. If you use this tactic as a second intention action you can attack them on the preparation.

PREPARATIONS FOR ATTACK

There are three types of preparation for attack: attacks on the blade; prise de fer; and gaining and breaking of ground. The first two categories have three sub-headings.

Attacks on the Blade:

Definitions: A beat is a crisp movement of the blade made against the opponent's blade with the object of knocking it aside or obtaining a reaction.

A pressure is the action of pressing upon the opponent's blade in order to deflect it or obtain a reaction from it.

A froissement is the action of grazing the opponent's blade very strongly and sharply by bringing the forté of one's own blade diagonally down from the foible to the middle of your opponent's blade, thus deflecting it sharply.

Andy's Note:

The beat is made by smartly opening and closing the last fingers; the fencer detaches their blade from that of their adversary and brings it back crisply and neatly in contact with it, thus knocking it aside. The trick to executing a successful beat is to not use the wrist. Using the wrist makes the movement of your blade large and exaggerated, giving your opponent the opportunity to avoid it. When executed well, the reaction provoked from your opponent may well be a return beat. Used as a tactic, the avoidance of the return beat may expose an opening.

The pressure is achieved when the blades are engaged. By a combination of the last fingers of the sword hand and a slight flexing of the wrist, a pressure is exerted on your opponent's blade. Like the beat, the pressure is used to provoke a reaction from your opponent. By using pressure on their sword, you may well open a fencing line enough to attempt an attack or you may well provoke a totally different response of a pushing back of your sword, which creates the ideal conditions for you to then execute a disengagement.

The froissement, the last of the attacks on the blade, is achieved when the blades are engaged. A slight extension of the sword arm and simultaneous flexing of the wrist, down and into a pronated position across your opponent's blade forté to foible, moves your opponent's blade out of line, exposing the target area. The force of the movement makes it difficult to control and it is the least used of the attacks on the blade. The froissement, in the days of duels of honour, was often used as an attempt to disarm an opponent.

Takings of the Blade (Prise de Fer):

Definitions: The envelopment is the action of taking the foible of the opposing blade in the forté of one's own and, by describing a circle with both blades in contact, returning to the original line of the engagement.

The bind, with the blades engaged, is the action of carrying the opponent's blade diagonally across from a high to a low line, or vice versa.

The croisé carries the opponent's blade from high to low line on the same side as the engagement and does not, as in the bind, carry it diagonally across. It is never executed from low to high line.

Andy's Note:

All prise de fer actions require your opponent to have what is commonly called a 'susceptible hand'. That is to say, the prise de fer requires you to move your opponent's blade in various directions before the final line of the attack is established. If their hand is stiff and rigid, the prise de fer can quickly turn into a battle of strength rather than finesse. On the other hand, if their hand is loose and weak, by nature the prise de fer will collapse during the movement.

Therefore, assuming our opponent has a 'susceptible hand', the bind which starts in sixte would finish in the line of septime. If the bind starts from quarte, the finish line of the bind will be octave and vice versa. There is no reason why two prise de fers cannot follow one another. If there is a detachment of blades prior to a re-attachment of the blades, it is called a double prise de fer. If there is no loss of contact between the prise de fers it is called a compound prise de fer.

The croisé is normally carried out on an opponent's threatening blade, i.e. their sword arm is either extending or is already extended.

The envelopment is a fast prise de fer, which normally results in the executant performing a simple straight-thrust attack.

RENEWED ATTACKS

Definition: Remise, redoublement and reprise. The remise is a renewed attack in the same line as the parry, the redoublement is a renewal of the attack in a new line and can be indirect or compound and a reprise is a renewal of attack by first coming through the on guard position.

Andy's Note:

Generally speaking, renewed attacks are done on an opponent who parries and fails to or delays in riposting.

The best way I've found of remembering the varieties of renewed attack is this: a remise is in the same line; a redoublement is in a new line and the reprise is the method of placing the other two, i.e. same line, new line, the means.

The remise is the replacing of the point or cut on the target, while on the lunge, in the line in which the attack was parried and does not comprise of any additional blade or arm movement. It is executed against an opponent who parries incompletely and fails to riposte or parries and delays their riposte. It is quite often the case that after a successful parry an opponent delays or fails to riposte immediately and their guard, which successfully stopped your original attack, weakens allowing a renewed attack by remise to score a hit. It is also worth mentioning that a remise with a degree of angulation, i.e. circumventing the guard by a combination of wrist and foot movement, is also very effective.

The redoublement is a renewal of the attack while on the lunge requiring an additional blade and arm movement. Once again, the original attack has been successfully parried, and there is a delay or no riposte; however your opponent's covered guard is still good. By the use of finger play and a small arm movement, the point or cut can be placed in an open line.

The reprise is a renewal of attack by first going through the on guard position, either forward or backward. As I stated earlier, the reprise is the means by which you use a remise or redoublement on an opponent who either steps out of distance once they have parried and fails to or delays in riposting or who parries and steps forward, forcing you to return to guard, then renewing your attack by either remise or redoublement.

The most important factor to remember when executing a renewed attack is that you must retain the original priority of attack by keeping your point or edge of your blade threatening the target throughout the renewed attack. By having an extended sword arm you retain the priority. To withdraw your sword arm totally means the loss of priority.

RIPOSTE

Definition: A riposte is an offensive action following the successful parry of your opponent's attack.

Andy's Note:

Ripostes can be either simple or compound. A simple riposte, like the simple attack, comprises a single blade movement and can be either direct or indirect, i.e. disengagement, cut-over or counter-disengagement.

A compound riposte must comprise one or more feints.

In modern fencing it is deemed an error to delay in riposting, unless it is part of your tactical plan. A failure to riposte or a delay in riposting may result in your opponent renewing their attack. This eventuality, the delay in riposting, is defined by the FIE rule 234 (b):

"The parry gives the right to riposte: the simple riposte may be direct or indirect, but to annul any subsequent action by the attacker, it must be executed immediately, without indecision or delay."

The simple direct riposte is achieved by detaching from your opponent's foible immediately after the successful parry of the attack. With an extension of the sword arm and using finger play, you place the point, or in sabre the cut, in an open line. If the attacker executed the attack on the lunge, the riposte may be executed into their recovery. The depth of your lunge depends on the speed of your opponent's recovery.

An indirect riposte requires a single movement of the blade, by use of finger play, so that you can place the point or the cut in an opening line.

The attacker, having failed in their attack, may instinctively cover their exposed target by closing out the line by moving their blade to cover the open line. By extending your sword arm in the same line as your parry, you will feel a pressure exerted on your blade as your opponent attempts to close the open line. This is the signal to execute an indirect riposte, by either passing beneath your opponent's blade as in a disengagement or passing over the top of it as in a cut-over. If your opponent closes the line while recovering, the indirect riposte must be executed while your sword arm is extending, placing the hit by the execution of a lunge, the depth of which is governed by the speed of your opponent's recovery.

As in compound attacks, the compound riposte must comprise one or more feints. It too must be a progressive action. In this event it is being used as a counter-offensive action, so the chances are you will be executing a compound riposte on your opponent's recovery, after their failed attack. As in compound attacks, the compound riposte, if executed poorly, is prone to a counter-offensive action too, i.e. the stop-hit or time-hit.

By definition, the riposte is the action that follows the successful parry of an attack. If the attack is compound the defence is successive parries, i.e. in an attempt to find your opponent's blade while they are executing the feint(s). If you are successful in finding your opponent's blade while they are executing their compound attack or compound riposte, you have the right to riposte or counter-riposte, as stated in the FIE rule 419 (f): "If during a compound attack the opponent finds the blade during one of the feints, the opponent has the right to riposte."

In my experience it can be an advantage to parry while on the rear foot while retreating from an attack. This gives you as the defender two distinct advantages over the attacker:

a. Distance and
b. Time

Changing the distance makes your opponent come after you, which may cause them to adjust their attack at the last instance giving you time to select a suitable parry or counter-offensive action to their attack, which in turn gives you time to select the riposte you wish to execute.

I think it is important, in this section, to talk about the 'right of way' or 'priority of attack'. In foil and sabre fencing there is clearly defined phrasing, which basically translates into 'Your go – my go'. The fencer starting the phrase is the fencer whose sword arm is extending or is already extended. This fencer is deemed to have the 'right of way'.

If their attack is successful, they get a valid hit scored. However, if their attack is parried successfully, they lose the 'right of way' and the 'right to riposte' goes to the defender. Assuming that the riposte is immediate, the original attacker must now defend themselves. They too may parry the riposte, the 'right of way' now going back to the original attacker who counter-ripostes, and so on. To return to guard automatically revokes the 'right of way'.

Problems in defining phrasing usually occur when simultaneous attacks or double-hits arrive on both fencers.

Simultaneous attacks occur when both fencers conceive and execute the same attack. In foil and sabre this is not allowed. No points are scored.

In view of the 'right of way' and phrasing in foil and sabre, simultaneous attacks are not allowed. If double-hits occur, one fencer will be at fault. If, for example, a fencer is deemed to have the 'right of way' and executes an attack that is successfully parried followed by an immediate riposte, however the original attack continues with the original attacker scoring a hit while the defender also scores a hit with the riposte. The attacker is deemed to be at fault because the 'right to riposte' was taken and was immediately executed. The attacker loses the priority as soon as their attack is parried and must, therefore, be prepared to defend themselves. In the example above, the defender scores the hit.

In épée fencing, there is no phrasing. If both competitors are hit, the question of the 'right of way' of hits is raised only when there is an appreciable difference of time between the hits; if no such difference exists there is a double-hit, that is to say a hit is scored against each fencer.

SIMPLE ATTACKS

Definition: An attack that requires only one movement of the blade. There are four simple attacks: straight thrust; disengagement; cut-over and counter-disengagement.

Andy's Note:

Attacks are divided into two categories, simple and compound. Attacks on the blade are deemed to be a preparation for an attack.

A common misconception when discussing simple attacks is the precursory term 'simple'. In fencing the word 'simple' refers to the single blade movement required to achieve the stroke and not, necessarily, to the simplicity of the attack. There are four simple attacks that apply equally to all three weapons. They are: the straight thrust; the disengage; the cut-over and the counter-disengage.

Each of the above attacks has a different blade action and in consequence its own particular technique.

a. The straight thrust or direct attack is an attack directed at an open or opening line. The straight thrust is an opportunist's attack. The fencer executing the stroke will attack immediately on seeing an opening or will take full advantage of an opponent's momentary lack of concentration in keeping a good covering guard.

There are two essential qualities to achieving the straight thrust; firstly, the attacker must have speed of execution and secondly accuracy. The straight thrust is executed with the lunge and becomes one flowing movement.

b. The disengagement is an indirect simple attack. It consists of passing the point of your sword under that of your opponent, from the line of engagement into the opposite line.

Fencers often have moments of slackness in their covering and, realising the weakness of their position, cover up. This means that their sword and sword arm travel across their target. Assuming the blades are engaged, your opponent will be exerting a pressure upon your blade, creating an ideal condition to execute a disengage attack.

From a technical standpoint the disengage requires some degree of skill to achieve. It requires blade manipulation by the use of the thumb and index finger (finger play) to lower the point of your sword so that it passes freely under the opposing blade, describing a broad-based 'U' shape, and to raise it up again in line with your opponent's target, while executing an arm extension giving the attacker the right of way for the attack.

All of these actions, the passing under of your opponent's point and the extension of the sword arm combined with a lunge, must form a single, smooth-flowing movement.

c. The cut-over is a form of disengagement which, instead of passing under the blade, passes over it to end in the line opposite to that of the engagement. Again, it is an indirect action.

   The principles of attack are the same for the cut-over as they are for the disengagement. However, in the initial execution of the attack the wrist and hand replace the finger play of the disengagement.

   It is essential that once your blade has cleared the point of the opposing blade, you extend your arm and threaten the target. Finger play can now be utilised to control the point and aid in the accuracy of the stroke.

   Once again, all of the above-mentioned actions combined with a lunge must form a single smooth movement. The cut-over is unique in that it requires the attacking fencer to remove their point from the target before re-establishing the threat. It is vital, therefore, that the attacking fencer has a fully extended arm prior to completing the attack with a lunge. Otherwise there is a very real danger of falling onto your opponent's blade.

d. To counter-disengage is to deceive the opponent's change of engagement, or to deceive their attempt to parry with a circular parry.

   As your adversary makes their change of engagement your blade must follow theirs round and back into the original line of the engagement. That is to say unlike the disengage or the cut-over, the counter-disengage does not end in the line opposite to that of the engagement, but remains in the same line.

   However, like the disengage, the blade manipulation is achieved by using the thumb and index finger, your sword arm must then extend, threatening the target, which in turn gives you the priority of attack (right of way).

It is also important to note that the counter-disengage does not deceive a lateral opposition, i.e. a pressure, but a circular movement of your opponent's blade.

When mastered, the counter-disengage is a very effective attack requiring great skill to defend one's self against successfully.

SUCCESSIVE PARRIES

Definition: A series of parries that immediately follow each other until the attacker's blade is found.

Andy's Note:

Successive parries are the defence against compound attacks. A combination of lateral, circular or semi-circular parries will increase your chances of collecting your opponent's feint(s) or attack before it has a chance to arrive in the final line. Remember that a parry or successive parries taken on the rear foot while retreating gives the defender two distinct advantages:

a. Forces your opponent to correct their distance for the attack accordingly

and

b. Gives the defender additional time and distance to select a suitable second or third parry and riposte.

Practise parrying on the rear foot while retreating, used normally against a marching compound attack, that is to say when your opponent executes their feints while stepping into distance or an opponent who has the advantage of reach.

TROMPEMENT

Definition: Tromper is to deceive. A trompement is, therefore, a deception. In fencing it is the term used to describe the blade actions that deceive an opponent's parry.

Andy's Note:

It is important not to confuse the trompement with a dérobement. The trompement is the deception of your opponent's parry. We have established that attacks on the blade and prise de fers are all preparations for attack; therefore we can safely say that all attacks, except the straight thrust, are attacks by trompement, indirect and compound, i.e. by deception of your opponent's blade.

CONSTITUTION OF A JURY

A fencing jury comprises of a President and four judges. Rules 53–55 of the FIE rulebook state that:

Rule 53   The President

All bouts at fencing are directed by a President who has many duties:

- *Calls the roll of competitors (Cf. 604, 615, 641).*
- *Directs the bout (Cf. 63).*
- *Checks that the material and equipment, especially that concerned with safety, properly carries the marks applied by the controls according to the special regulations for each weapon. Checks the insulation of the wiring, particularly inside the guard (Cf. 18, 217, 314, 425).*
- *Supervises his assistants (judges and ground judges and arm judges, time-keepers and scorers, etc.).*
- *Maintains order (Cf. 615).*
- *Penalises faults (Cf. 615).*
- *Awards the hits (Cf. 67, 69, 75).*

Rule 54   The jury, judges and ground judges

The President fulfils his duty of judging hits, either with the help of four judges, or with the assistance of an apparatus for the automatic registering of hits; with the latter the President may be assisted by two ground judges or two judges looking out for the use of the unarmed hand or arm (Cf.31).

Ground judges are obligatory when there is no metallic piste. The President and the judges (or ground judges) constitute the jury. For all bouts in the final the President must be assisted by two judges each watching one of the fencers in order to draw attention to any use of the non-sword arm or any other off target part of the body (Cf. 30, 31) as follows:

- *at foil, either to parry the opponent's blade or to cover part of the target;*
- *at épée, to parry the opponent's blade and to fulfil the functions of ground judges (Cf. 30, 31, 71, 640);*
- *at sabre, to replace the valid target by other parts of the body where hits do not score.*

Rule 55

By accepting a position on a jury, each of the members concerned pledges on their honour to respect the rules and to cause them to be respected, and to carry out their duties with the strictest impartiality and most sustained attention.

NAMES FOR PARTS
OF THE WEAPON

From the point of the sword:
 Rubber button – foible – middle – forté – tang – guard –
finger cushion – grip – martingale pommel.

PENALTIES – YELLOW, RED AND BLACK CARDS

Article 642 of the FIE rulebook covers the offences and penalties relating to competitors and their coaches. For each offence a coloured card is produced. A YELLOW card is a warning, valid for the bout. A RED card is a penalty hit and a BLACK card means exclusion or expulsion from the competition. The offences are categorised into FOUR groups.

Group One Offences	Article	1st	2nd	3rd
Without a national armband in official events, equipment not working or conforming, absence of 2nd regulation weapon	21A/1 &3.b, 27/3	Yellow card	Red card	Red card
Simple corps-a-corps (foil and sabre)*	34,224,412			
Corps-a-corps to avoid being hit, jostling, falling, disorderly fencing, reversing shoulders (foil)*	28, 34, 224			
Taking off mask before the President calls halt	28			
Covering, substitution of valid target area	30,411			

Irregular use of the non-sword arm/hand	30,411			
Touching, taking hold of electrical equipment	30			
Leaving piste without permission	32			
Turning back on opponent*	35			
Leaving piste to avoid being hit	43			
Unjustifiable interruption of bout	48			
Placing, pressing weapon point on metal piste	211, 316			
Bringing weapon in contact with lame jacket*	230			
Deliberate hit not on opponent	230, 325			
At sabre, hit made with the coquille*	409			
Refusal to obey the President	602/3/6/9			
Unjustified appeal	661			
Group Two Offences	Article	1st	2nd	3rd
Absence of weapon control markings* Dangerous, violent or vindictive action, blow with guard or pommel*	21A, 30 28	Red card	Red card	Red card
Interruption of bout for claimed injury not confirmed by doctor	50			
Deliberate hit not on opponent in the last minute	230, 325			
Group Three Offences	Article	1st	2nd	3rd
Faking markings of weapon control, intentional modification of equipment*	21N3.c,d	Red card	Black card	–
Dishonest fencing*	28			
Fencer disturbing order when on piste (4)	602			
Offence against publicity code	Publicity Code			

Supporter, trainer, spectator, fencer not on piste disturbing good order	602	Red card warning		
Group Four Offences	Article	1st	2nd	3rd
Non-presentation when called by the President at the start of the competition/round/bout/match after three calls at one minute intervals (1)	604	Black card	-	-
Manifest cheating with equipment (2)	21N3.e			
Deliberate brutality (1)*	28			
Offence against sportsmanship (l) or (2)* Profiting from collusion	605			
Favouring an opponent (1)*	607			
Doping (2)	608			

Key

* * – Annulment of any hit scored by the fencer at fault.
1. Exclusion from the competition.
2. Exclusion from the whole tournament.
3. Expulsion from the competition venue.
4. In serious cases, President may exclude/expel immediately.

If a fencer commits an offence in the first group after having been penalised by a red card, for whatever the reason, they receive a further red card. A fencer only receives a black card in the third group if they previously committed an offence in the third group (demonstrated by red card).

REPLIES A JUDGE MAY GIVE TO A PRESIDENT

When judging by a jury, that is to say with no electrical apparatus to assist the President, the judges are placed in the following manner:

Two judges are placed on each side of the piste on the President's right and left respectively and slightly behind the competitors.

The two judges placed on the President's right hand should watch the fencer who is placed on the President's left hand and especially verify the arrival of hits which this competitor may receive.

Similarly, the two judges placed on the President's left hand should watch the fencer who is placed on the President's right hand and especially verify the arrival of hits which this competitor may receive.

The President, who alone is responsible for the direction of the bout, gives the orders. However, any other member of the jury may give the command 'HALT', but only if they think that there is an accident. Similarly, the time-keeper stops the bout by calling 'HALT' when time expires.

As soon as a judge sees a hit (whether on a valid surface or not) arrive on the fencer whom they are watching they must raise their hand in order to advise the President.

All judging is carried out aloud and without the members of the jury leaving the position which they occupy.

The jury is not bound to take account of the acknowledgement of a hit properly made by a competitor, i.e. if the fencer themselves acknowledges that they have been hit.

The jury first decides as to the materiality of the hit or hits. The President then alone decides against which fencer a hit shall be scored by applying the conventional rules for each weapon.

As soon as the bout has stopped, the President reconstructs briefly the movements which composed the last fencing phrase before the order 'HALT' (this formality is not obligatory at épée) and in the course of their analysis they question the two judges watching one fencer in order to ascertain whether in their opinion any of the movements occurring in their analysis of the phrase has resulted in a hit on the competitor; the President then follows the same procedure with the two judges of the other competitor. (This formality must be observed at all three weapons.)

When the judges are questioned, they must reply in one of the following ways:

- Yes
- Yes, but not valid
- No
- I abstain

The President votes last.

The President then aggregates the votes thus made from each side; the opinion of each judge counts as one vote, the opinion of the President as one and a half votes, while abstentions are not counted at all.

If both judges on the same side agree in a positive opinion (either both say YES or both say NO or both say YES, BUT NOT VALID) their judgement prevails.

If one of the judges has a definite opinion and the other abstains, the opinion of the President prevails since their vote is over-riding; if he also abstains, the decision of the judge who has the definite opinion prevails.

If the two judges concerned are positive but contrary in their opinions or if both abstain, the President may decide according to his own observations. If the President abstains, the hit is regarded as doubtful. For example, Judge A says NO; Judge B says YES, BUT NOT VALID; even if the President considers the hit valid, the judgement must be 'no hit'.

In the case of a double abstention, the President may, as an exceptional measure, ask the opinions of the two other judges if he considers that they were better placed to see the hit, for example, a riposte on the back made on a fencer who has made a flèche attack and has passed his opponent.

A doubtful hit is never scored against the competitor who might have received it; but on the other hand, any hit made subsequently or simultaneously in the same phrase by the fencer who has thus been granted the benefit of the doubt must also be annulled. (Except in the case when one of the fencers leaves the boundary of the piste. Any hit scored by the fencer remaining on the piste is valid, any hit from the fencer off the piste is not valid, even in the case of a double-hit.)

As regards a hit made subsequently by the fencer who originally made the doubtful hit, the following courses will apply:

I. If the new hit (remise, redoublement, or riposte) is made by a fencer who made the doubtful hit without any hit having been made by his opponent, this new hit must be scored.

II. But if the doubt concerns the surface on which the hit arrived (one YES and one YES, BUT NOT VALID) no other hit in this phrase can be scored.

III. This is also the case if the opponent has made a doubtful hit between the doubtful hit and the new hit made by the same competitor.

RULES AND DIMENSIONS OF THE PISTE

The field of play that is used for fencing is called the piste. The piste may be made of various materials: earth, wood, linoleum, cork, rubber, plastic, metallic mesh, metal or a compound with a metal base.

The piste is 14m long and from 1.80m to 2m wide.

The piste should in practice be extended at each end by a distance of 1.50 to 2m, to enable a competitor who is about to cross the limit of the piste to retire over a continuous and even surface.

If the piste is mounted on a platform, the latter must not be higher than 0.50m.

When a competitor crosses one of the boundaries of the piste with both feet, the President must immediately call 'HALT' and annul everything which has occurred after the boundary has been crossed. The only exception is a hit received by a competitor who has crossed the boundary (even after he has crossed it), provided that this hit is made immediately as part of the movement in the course of which the competitor crossed the boundary.

When one of the competitors leaves the piste only a hit made by the fencer who remains on the piste can be counted valid, even in the case of a double-hit.

Should a competitor cross the rear limit of the piste completely – i.e. with both feet – a penalty hit will be scored against them. No verbal warning shall be given to the fencer as to the proximity of the rear limit.

When one of the competitors crosses the lateral boundaries of the piste with one foot, they are not penalised but the President must immediately call 'HALT' and replace the competitors on guard on the piste.

A competitor who crosses one of the lateral boundaries of the piste with both feet is penalised. When the competitors are replaced on guard, the opponent of the competitor who has crossed the lateral boundary will step forward one metre from the position they occupied when his opponent left the piste; the competitor who is penalised must retire in order to resume the correct fencing distance.

When the infliction of this penalty places a competitor with both feet beyond the rear limit of the piste, that competitor is considered as having been hit.

A competitor who crosses one of the boundaries of the piste with both feet, e.g. when making a flèche attack – to avoid being hit, will be penalised as specified in Articles 641 (1st group – yellow card).

SAFETY

Safety in fencing is the responsibility of every individual fencer.

Following the 'golden rules', along with some common sense, will help keep you and others safe while fencing.

The golden rules:

Never fence or demonstrate fencing without wearing correctly fitting fencing masks.

Never fence someone who is not wearing a fencing mask.

Never carry a sword over your shoulder or under your arm.

Never talk expressively with a sword in your hand.

Never put a fencing mask on while holding a sword in the same hand.

Always wear an under-plastron.

Always wear breast protectors (females only).

Always wear your fencing jacket correctly fastened. Ensure that if you are wearing a front zip-fastening jacket, that the zip lies on the non-sword arm of the body, i.e. if right-handed the zip should be on the left with the zip cover lying away from your opponent's blade.

Always wear a glove over your fencing hand with the sleeve of your jacket inside the gauntlet of the glove.

Make sure that your sword meets all the FIE safety regulations, i.e. good condition of the blade, no rust, kinks or sharp edges, a rubber button, hilt assembly is secure.

Make sure your mask is a good fit with an elastic strap attached to the back, which you must wear on your head and not left 'resting' on your mask, and that the bib is also fully attached.

Make sure there are no rips or holes in your jacket.

Make sure all your equipment is clean and well maintained. Safety checks should be carried out on all your equipment prior to every fencing bout.

Maintain good behaviour and discipline while fencing and listen carefully for any safety warnings or instructions from the qualified coach, club leader or from the officials at a competition.

THE DUTIES OF A TIME-KEEPER

The duration of a bout is held to mean 'the effective duration', that is the total of the intervals of time between the orders 'PLAY' and 'HALT'. The time taken for the deliberations of the jury and for other interruptions is therefore not counted.

The duration of the bout must be registered exactly by a time-keeper appointed by the organising committee (obligatory for official competitions of the FIE).

For the finals of all official competitions, as well as for all bouts for which a chronometer is visible to the spectators, the chronometer must be so placed that it is visible to the two fencers on the piste and to the President.

The effective duration of a bout is:

At épée for one hit: five minutes.

At all weapons four hits: five minutes; for five hits: six minutes; eight hits: eight minutes; ten hits: ten minutes.

One minute before the expiry of the time allowed for actual fencing the time-keeper must stand up and call 'one minute' (without stopping the clock). This warns the President who should stop the fight and warn the fencers that they have approximately one minute before the expiry of the time allowed for actual fencing.

Any hit arriving 'coup lance' at the moment of the President's 'HALT' is valid. At any interruption during the last minute of the bout, the fencer may be told, when they are placed back on guard, how much time they have left to fence.

At the expiry of the regulation fencing time, the time-keeper must shout 'HALT' (or operate a sound signal) which stops the fight; in this case even a 'coup lance' is not valid.

THE PRINCIPLE OF DEFENCE

The principle of defence refers to the part of the sword used to parry.

The forté of the defender's blade against the foible of the attacker's blade is the principle of defence – strong against weak.

THE TARGET AREA

Foil:

The target at foil, for ladies as for men, excludes the limbs and the head. It is confined to the trunk, the upper limit being the collar up to 6cm above the prominences of the collar bones; at the sides to the seams of the sleeves which should cross the head of the humerus; and the lower limit following a horizontal line across the back joining the tops of the hip bones thence by straight lines to the junction of the lines of the groin.

The meeting of the 1994 FIE Congress confirmed that the bib became part of the valid target from January 1, 1995.

Épée:

At épée the target includes the whole of the fencer's body including their clothing and equipment.

Thus, any point which arrives counts as a hit whatever part of the body (trunk, limbs or head), the clothing or the equipment it reaches.

Sabre:

The target comprises any part of the body above a horizontal line drawn between the top of the folds formed by the thighs and by the trunk of the fencer when in the on guard position.

WHAT CONSTITUTES
A VALID HIT?

In foil and sabre fencing only hits that arrive on the target area are valid.

In foil and épée, the thrusting weapons, the blade must show to some degree the 'character of penetration', that is to say a bend in the blade as the hit is made.

In sabre fencing, the cut and thrust weapon, all hits made with the cutting edge, the flat or back of the blade are counted as good. Hits made with the point (thrusts) are also counted as good so long as the blade shows to some degree the 'character of penetration'.

TACTICS

An entire guide could be taken up solely on the subject of tactics. When people first meet me and discover that I coach fencing, they often ask, "What is fencing like?" Without hesitation I reply, "Physical chess." For every action there is a counter-action and for the counter-action there is also an action and you must have the means both physical and mental to apply them.

Below is an easy to remember 'trick' which may help you to draw up a tactical plan to defeat your opponent. I have called it TOTAL:

T – Think:	Switch on to the task ahead.
O – Observation:	Watch your opponent fence. Look for their strengths as well as their weaknesses, footwork, blade work, distance, etc.
T – Tactical plan:	After observing your opponent, make a mental tactical plan of three moves, comprising attacks or counter-attacks or combinations thereof.
A – Adaptability:	Be prepared, just in case your tactical plan fails. Be flexible and utilise all your fencing knowledge and experience.
L – Learn:	Every opponent will give you new and different challenges. Whether you win or lose, learn from your bout. Ask yourself; what worked and what do I need to do to improve.

TOTAL

A GLOSSARY OF FENCING TERMINOLOGY

Absence of blade	When the blades are not in contact, i.e. not engaged.
Academic assault	A display bout in which hits are not normally counted.
Advance	To step forward.
Aids	The last three fingers of the sword hand.
Angulation	Bending the wrist when placing a hit, so as to present the point at right angles to the target.
Assault	A bout between two fencers.
Attack	An offensive movement designed to hit an opponent.
Attack on the blade	A preparation for an attack by beat, pressure or froissement.
Attack on the preparation	An attack launched when the opponent is making a preparation for an attack.
Backward spring	A leap backwards, out of distance, from the lunge.
Balestra	A short jump forward during an attack.
Barrage	A tiebreaker, in a competition bout.
Beat	A preparation for attack.
Bind	A preparation for attack which carries the opponent's blade diagonally across from the high line to the low line, or vice versa.
Bout	An assault between two fencers in which hits are counted.
Breaking ground	Retiring by stepping backwards.

Broken time	A pause deliberately made between two movements, which normally follow each other immediately.
Cadence	The rhythm in which a sequence of movements is made.
Ceding parry	A parry formed by giving way to an opponent who is taking the blade.
Central guard	A position on guard when the hand is placed between two lateral lines and thus not completely covered in any line.
Change beat	A beat made after a change of engagement.
Change of engagement	Engaging an opponent's blade in a new line.
Circular parry	A parry in which the defender's blade describes a circle to gather the attacker's blade.
Close quarters	When two fencers are close together but can still wield their weapons.
Compound attack	An attack that comprises one or more feints.
Compound riposte	A riposte comprising one or more feints.
Coquille	The bell-shaped guard of a foil or épée.
Corps à corps	When two fencers are touching so that they cannot wield their weapons correctly.
Coulé	A thrust in the line of the engagement while keeping contact with the opponent's blade.
Counter-disengagement	The action if deceiving a change of engagements or a circular parry.
Counter-offensive actions	The stop-hit and time-hit.
Counter-riposte	An offensive action following the successful parry of your opponent's riposte or counter-riposte.
Counter-time	A movement by second intention.
Covered	A position of sword hand and weapon, which closes the line of engagement against a direct thrust.
Croisé	Taking the opponent's blade from the high line to the low line on the same side as the engagement.
Cut	A hit made with the front edge, or the first third of the back edge of the sabre.
Cut-over	A disengagement made by passing over the opponent's blade.
Cutting the lines	Circular parries made otherwise than in the line of engagement.

Delayed	An attack or riposte made after a pause.
Dérobement	Evading an opponent's attempts to beat or take the blade while your sword arm is extended.
Detachment parry	A crisp parry, in which the defender's blade quits the attacker's blade immediately it has deflected it.
Development	The extension of the arm and the lunge.
Direct	An attack or riposte made in the line of engagement.
Disengagement	Moving the weapon from the line of engagement into an opposite line by passing under the opponent's blade.
Doigté	Finger play.
Double	An attacking movement during which the blade performs a complete circle in order to deceive the opponent's circular parry.
Double prise de fer	A succession of takings of the opponent's blade.
Engagement	The crossing of the blades.
Envelopment	Taking the opponent's blade and describing a circle returning to the original line of the engagement without losing contact of blades.
En marchment	Movement made with one or more steps forward.
Épée	The duelling sword.
Evasion	A dérobement.
False attack	An offensive movement that is not intended to score a hit.
Feint	An offensive movement made to resemble an attack in order to draw a reaction from the opponent.
Fencing measure	The distance which exists between two fencers.
Fencing positions	The position in which the sword arm and weapon may be placed to cover the lines of the target.
Fencing time	The time required to perform one simple fencing action.
FIE (the)	Federation Internationale D'Escrime.
Field of play	The piste and its extensions on which fencing takes place.
Finger play	The method of manipulating the weapon with the fingers.
Flèche	An attack made by a succession of running steps, instead of by the lunge or steps forward.

Foible	The half of the blade nearest the point of the weapon.
Foil	The basic weapon with which the art of fencing should be learned.
Forté	The half of the blade nearest the guard of the weapon.
Froissement	A preparation for attack made by deflecting the opponent's blade with a strong, sharp grazing movement along it.
Gaining ground	Stepping forward.
Gaining on the lunge	Bringing the rear foot up to the leading foot before making a lunge.
Graze	A coulé along the opponent's blade.
Grip	The part of the handle normally held by the sword hand. Also, the manner in which the sword is held.
Ground judges	Two judges who look for hits made on the ground during electrically scored fencing bouts and to assist the President in looking for other offences such as the use of the unarmed hand.
Guard	The portion of the hilt assembly between the blade and the handle designed to protect the hand.
High lines	The parts of the opponent's target visible above his sword hand when on guard.
Hit	The offensive action which lands with the point or edge on the opponent's valid target area.
Immediate	An action made without pause.
Indirect	A simple attack or riposte made in another line.
Inside lines	The parts of the target furthest from the sword arm.
Insufficient parry	A parry that does not close the line completely and through which the opponent can score a hit.
Invitations	Opening a line to offer a path to an opponent's offensive movement.
In quartata	An offensive movement made while removing the body out of line by a side step.
Jury	The president and judges who officiate at a fencing event.
La belle	The deciding hit during a fencing bout.
Lines	Theoretical divisions of the target corresponding to the fencing positions.

Low lines	The parts of the opponent's target visible below their sword hand when on guard.
Lunge	The extension of the arm, body and legs used to reach an opponent.
Manipulators	The first finger and thumb of the sword hand.
Martingale	A loop of leather used to prevent a foil or épée from flying out of the hand during a bout.
Match	A contest between two teams.
Measure	See fencing measure.
Molinello	A circular cut at the head made from the sabre parry of prime.
On guard	The position of the arms, body and feet adopted by a fencer when prepared for a bout.
Opposition	A movement made without quitting the opponent's blade.
Orthopaedic grip	A handle moulded to the shape of the fingers (otherwise known as a pistol grip).
Outside lines	The parts of the target nearest the sword arm.
Parry	A defensive action made with the blade to deflect an attacker's blade.
Passata sotto	The action of avoiding an attacker's blade by ducking below it.
Period of fencing time	See fencing time.
Phrase	A sequence of fencing movements exchanged between two fencers leading to a hit.
Pied ferme	A movement made while the feet remain immobile.
Piste	The part of the field of play within which a bout takes place.
Plastron	An undergarment worn as a safety precaution for all weapons.
Pommel	A piece of metal screwed to the end of the hilt to lock the parts of the weapon together and to aid in the balance of the blade.
Pool	A grouping of fencers or teams in a competition.
Preparation for attack	A blade, body or foot movement made prior to an attack.
President (referee)	The referee in a fencing bout.

Pressure	A preparation for attack made by pressing on the opponent's blade.
Principle of defence	The opposition of the forté of the defender's blade against the foible of the attacker's blade.
Prise de fer	A preparation for an attack in which the opponent's blade is taken by an envelopment, a bind or a croise.
Progressive attack	A method of executing the various movements of a compound attack, while continuously approaching the target in order to cut time and distance to a minimum. The opposite to a pied ferme.
Pronation	The position of the sword hand with the fingernails downwards.
Rassemblement	Bringing the leading foot back to the rear foot while rising to full height.
Recovery	Returning to the on guard position after a lunge.
Redoublement	A renewal of attack while remaining on the lunge, which includes one or more blade movements.
Remise	A renewal of attack while remaining on the lunge by replacing the point on the target in the same line without withdrawing the arm.
Renewed attack	A remise, redoublement or reprise.
Reprise	A renewal of the attack by first coming through the on guard position, either forward or backward, maintaining priority throughout by keeping the sword arm extended.
Retire	To step back.
Reverse beat	A change beat or, at sabre, a beat made with the back of the blade.
Riposte	An offensive action following the successful parry of your opponent's attack.
Sabre	The cut and thrust weapon.
Salute	The acknowledgement with the weapon that the fencer extends to their opponent at the commencement and conclusion of a bout.
Second intention	A premeditated offensive action to provoke a response.
Semi-circular parry	A parry during which the blade describes a half-circle from the high line to the low line or vice versa.

Sentiment du fer	Feeling an opponent's reactions through contact of the blades.
Simple attack	An attack made with one movement, either direct or indirect.
Simultaneous actions	Where both fencers conceive and execute the same action simultaneously. Any hits incurred by fencers during simultaneous actions are annulled at foil and sabre.
Sitting down	Bending the knees when in the on guard position.
Stance	The position of the feet and legs while in the on guard position.
Stop-hit	A counter-offensive action made on an opponent's attack.
Straight thrust	A simple and direct offensive movement.
Successive parries	A series of parries that immediately follow each other until the attacker's blade is found.
Supination	The position of the sword hand with the fingernails facing upwards.
Taking the blade	A preparation for attack by prise de fer.
Target	The area within which a hit counts as valid.
Terrain	The field of play. Also, the measured piece of ground on which a duel is fought.
Time hit	A counter-offensive action, which anticipates and closes the final line of the opponent's attack as it is made (also known as the stop-hit with opposition).
Timing	The execution of a fencing movement at the correct moment.
Touché	The word used to acknowledge a hit.
Trompement	Offensive blade movements that deceive the opponent's parries.
Two-time	A movement made of two periods of fencing time.
Uncovered	A position of the sword hand and blade where the line of engagement is not closed.
Valid hits	Hits that arrive on the target.
Warning lines	Lines drawn at the rear limits of the piste.

INDEX